Lecture Notes in Computer Science 2299

Edited by G. Goos, J. Hartmanis, and J. van Leeuwen

T0223689

Springer
Berlin
Heidelberg
New York
Barcelona
Hong Kong
London
Milan
Paris
Tokyo

Hartmut Schmeck   Theo Ungerer
Lars Wolf (Eds.)

Trends in Network and Pervasive Computing – ARCS 2002

International Conference on Architecture of Computing Systems
Karlsruhe, Germany, April 8-12, 2002
Proceedings

Springer

Series Editors

Gerhard Goos, Karlsruhe University, Germany
Juris Hartmanis, Cornell University, NY, USA
Jan van Leeuwen, Utrecht University, The Netherlands

Volume Editors

Hartmut Schmeck
Inst. of Applied Informatics and Formal Description Methods - AIFB
University of Karlsruhe (TH), 76128 Karlsruhe, Germany
E-mail: schmeck@aifb.uni-karlsruhe.de

Theo Ungerer
University of Augsburg, Institute of Informatics
86159 Augsburg, Germany
E-mail: ungerer@informatik.uni-augsburg.de

Lars Wolf
Inst. of Telematics, Faculty of Informatics and Computing Center
University of Karlsruhe (TH), Zirkel 2, 76128 Karlsruhe, Germany
E-mail: lars.wolf@uni-karlsruhe.de

Cataloging-in-Publication Data applied for

Die Deutsche Bibliothek - CIP-Einheitsaufnahme

Trends in network and pervasive computing : proceedings / ARCS 2002,
International Conference on Architecture of Computing Systems, Karlsruhe,
Germany, April 8 - 12, 2002. Hartmut Schmeck ... (ed.). - Berlin ;
Heidelberg ; New York ; Barcelona ; Hong Kong ; London ; Milan ; Paris ;
Tokyo : Springer, 2002
  (Lecture notes in computer science ; Vol. 2299)
  ISBN 3-540-43409-7

CR Subject Classification (1998): C.2, C.5.3, D.4, D.2.11, H.3.5, H.4, H.5.2

ISSN 0302-9743
ISBN 3-540-43409-7 Springer-Verlag Berlin Heidelberg New York

Springer-Verlag Berlin Heidelberg New York
a member of BertelsmannSpringer Science+Business Media GmbH

http://www.springer.de

© Springer-Verlag Berlin Heidelberg 2002
Printed in Germany

Typesetting: Camera-ready by author, data conversion by DA-TeX Gerd Blumenstein
Printed on acid-free paper   SPIN 10846458   06/3142   5 4 3 2 1 0

Dedicated to the memory of Jochen Liedtke
who died much too early on June 10, 2001

Preface

Future processors will become smaller, provide higher performance, and consume less power than today's devices. Such processors will spark off new applications in particular in the area of everyday consumer devices. Personal digital assistants, mobile consumer devices, and various smart personal appliances will soon be widely used. Mobile telecommunication systems will increase their bandwidth and will yield highly connected, ubiquitous computing appliances. Ubiquitous computing induces a new way of thinking in system design: computers vanish into the background hidden behind the habitual human environment.

These trends are the major topics of ARCS 2002, the "International Conference on Architecture of Computing Systems", which continues and replaces the biennial series of German Conferences on Architecture of Computing Systems, organized by the special interest group on "Computer and System Architecture" of the GI (Gesellschaft für Informatik – German Informatics Society) and the ITG (Informationstechnische Gesellschaft – Information Technology Society). The fifteen predecessor conferences (except the EuroArch in 1993) were national conferences only, this is the first German conference on computer architecture addressing the international research community. It serves as a forum to present current work by researchers from around the world, this year being focused on topics that are truly changing our perception of information processing – "Trends in Network and Pervasive Computing".

The call for papers resulted in a total of 42 submissions from around the world. Every submission was reviewed by four members of the program committee or additional reviewers. The program committee decided to accept 18 papers, which are arranged into 6 sessions with the result of a strong program. The two keynote talks by Ralf Guido Herrtwich (DaimlerChrysler Research) and Marc Fleischmann (formerly Transmeta, now Pixelworks) focus our attention on an innovative application area ("Communicating Cars: A Case for Ubiquitous Computing in the Automotive Domain") and on innovative architectures ("Microprocessor Architectures for the Mobile Internet Era").

The organizers gratefully acknowledge the support by ACM, IEEE, IFIP TC10, CEPIS, and EUREL, and, in particular, the financial support by PEP Modular Computers and by SAP.

The preparation of this conference has been heavily influenced by our colleague Jochen Liedtke, who died much too early in June 2001. He strongly advocated the international orientation of this conference, he was a major contributor in shaping its thematic focus, and he helped significantly to form a truly international program committee. The research community on computer and system architecture deeply regrets the loss of such an energetic and enthusiastic colleague, who contributed numerous stimulating concepts and ideas, in particular on the design of micro kernel architectures.

We would like to thank all who contributed to the success of this conference, in particular the members of the program committee and the additional referees for carefully reviewing the contributions and selecting a high quality program. Our Workshop and Tutorial Chair Uwe Brinkschulte did a perfect job in organizing the tutorials and coordinating the workshops. Our special thanks go to the General Co-chair Lars Wolf and to the members of the organizing committee, namely Michael Beigl and Martina Zitterbart, for their numerous contributions as well as to Daniela Müller and André Wiesner for setting up the conference software and for designing and maintaining the conference web-site. Faruk Bagci and Jan Petzold did a perfect job concerning the preparation of this volume.

We hope that all participants enjoy a successful conference, make a lot of new contacts, engage in fruitful discussions, and have a pleasant stay in Karlsruhe.

January 2002   Hartmut Schmeck
                                                                      Theo Ungerer

Organization

Executive Committee

General Chair:	Hartmut Schmeck	University of Karlsruhe (TH)
General Co-Chair:	Lars Wolf	University of Karlsruhe (TH)
Program Chair:	Theo Ungerer	University of Augsburg
Workshop and Tutorial Chair:	Uwe Brinkschulte	University of Karlsruhe (TH)

Program Committee

Nader Bagherzadeh	University of California Irvine, USA
Michael Beigl	TecO, Karlsruhe, Germany
Frank Bellosa	Univ. of Erlangen & IBM Watson, USA
Arndt Bode	Technical University of Munich, Germany
Gaetano Borriello	University of Washington, USA
Uwe Brinkschulte	University of Karlsruhe (TH), Germany
Kemal Ebcioglu	IBM T.J. Watson, USA
Reinhold Eberhardt	DaimlerChrysler, Ulm, Germany
Werner Erhard	University of Jena, Germany
Hans Gellersen	University of Lancaster, GB
Orran Krieger	IBM T.J. Watson, USA
Jochen Liedtke*	University of Karlsruhe (TH), Germany
Erik Maehle	Medical University of Lübeck, Germany
Friedemann Mattern	ETH Zürich, Switzerland
Christian Müller-Schloer	Univ. of Hannover, Germany
Wolfgang Rosenstiel	Univ. of Tübingen, Germany
Bernt Schiele	ETH Zürich, Switzerland
Alexander Schill	Techn. Univ. of Dresden, Germany
Hartmut Schmeck	University of Karlsruhe (TH), Germany
Karsten Schwan	Georgia Tech, USA
Peter Steenkiste	Carnegie-Mellon University, USA
Djamshid Tavangarian	Univ. of Rostock, Germany
Rich Uhlig Intel	Microprocessor Research Lab, USA
Theo Ungerer	University of Augsburg, Germany
Klaus Waldschmidt	University of Frankfurt, Germany
Lars Wolf	University of Karlsruhe (TH), Germany
Hans Christoph Zeidler	Univ. Fed. Armed Forces, Germany
Martina Zitterbart	University of Karlsruhe (TH), Germany

---

* died June 10, 2001

Local Organization

Michael Beigl	University of Karlsruhe (TH)
Uwe Brinkschulte	University of Karlsruhe (TH)
Hartmut Schmeck	University of Karlsruhe (TH)
Theo Ungerer	University of Augsburg
Lars Wolf	University of Karlsruhe (TH)
Martina Zitterbart	University of Karlsruhe (TH)

Reviewers

Stavros Antifakos	ETH Zurich
Faruk Bagci	University of Augsburg
Nader Bagherzadeh	Univ. of California Irvine
Marc Bechler	Univ. of Karlsruhe (TH)
Michael Beigl	Univ. of Karlsruhe (TH)
Frank Bellosa	Univ. of Erlangen & IBM
Arndt Bode	Technical Univ. of Munich
Gaetano Borriello	Univ. of Washington
Markus Braun	Univ. of Tübingen
Uwe Brinkschulte	Univ. of Karlsruhe (TH)
Fabian Bustamante	Georgia Tech
Vlad Coroama	ETH Zürich
Erik Cota-Robles	Intel Labs
Christian Cseh	DaimlerChrysler
Svetlana Domnitcheva	ETH Zürich
Kemal Ebcioglu	IBM T.J. Watson
Reinhold Eberhardt	DaimlerChrysler
Greg Eisenhauer	Georgia Tech
Werner Erhard	Univ. of Jena
Frank Eschmann	Univ. of Frankfurt
Fridtjof Feldbusch	Univ. of Augsburg
Christian Flörkemeier	ETH Zürich
Walter Franz	DaimlerChrysler
Hans Gellersen	Univ. of Lancaster
Christoph Grimm	Univ. of Frankfurt
Albert Held	DaimlerChrysler
Udo Heuser	Univ. of Tübingen
Verena Kahmann	Univ. of Karlsruhe (TH)
Nicholas Kern	ETH Zürich
Bernd Klauer	Univ. of Frankfurt
Orran Krieger	IBM T.J. Watson
Alain Kägi	Intel Labs
Marc Langheinrich	ETH Zürich
Jochen Liedtke*	Univ. of Karlsruhe
Erik Maehle	Medical Univ. of Lübeck

---

* died June 10, 2001

Friedemann Mattern	ETH Zürich
Florian Michahelles	ETH Zürich
Christian Müller-Schloer	Univ. of Hannover
Trevor Pering	Intel Labs
Matthias Pfeffer	Univ. of Augsburg
Philip Robinson	Univ. of Karlsruhe (TH)
Michael Rohs	ETH Zürich
Wolfgang Rosenstiel	Univ. of Tübingen
Christian Ruess	DaimlerChrysler
Bernt Schiele	ETH Zürich
Alexander Schill	Techn. Univ. of Dresden
Hartmut Schmeck	Univ. of Karlsruhe (TH)
Albrecht Schmidt	Univ. of Lancaster
Stephen Schmitt	FZI Karlsruhe
Carsten Schulz-Key	Univ. of Tübingen
Martin Schwab	DaimlerChrysler
Karsten Schwan	Georgia Tech
Frank Siegemund	ETH Zürich
Martin Stark	Univ. of Tübingen
Peter Steenkiste	CMU
Djamshid Tavangarian	Univ. of Rostock
Rich Uhlig	Intel Labs
Sascha Uhrig	Univ. of Augsburg
Theo Ungerer	Univ. of Augsburg
Harald Vogt	ETH Zürich
Nick Wade	Intel Labs
Klaus Waldschmidt	Univ. of Frankfurt
Patrick Widener	Georgia Tech
Christian Wilk	DaimlerChrysler
Lars Wolf	Univ. of Karlsruhe (TH)
Hans C. Zeidler	Univ. Fed. Armed Forces
Martina Zitterbart	Univ. Karlsruhe (TH)

Supporting/Sponsoring Societies

Organized by GI-Fachausschuss 3.1 / ITG-Fachausschuss 6.1 and GI-Fachausschuss 3.3, Fachgruppe 3.3.1
Supported by CEPIS and EUREL
In cooperation with ACM, IEEE, and IFIP TC10

Sponsoring Companies

CEC Karlsruhe – Corporate Research

Table of Contents

IV Processor Architecture

V Middleware and Verification

VI Networking 2

Invited Program

Keynote
Communicating Cars: A Case for Ubiquitous Computing in the Automotive Domain

Ralf Guido Herrtwich

DaimlerChrysler AG
Alt-Moabit 96a, 10559 Berlin, Germany
ralf.herrtwich@daimlerchrysler.com

Abstract. Examples for ubiquitous computing applications usually come from the household domain. Typical lists include microwave ovens with integrated web-pads, refrigerators or washing machines with remote Internet connections for maintenance access, and even instrumented coffee mugs or clothes. While many of these examples have substantial entertainment value, the likelihood of their realization and pervasive deployment in the not too distant future is questionable. There is, however, another application domain for ubiquitous computing which holds substantial promise, but is often overlooked: the automotive sector.

Cars are fairly attractive protagonists for ubiquitous computing: They are large enough to have communication devices integrated in them, in fact, a substantial portion of them has integrated phones today. They come with their own power source which can also feed their communications equipment. Their price is some orders of magnitude higher than that of the device to be included, so the relative price increase to make them communicate is small. And, perhaps most importantly, some services such as mayday, remote tracking, or tele-diagnosis make vehicle connectivity desirable for car buyers and car manufacturers alike.

In this talk, we discuss how ubiquitous computing in the automotive domain can become a reality. We investigate the principal services resulting from network-connected cars, focussing on vehicle-originated rather than passenger-related communication as we believe that ubiquitous computing is more about communicating machines than communicating humans. Within the vehicle-centric services identified, we distinguish between client/server and peer-to-peer applications, resulting in different communication requirements and system setups. We outline some network solutions to meet these requirements, including technologies for car-to-infrastructure and car-to-car communication in different regions of the world. We conclude by discussing the overall effect which these developments may have on the automotive industry.

H. Schmeck, T. Ungerer, and L. Wolf (Eds.): ARCS 2002, LNCS 2299, p. 3, 2002.
© Springer-Verlag Berlin Heidelberg 2002

Keynote
Microprocessor Architectures for the Mobile Internet Era

Marc Fleischmann

Vice President of Engineering, Pixelworks
7700 SW Mohawk St., Tualatin, OR 97062, USA
marcf@pixelworks.com

Abstract. The mobile Internet era is characterized by three core technology trends: First, wireless bandwidth growth is outpacing Moore's Law by an order of magnitude. Second, Moore's Law itself is becoming constrained, as continuously increasing chip transistor densities lead to prohibitive heat density levels. And third, mobility, anytime, anyplace and on any device, is rapidly becoming a key design requirement, calling for smart, energy-aware placement of transistors across the network.

In the periphery of the Internet, these trends culminate in ubiquitous Internet appliances that deliver dynamic content over persistent real-time connections. Their requirements define the design imperatives of future Internet microprocessors: high integration - to minimize form factors; high energy efficiency - to maximize battery life or computational density; compatibility - with the full PC and Internet experience; and flexibility - to quickly adapt to new devices, content types and usage models.

The Crusoe microprocessor is an example for how these design imperatives can be realized. It uses a hybrid hardware/software architecture. The hardware consists of a highly efficient VLIW core, which is complemented by the Code Morphing Software. The latter currently implements the x86 instruction set and a Java Virtual Machine. This architecture can be extended into a self-optimizing, largely instruction set agnostic, "soft" core.

H. Schmeck, T. Ungerer, and L. Wolf (Eds.): ARCS 2002, LNCS 2299, p. 4, 2002.
© Springer-Verlag Berlin Heidelberg 2002

Session I

Context-Aware Systems

An Architecture for the Integration of Physical and Informational Spaces

Scott M. Thayer and Peter Steenkiste

Carnegie Mellon University
5000 Forbes Avenue Pittsburgh, PA 15213
{sthayer,prs}@cs.cmu.edu
http://www.cs.cmu.edu/~aura

Abstract. While computer processing power, storage space, and bandwidth capacities are experiencing exponential growth, individual human processing capabilities are not increasing significantly. Pervasive computing creates an environment that offers a wealth of computing resources, I/O capabilities, and sensors. This offers an opportunity for applications to interact with and monitor the physical environment and to provide a task-centric and mobile infrastructure for the modern user. However, this rich environment can also be overwhelming and distracting to users, in part because of a disconnect between the physical infrastructure observed by users and the information space seen by applications. In this paper we introduce AIPIS, an architecture for a technological bridge between the physical and informational realms of the human and the computer, respectively. The purpose of this bridge is twofold: (1) to provide to users a hands-free computing environment that automates much of the drudgery associated with use of computers, and (2) to focus human attention to only the critical aspects of task execution that require their input. We also describe the implementation of the Aura desktop, a first prototype of the AIPIS architecture.

1   Introduction

Much of today's computing systems and software are application centered. Commercial pressures demand well-defined, shrink-wrapped products that can be readily and repeatedly marketed to consumers in part drive this situation. With great diversification in the software market, the typical computer is loaded with software from dozens of different vendors. Some application integration is available, but typically it is within a select bundle of applications from a major vendor with proprietary interfaces. The problem with this model is that while performing tasks, users typically do not work within the framework of a single application or even an application bundle. On the contrary, users typically coordinate diverse applications in the daily execution of tasks and projects under their charge. For example, the preparation of a multi-author conference paper typically involves email and phone applications, spreadsheets, word

H. Schmeck, T. Ungerer, and L. Wolf (Eds.): ARCS 2002, LNCS 2299, pp. 7-20, 2002.

processors, schedulers, scientific simulation and mathematics packages, photo editing, typesetters, etc. The user wants a seamless interface between applications that can be tailored to each particular task and configured with the current set of user preferences. Even with the recent, rapid progress resulting in increasingly powerful computing platforms and software, the state-of-the-art in system-wide, task-level interfaces to computing and software applications from distinct vendors is somewhere between ftp and file copy. The level of distraction and frustration associated with using a computer to coordinate a reasonably complex task can be disconcerting for the veteran and novice user alike.

An application-centered approach can never achieve the level of efficiency and utility necessary to liberate people from computer drudgery in a task-based world. This is a natural consequence of an approach that attempts to satisfy the needs of an average user base with a common, commercial software base. In Aura [1,2,3], we embrace an approach that attempts to weave applications into an infrastructure that is pliable enough to represent user preferences and mobile enough to support user on the go and intelligent enough to operate as viable resource in the execution of day-to-day tasks [12]. Our approach to realizing this vision centers on the following principles:

Embedded Users. Users are embedded in a physical world and Aura must operate within the limitations, constraints, and distractions of that world.

Mobile Users. Users are mobile and move within the physical world during the execution of tasks.

Task-Centered. Most users are not application or even bundle centered – they are task centered and currently lack an intelligent interface that helps in the automated execution of comprehensive user tasks.

One challenge is that we have to bridge the gap between two currently distinct domains: informational and physical. Applications interact various sources and sinks of information streams, while users interact with devices that have certain properties (physical location, capabilities). Typically, these domains are not tightly coupled and as a consequence, current computer interfaces inhibit the optimal benefit to the user. In this paper we present an architecture called AIPIS, for Architecture for Integrating Physical and Informational Spaces, that bridges the physical and informational spaces in such a way that it becomes easier to develop applications that can interact with humans in a more natural manner. In the next section we first give an overview of the CMU Aura project, which provided the motivation for AIPIS. We then present the AIPIS architecture and we describe a prototype implementation. We conclude with related work and conclusions.

2   Aura: Ubiquitous Invisible Computing

The Aura project is evolving a ubiquitous invisible computing infrastructure that supports mobile users in performing every day tasks. Ubiquitous means that Aura is present everywhere, although the level of support may vary significantly. For example, device-rich smart rooms will offer a wider range of modes of interaction than elevators and parks. Invisible means that Aura will minimize the level of distraction that it imposes on users. For example, it will only interrupt the user when necessary.

In this section we give a short overview of Aura, starting with a motivating example. The remainder of the paper focuses on one aspect of Aura, the integration of physical and informational space.

2.1   Motivating Example

Bob is on a plane, working on a large project that involves multiple documents. When the captain announces that they are about to land, he logs out. Aura automatically saves all the documents that are part of the task, and transmits them to a server.

When Bob walks into his office, he uses a finger print reader to authenticate himself. Aura knows that he is alone in the office and restores the files that he was working, opening them at the right point, on the large display in his office. Aura also opens his mail, since Bob always reads mail first. While Bob was using a keyboard and mouse on the plane, Aura switches to voice control since it is more appropriate for the current task executed in the privacy of his office. Aura can synthesize speech to provide an audio alert to Bob of certain events or even for more complex operations such as reading back e-mail so Bob can have additional interaction with Aura while moving around in his personal space.

At this point, Bradley walks towards Bob's office. Aura recognizes Bradley since he is wearing an RF badge, but since badges do not provide strong authentication[1], Aura decides that the physical environment is no longer secure, and it iconifies Bob's e-mail client, thus hiding the confidential message that was being displayed.

Bradley drops by to work with Bob on a presentation that accompanies his project. Bob and Bradley continue to use voice control to navigate the PowerPoint presentation, but Bob uses the touch screen for modifications, while Bradley uses his PDA to annotate Bob's changes. When Bob and Bradley leave for lunch, Aura captures the state of the project and stores it on a server so it is ready to be restored wherever Bob decides to work on it next.

The current Aura prototype supports this scenario in a controlled environment. In the remainder of this paper we elaborate on the specific mechanisms used.

2.2   Overview of Aura

The motivating example shows some of the features of Aura. First, we want to support a rich set of I/O interfaces for users to interact with the computer system. This makes it possible to pick the most appropriate form of interaction for the job at hand (voice, keyboard/mouse, touchscreen, PDA). However, the change between modes of interaction should be seamless. Second, the system should be "context aware", i.e. it should know about the environment so it can automatically take appropriate actions, e.g. select the appropriate I/O device or hide confidential information. Third, the system has a notion of what the user is trying to achieve. In Aura this is explicitly

---

[1] RF badge identification is only effective if each individual is wearing an appropriate badge. We are extending Aura with video capabilities so we can detect people not wearing badges.

represented in the form of a task, which is a first class object. Finally, Aura has a number of goals that are not explicit in the example and that are not central to this paper. For example, applications in Aura automatically adapt to resource availability, e.g. by using servers if the cycles are not available locally. Similarly, QoS support can be used to improve predictability in a resource-poor environment.

Figure 1 shows the Aura architecture. The bottom layers are concerned with identifying and managing the resources in the computing and physical environment. This includes support for networking, including network monitoring [20], and node management. At a slightly higher level, Aura also supports intelligent information access through Coda [18] and Odyssey [18], and adaptive remote execution capabilities through Spectra [21]. The top of the picture represents user tasks and preferences. The combination of low level system input and high-level user input allows the Aura system to make decisions about what to do (what operations could be of help to the user) and how to do it (what I/O devices to use, what CPUs to use, etc.) In this paper, we focus on the middle layer, i.e. the application support, which ties the physical environment to the computing environment in the context of executing an everyday task, such as preparing a presentation.

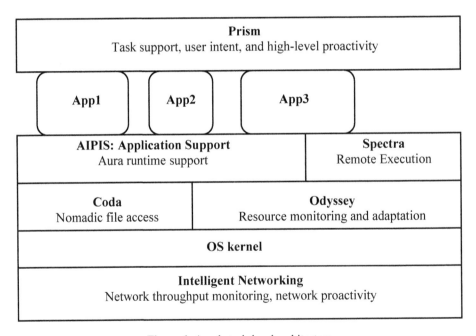

Figure 1. Aura's task-level architecture

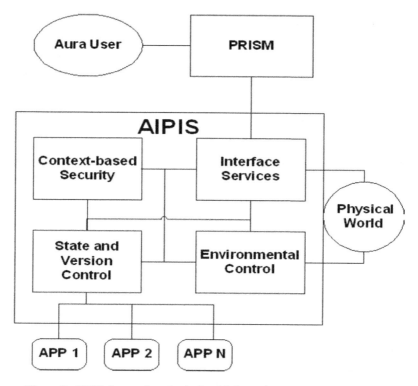

Figure 2. AIPIS: Integrating physical and information spaces

The application support component interacts with the physical environment in several ways:

- It has to handle I/O from a variety of devices and channel that information to the right application or to the system itself. Specifically, our prototype supports voice control, touch screen, and PDA input, besides the usual keyboard and mouse input.
- It channels input from sensors in the environment to applications that are interested in the information. In our current system, examples include input from badges, finger print readers, motion detectors, etc.

In the remaining sections, we describe how we coordinate the flow information between the physical environment and the computing systems.

3   Application Services

Aura is concerned with the automation of everyday tasks for the mobile user. This concept is distinct from application and application-bundle automation services that many vendors provide. For example, Microsoft provides common API's that allow the seamless transfer of information and control between application bundles, e.g. MS

Office. What is missing from these is a set of rich automation services that provide run-time support to applications such that they can leverage information provided by a task-level support engine, e.g. user intent and preference within the current context, the proactivity needed to support mobile users, and QoS support during infrastructure transitions.

3.1   AIPIS Architecture

The value of providing applications with a context-based or task-based mechanism for application support is well understood [4, 11, 8]. In Aura, task level support is provided by Prism. Prism provides support for saving and restoring of a task in different environments, where a task is a set of documents that are needed as a group to meet a certain goal. An early version of Prism for the Windows environment is described in [4]. Aura's Architecture for the Integration of Physical and Information Spaces, AIPIS, extends these results by providing task-focused, context-based run-time support to Aura aware applications and application bundles. The four fundamental blocks of AIPIS, shown if Figure 2, coordinate between the Aura task layer, Prism, and the individual applications to provide the following:

Application Interface Services. This component supports inter-application data exchange and control protocols. It is also responsible for the human-machine interface component.

Environment Control Services. This component realizes Aura's bridge from the information domain to the physical environment, e.g. lighting, temperature control, access control, external displays, etc.

Context-Based Security Services. This component provides an integrated control mechanism that provides context-aware access to physical, computational, and information-based resources.

State and Versioning Services. This component manages the allocation/de-allocation, transport, crash recovery, merging, and configuration of Aura aware applications.

The modules work in a loosely coupled, agent-based framework centered on the application interface, which monitors control input from the physical world, including user inputs, and the other AIPIS modules and provides this information to Aura's task-layer, Prism. An example of such information, provided by the security module, would be the privileges and identities of the set of known viewers of a presentation, which contains some classified data. The state and versioning module also provides to AIPIS the classification of each data set that is to be displayed in Aura, before it is displayed and also the current suite of information protection modes available within AIPIS, e.g. data hiding. The environmental module provides the set of devices, e.g. displays, physical locks, notifications, etc. that Aura can leverage to protect the data from the unauthorized viewers. The application interface aggregates this information and relays application, environmental state, context, and security information to Prism. These control signals are reconciled by Prism with attention to minimizing impact on the current task and routed to AIPIS through the Application Interface and on to versioning, environment, and security modules such that the appropriate actions are executed such that the classified data is not exposed to unauthorized viewers. For example, Prism could relay to AIPIS that sensitive data must not be shown in its current form to a subset of users without proper privilege. AIPIS's security module could then chose instruct the application to remove the data from the presentation, the environmental manager could be notified to switch displays, or the state manager instructed to terminate the application depending on the high-level direction from Prism.

3.2   Application Interface & Environmental Control

Application interface & environmental service modules provides a uniform access to input, output, and external control functions for Aura applications. The associated capability that any application can include for each of the managers provides is:

Application Input Manager. Speech recognition, handwriting recognition, gestures, eye tracking, data mining, etc.

Application Output Manger. Speech synthesis, display management, environmental settings, mobile messaging

The input manager coordinates a set of data sources that can provide input to applications. Input data is typed and data sources of the same type are basically indistinguishable from the perspective of the application. For example, keyboard input, speech synthesis, and handwriting recognition all provide ASCII input. Similarly, gesture recognition or eye tracking will provide input of type "location". The application input manager controls what input source is used for an application. This decision can be based on many factors, e.g. user preferences, availability of specific devices in the environment, explicit user specification, etc. Note that users can use a specific data source for input to several applications. For example, speech input can be used control PowerPoint, a mail client, and the OS (e.g. application selection). It is up the input manager to keep track of what application is active. We elaborate on this in the next section when we discuss our prototype.

The output manager has a similar role as the input manager, but it controls the output mode for applications. For example, it controls what display to use for screen output.

One can think of the data sources and output devices as I/O services. The input and output managers are basically responsible for deciding dynamically which I/O services applications should currently use based on user level and context information. They can on the fly reconfigure the I/O services as desired.

3.3   Context-Based Security & State and Versioning

The security issues in a pervasive computing environment are fundamentally different from those in a traditional distributed computing environment. The reason is that various ubiquitous I/O devices create new opportunities for privacy and security violations. For example, large touch screens provide a convenient way for users to interact with the system, but they make it easier for third parties to get unauthorized access to information. Similarly, speech synthesis can be a convenient output device, but it also similar privacy concerns.

Fortunately, devices can also help in addressing some of these new security and privacy risks. For example, fingerprint devices can provide convenient strong authentication while cameras, motion detectors, and badges can be used to identify the presence of other people. The challenge is to make this sensor information available to the applications that need it.

Security in Aura is concerned with access to resources, e.g. space, devices, applications, and data. The current instance of the security monitoring systems has three fundamental components that provide context-based security to Aura. They are:

Resource Monitor. Controls access to physical spaces, devices, and applications. Access to resources in AIPIS is usually provided by a challenge of the person requesting resources with a password or ID badge –based verification

Information Monitor. The information monitor provides the same level of protection for information that the resource monitor provides. The most advanced levels of security in Aura assume the lowest common denominator from the group that is to view Aura data and will employ data hiding or fuzzification to protect the release of unauthorized data to the group

Context-Monitor. AIPIS currently employees a simple context awareness that aggregates group permissions and then decides the optimal sub-set of resources that AIPIS is allowed to engage. In cases where security violations are present (sensitive data is exposed to unauthorized viewers), AIPS adapts resources and information to fit the current group security profile. The mechanisms employed are:

- *Display.* Transport and hiding
- *Input.* Mode suppression
- *Control.* Soft lockout of sensitive applications.

AIPIS uses an application state and transport mechanism that is described by Wang and Garlan in [4]. We describe how we use its capabilities in the next section.

4   Prototype Implementation: Aura Desktop

The Aura Desktop is a PC application that provides a hands-free gateway to many of the features and capabilities of an Aura environment, including AIPIS run-time support. In its current manifestation, the Aura Desktop provides voice-control of four common Microsoft applications, PowerPoint, Outlook, Word, and Excel. These applications support a wide range of documents. The user can also select from a suite of optional physical security devices including RF and IR tags, fingerprint readers, and context-based security services provided directly by AIPIS. Security options are configured during compilation. In addition, a context preserving mechanism is provided that allows users to maintain the state of applications across Windows machine boundaries, including PDAs, and infrastructure transitions thus enabling mobile users to work from any resource equipped with the Aura Desktop.

4.1   Application Interface & Environmental Control

Besides keyboard input and textual output on the screen, the Aura Desktop uses state-of-the-art speech recognition and synthesis to provide both application navigation capabilities and to provide feedback to the user in a hands free context. Speech recognition is accomplished using a native Sphinx II OCX [15] with a small dictionary. The top-level voice interface is designed to reliably provide the control of email and presentations at the expense of generality. This allows Bob to us voice control for working on this presentation in his office in the scenario of Section 2.1. Applications such as MS Word require continuous recognition with a much larger dictionary; they are currently not supported but they could be added easily to the AIPIS framework. Speech synthesis was implemented using a client/server implementation of the popular Festival speech synthesis system [16].   This is used to read back e-mail to Bob in the scenario of Section 2.1

The services provided to applications that leverage our voice-control interface are:

PowerPoint Services. The Aura Desktop implements speech-based presentation navigation, editing, and creation features such that drudgery of a large number of manual tasks associated with these capabilities is eliminated.

Document Archive. The Aura Desktop can be configured such that user documents (presentations, images, word and excel files, etc.) are stored in any network accessible file folder.

Outlook Services. The Aura Desktop provides the user with a voice-controlled interface to email as well. It also provides the ability to synthesize the email text and to recite each email to the user. In speech control mode, the user is freed to perform other tasks while sorting emails. In addition to recitation, a baseline set of sorting features is implemented.

Excel & Word. The Aura Desktop has minimal support in the form of (1) transport, (2) instantiation, (3) document hiding for security purposes, and (4) termination.

Digitized speech is provided asynchronously to the AIPIS application interface module from Sphinx. This speech is then parsed for clues relating to the application and the associated action(s) the user is trying to effect. Once application-context is decoded speech strings are sent to an application specific analysis routine that extracts any necessary data and action contexts from the string or inserts any implied data into the action sequence. For example, the integrated AIPIS application interface module may receive the command string, "Open the Aura Presentation" from the Sphinx OCX. AIPIS parses the string for context: (1) the presence of the keyword "presentation" implies PowerPoint is the application to use on a Windows system, and (2) from the keyword open in conjunction with the application context, AIPIS searches the set of known presentation directories for presentations that contain references to "Aura". AIPIS then selects the best match and engages the state and versioning module to transport the application to the appropriate combination of location, processor, and display.

For graphical input and mouse control, the Aura desktop also supports PowerPoint Commander and Pebbles interfaces [13, 14], besides the usual mouse and keyboard control. This makes it possible to support basic navigation and annotation of PowerPoint from a PDA. This mode of interaction is sometimes more appropriate than the keyboard and mouse mode, for example, when mobility is important such as during a presentation. In our scenario of Section 2.1, this allows Bob and Bradley to work together on a presentation using (besides voice) three different modes of interaction: keyboard and mouse, touch screen capabilities, and a handheld PDA. They can pick their most appropriate mode of interaction based on what operation they plan to perform and where they are physically present.

AIPIS makes extensive use of the Microsoft COM/D-COM interfaces to implement application control within the MS Office suite. Speech recognition and synthesis modules are controlled through a sockets-based interface using client/server architecture. In both cases, the implementation of the communication between applications in AIPIS resides in C++ wrapper classes such that details are hidden from the main AIPIS control loop.

4.2   Context-Based Security

AIPIS employs an integrated security mechanism that leverages passwords, RF-based authentication [17], motion detection, and finger print readers. The security module uses a two-tiered system for access where maximum access is provided by reliable security mechanisms such as passwords or fingerprint ID readers. The RF badge is treated strictly as a weak form of access that allows applications with sensitive information to be suppressed when a weak user is identified. For example, an accountant is reviewing a spreadsheet with current and recommended salaries for university staff. The Aura Desktop can be configured to automatically suppress (un-map it from the display) when an unauthorized employee enters the viewing space. This was also demonstrated in our scenario in Section 2.1. Since Bob used a fingerprint reader for authentication, so he had unlimited access to all information and applications. However, since Bradley was only identified using a badge (weak security), confidential information was hidden. Of course, once Bob recognizes Bradley, he can use the touch screen or voice control to display any information that he thinks is appropriate.

Security in AIPIS uses an asynchronous, event-driven scheme coupled with a security state matrix that encodes all the relevant relationships between user and application. For example, a user with weak access might be granted navigation privileges in PowerPoint, but would be blocked out from Outlook until he/she provides password or fingerprint ID. Each new event is decoded and the state matrix is updated. The security state vector for any affected application is then reconciled by taking an action that alleviates the violation, e.g. the email application is terminated and the unauthorized user is blocked from trying to access it.

A Security Warning Indicator (SWI), see Figure 3, is provided that warns the user when an unauthorized person has entered a private workspace. The SWI has hooks for the RF badge reader as well as external devices that the user might integrated, e.g. a video camera running motion detection, for example. Also, a text list of current users is displayed in the User Access Panel. In this panel, three levels of access are represented:

Maximum. The specified user has been authenticated through a physical device such as password or fingerprint ID. Full access to all Aura Desktop features is provided.

Weak. The specified user has been identified with an external authentication device such as RF/IR tags or video recognition. Access to a navigation features is provided.

Unauthorized. An unidentified or identified but unauthorized individual has entered a private workspace. No access to the Aura Desktop features is provided to that individual.

4.3   State and Versioning Support

Aura's current state services center on the task transport necessary to support a mobile user such that application state, including preferences and data, track the physical movement of the user through an Aura enabled space [4]. Users can define a task as a set of documents that belong together. Aura keeps track of the task state, including not only the contents of the documents, but also information such as cursor position and window layout. Aura can then restore the task on any Aura-capably Windows platform, using one of four applications (MS Word, Powerpoint, Excel, and Outlook) to handle the documents. Even the current prototype is restricted to Windows, this is already a powerful capability. For example in our scenario, Bob's tasks are automatically moved from his laptop to his office desktop system. Aura's state manager provides the seamless transition necessary, as application transport is trigger by movement in or out of Aura cells or user request. In the default case, Aura will try to maintain the default status of the user's computing environment as closely as it can across platform boundaries providing ubiquitous access to applications for the mobile user.

Work is in progress in extending task support so it works across heterogeneous platforms, e.g. Windows and Linux. This is a lot more challenging since often different applications may have to be used and document translation may be necessary.

4.4   GUI and Configuration

Figure 3 shows a screen shot of the Aura Desktop management GUI. It provides a fairly minimal interface for managing speech synthesis and security and it is designed primarily to support experimentation and evaluation.

Users can customize a remote Festival server with a favorite voice model by setting the IP address and port name in the "Festival Speech Synthesis Server IP Address" box (lower right corner of Figure 3). The Aura Desktop will then send all future synthesis requests to this preferred service provider.

Users can select the RF badge service by specifying its IP address in the lower left corner. The top of the window shows the security of the user's current physical context. The window in the middle lists all nearby users and their status. The rectangle in the top right hand corner turns red if any unauthenticated users are in the vicinity and is green otherwise.

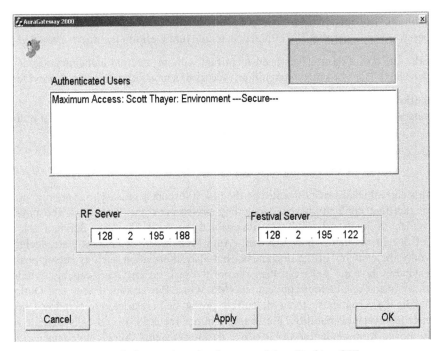

Figure 3. Screen shot of an instance of Aura Desktop GUI

5   Related Work

Besides Aura, a number of other projects are exploring pervasive computing. MIT's Project Oxygen aims to "communicate with people using natural resources, such as speech and vision", to support users on the move, and to monitor and control the environment [6,7]. Georgia Tech's InfoSphere endeavors to "achieve nothing less than radically enhancing human understanding through the use of information technology, by making it dramatically more convenient for people to interact with information, devices, and other people." They forward the idea of universal *Information Utility* and explore the architecture in areas of "rapid decision making" and learning. They define success in terms of the effectiveness of the "InfoSphere" to amplify human intellect [9]. University of Washington's Portolano project "seeks to create a test bed for investigation into the emerging field of invisible computing [10]. Aura is distinct from these efforts in that it seeks to service the needs of a mobile users engaged in everyday tasks as they move through infrastructures of varying quality.

This paper describes the infrastructure between Aura's task layer and the user applications that are registered within Aura. This infrastructure, AIPIS, provides context-based security, versioning, interface, and environmental services sufficient to coordinate the application base such the mobile user can continue to engage the world with relative independence from infrastructure.

6   Conclusions

We have presented an initial architecture and implementation of a system for hands-free computing that transforms the focus of computing architectures from application-based to task-based implementations. This is a critical first step in harnessing the tremendous potential of a truly human-centered approach to computing. In additional to a task bias, our architecture works to seamlessly integrate the physical-reality of humans and the information spaces that encode much of our identity, knowledge, and resources. Only with an efficient coordination of both physical and information domains can the full potential of computing be realized. We, as users, must be allowed to move throughout both the physical and information worlds with minimal constraints and burdens. Further, we require a personal infrastructure that is capable of taking maximal advantage of the modalities presented to us at each point in the physical-informational continuum such that we are empowered to engage tasks independent of location, bandwidth, and the chains of deskbound computing.

This Aura application architecture is a first step in the realization of ubiquitous, hands free, and mobile computing tailored to user needs. In this first implementation, both personal and desktop computing devices have been coordinated to automate a simple task level interface for the creation and delivery of presentation materials. This infrastructure utilizes speech-recognition and synthesis; MS PowerPoint, Word, and Excel; portable computing; personal location and identification services; and application transport software to generate the capability where a user working at a desktop computer can create and edit a presentation from a voice-driven interface. The user can then utilize the Aura infrastructure to tweak presentation material en route to the speaking engagement with either his personal computing resources or salient and Aura aware resources embedded in the environment. Upon arrival at the engagement, Aura will install an audience appropriate version of the presentation material and allow the user to navigate using a natural voice or PDA interface.

References

1.   Small, J., Smailagic, A., Siewiorek, D.,"Determining User Location For Context Aware Computing Through the Use of a Wireless LAN Infrastructure", December 2000
2.   Narayanan, D., Flinn, J., Satyanarayanan, M., "Using History to Improve Mobile Application Adaptation", Proceedings of the Third Workshop on Mobile Computing Systems and Applications, Monterey, CA, December 2000
3.   Satyanarayanan, M., "Caching Trust Rather Than Content", Operating Systems Review, Volume 34, No. 4, October 2000
4.   Wang, Z, Garlan, D. "Task-Driven Computing" Technical Report, CMU-CS-00-154, School of Computer Science, Carnegie Mellon University, May 2000
5.   http://www.cs.cmu.edu/~aura/
6.   http://oxygen.lcs.mit.edu
7.   Michael L. Dertouzos, "The future of computing", *Scientific American*, July 1999

8. Anind Dey and Gregory Abowd, "The Context Toolkit: Aiding the Development of Context-Aware Applications", IEEE 2000 International Conference on Software Engineering, Limerick, Ireland, June 6, 2000
9. http://endeavour.cs.berkeley.edu/
10. Esler, M., Hightower, J., Anderson, T., and Borriello, G. "Next Century Challenges: Data-Centric Networking for Invisible Computing: The Portolano Project at the University of Washington", Mobicom 1999
11. Dey, A.K., et. al. "The Conference Assistant: Combining context-awareness with wearable computing". Proceedings of the 3rd International Symposium on Wearable Computers (ISWC '99, pp. 21-28
12. Jim Waldo, "Mobile Code, Distributed Computing, and Agents", IEEE Intelligent Systems, pg. 10-12, Jan 2001
13. Brad A. Myers. "Using Multiple Devices Simultaneously for Display and Control." *IEEE Personal Communications*, Special issue on "Smart Spaces and Environments." vol. 7, no. 5, Oct. 2000. pp. 62-65
14. Brad A. Myers. "User Interface Software Tools," *ACM Transactions on Computer-Human Interaction*. vol. 2, no. 1, March, 1995. pp. 64-103
15. http://fife.speech.cs.cmu.edu/speech/sphinx/
16. http://www.cstr.ed.ac.uk/projects/festival/
17. http://www.versustech.com/
18. Braam, P. J.: The Coda Distributed File System, Linux Journal, Vol. 50, May 1999
19. Noble, Brain, System Support for Mobile, Adaptive Applications, IEEE Personal Communications, Vol. 7, No. 1, Feb. 2000
20. DeWitt, T. Gross, B. Lowekamp, N. Miller, P. Steenkiste, J. Subhlok, and D. Sutherland: *"ReMoS: A Resource Monitoring System for Network-Aware Applications"* Carnegie Mellon School of Computer Science, CMU-CS-97-194
21. Jason Flinn, Dushyanth, Narayanan, and M. Satyanarayanan, *"Self-Tuned Remote Execution for Pervasive Computing"*, Proceedings of the 8th Workshop on Hot Topics in Operating Systems (HotOS-VIII), Schloss Elmau, Germany, May 2001

A Context System for a Mobile Service Platform

Fritz Hohl[1], Lars Mehrmann[2], and Amen Hamdan[1]

[1]Sony International (Europe) GmbH, Advanced Technology Center Stuttgart
Heinrich-Hertz-Str. 1, 70327 Stuttgart. Germany
{hohl,hamdan}@sony.de
[2]Siemens AG, Corporate Technology, Software and Systems Architectures, CT SE 2
Otto-Hahn-Ring 6, 81730 Munich, Germany
Lars.Mehrmann@mchp.siemens.de

Abstract. The possibilities that can be achieved by context information, especially the location of mobile users, might lead to the attractive new mobile services technologies like UMTS desperately look for in order to foster the user demand for 3G networks. The EU IST research project "YOUNGSTER" is developing a mobile services platform that will employ a context subsystem that is able to handle (i.e. gather, process, store, and deploy) not only location information, but the whole variety of user context information in a generic way. In this article, the requirements of a mobile services platform for a context system and the design of this context subsystem are described.

1   Introduction

In order for the investments of several telecom operators in UMTS to pay off, a large number of customers have to be willing to periodically spend a considerable amount of money for the upcoming, new services. To this end these 3G services have to provide a significant benefit to the already available GSM or Internet based services. This can only be achieved if new mobile services are offered to the customers, services that are both attractive to a large number of people and that require the special abilities of UMTS. Apart from the promised ability of UMTS to being able to allow broadband multimedia access, especially personalization and location-awareness seem to be the most promising approaches that could enable these attractive services.

The European Union funded project "Youngster" [YOU01] is targeting these two aspects and focuses especially on a user-centric approach. The aim of Youngster is twofold. First, an innovative, open active Mobile Service Platform (MSP) will be developed that offers:

- accessibility from anywhere by a wide range of devices and networks
- personalized and highly adaptive delivery of services
- support of community functions
- support of context-aware features (including location-awareness)

H. Schmeck, T. Ungerer, and L. Wolf (Eds.): ARCS 2002, LNCS 2299, pp. 21-33, 2002.
© Springer-Verlag Berlin Heidelberg 2002

Second, a new generation of enhanced mobile services will be developed using the Mobile Service Platform. As the aimed target group consists of young people, the implemented services will be specifically tailored to the need of youngsters. As it can be anticipated that the current business models will not be ideal for the target group, new business models will be examined, as young people cannot afford premium services. To verify the services and the platform a field test will be conducted in Norway. The results of the trials will be evaluated and success will be assessed in terms of the response of the young people who participate and the use that they make of the services. The Youngster consortium consists of the Heriot-Watt-University (United Kingdom), NRK (Norway), Siemens (Germany), Sony (Germany), Steria (France), Telenor (Norway), and T-Systems (Germany).

As personalization relies on context information and location-awareness is in fact a form of context usage, one focus of the Youngster project lies on mechanisms to support gathering, storing, and deployment of context information for usage in a mobile services platform. In this article, the architecture of this context subsystem, TCoS, will be presented.

Although the general structure of the context subsystem is rather similar to the Context Toolkit approach (see [Dey00]), some differences exist that result mainly from of the intended usage area, the mobile service platform. While the Context Toolkit stemmed from a framework approach that intends to help an application to use context data (and is, therefore, part of the application), the Trivial Context System (TCoS) is a *context service*. A context service is an autonomous component that also can be used by any application, but that exists independently of the application. To allow a 24/7-type of operation, our architecture supports a dynamic association of sensors to the processing infrastructure as well as an automatic configuration of this infrastructure. As context data might be security and privacy sensitive, and as a mobile service platform intended for commercial use has to cope with the fears of the users, an access control component ensures that only authorized parties are able to access context data. Finally, our system supports the access also to past context data.

The rest of this article is structured as follows. The next section will examine the context concept and present a classification of context data. In the next section, the requirements will be listed that result from the usage of a context system in a mobile service platform. Then, the components of the context system architecture are presented. Related work is presented in the next section. The last section concludes the article and gives s brief overview over future work.

2   Context

A recent definition of context is due to [DA99] who defined it as "any information that can be used to characterize the situation of an entity, where an entity can be a person, place, physical or computational object". From this point of view, almost all information that occurs in the context of a specific system usage can be subsumed under the term "context" (e.g. the current time and date, the usage history, the user profile, the temperature at the user location, the position of the user, etc. pp.). Following on from this, context can be used in several areas in context-aware applications, including:

- presenting the context information itself as content to the user (e.g. a map showing the current position)
- adapting of presentation of information and services to a user (e.g. a GUI suitable for the mobile phone the user is using currently)
- triggering actions on the occurrence of a context "constellation"
- tagging context to information for later retrieval (e.g. weather information when taking a picture in order to let the photo lab adjust the development process)

While the term *context* denotes the set of all information characterizing the situation of a *focus entity*. The single context unit can be called *context element*, i.e. all context elements relating to a focus entity form the context of that entity. Context elements have a *context type* which characterizes the context element. Context elements occur in a certain context *format*, which denotes the structure of the context data at the surface.

The component of a mobile service platform that deals with context is called the *context service* or *context system*.

2.1   Classification of Context Data

Context data can be grouped into two pairs of excluding categories. These pairs are (entity-defined/system-defined data) and (constant/dynamic data).

Entity-defined data denote context data the focus entity can specify to adapt something to its wishes or abilities. Preferences change when the focus entity wishes to change them. *System-defined data* denotes context data that the system determines concerning the focus entity. This includes environmental data of the focus entity such as the location or the time at the location as well as the current areas of interest the system deduces from the documents the user accessed. One aspect of the distinction entity-/system-defined is that it does not apply to context data by nature, but by choice. The user e.g. might be able to specify his/her age, but this information might also be derived by other data by the system.

Constant data denotes context data that never (or only rarely) changes, e.g. the age of a user, his/her gender, the display resolution of a PDA, etc. In contrast to constant data, *dynamic data* changes frequently (like the location of the focus entity). In contrast to the distinction entity-/system defined, the distinction constant/dynamic applies to context data by the nature of this data.

Obviously the two pairs are orthogonal. Nevertheless, it is more likely for entity-defined context to be constant data as it is more likely for system-defined data to be dynamic. Constant system-defined context might also occur as it allows to determine constant data the entity does not specify. Dynamic entity-defined context also sometimes occurs (e.g. when a user enters his/her current location manually), and it helps to deal with the case that no sensors are available to sense certain context data, but this mode of operation normally is unsatisfying.

Most context-awareness approaches consider only the present context of the focus entity. A more general approach might also consider *past* context situations. Past context data might include e.g. the history of services a human user used.

3   Requirements for a Context System by a Mobile Service Platform

While the Context Toolkit ([Dey00]) supports applications that use context information, our approach is to be used as a part of a certain mobile service platform. In this section, the additional requirements of this platform towards the context system compared to the requirements described in [Dey00] will be briefly described.

In contrast to a general application, a service implies that some functionality is generated from a service provider for a service client (by using a system of a platform operator). In an environment where three and more parties interact, often (maybe not always) commercial aspects play a crucial role. Therefore, one requirement is to let the platform operate without the need of interruption due to minor events such as the availability of a new sensor. This means for the context system that is has cope with a rather dynamic environment (due to its extended operating time) where sensors connect and disconnect, where context of new focus entities needs to be supported, and so on, without the need of restarting the system.

As one of the aspects of the Youngster project is to support networked sensors, also the ability to cope with sensors that change as e.g. the user moves, needs to be supported.

To support the broadest range of mobile services, a context processing infrastructure is needed that is both modular, flexible, and that can be configured without manual work by a programmer.

Systems where context data producer, context data consumer, context data processors and focus entities are different parties have to cope with the fear of the focus entities to misuse their context data. Therefore an additional requirement is to allow both a working (i.e. technically sound) and user-controllable possibility to control the access to context data that is still easy to use even for non-technicians.

Finally, not only actual, but also past context needs to be supported as there are services that require this information, but which shall not bear the burden of having to implement this functionality themselves.

After having described the requirements, we will now have a look at an architecture that satisfies these needs.

4   The Components of TCoS

In the Trivial Context System (TCoS) the following components are used (see

Figure 1).

4.1   Context Servers

The context system consists of several context servers. A context server offers context data related to a number of focus entities. Therefore, it is necessary to find the corresponding context servers that store context data of a certain focus entity. This is done by means of a *context server lookup service*.

Context servers get context data from a number of sensors. Context clients query a context server for context data related to certain context entities. To ensure access control, an access controller unit accepts or rejects queries by the context clients. When an application queries the value of a context attribute and the access control accepts the query, the corresponding value is returned. Likewise the context client is informed when it subscribed for a certain context attribute when the value changes.

4.2   Context Attributes

Context attributes store single context elements. When an attribute is created, an infrastructure is generated by the Path Builder that connects the attribute logically with one or more sensors. This infrastructure allows later on context data to be delivered to the attribute. Context Attributes receive context data either from components called Context Sources or from components called Context Interpreters.

4.3   Context Clients

Context clients are the components that want to access context information on context servers. These clients can be application services, but also other components of the mobile service platform. Context clients are able to:

- create/delete context attributes inside context servers
- query context servers for context information related to a certain focus entity
- feed context attributes with certain information

Context clients are able to query context data either in a request-response or a publish-subscribe manner.

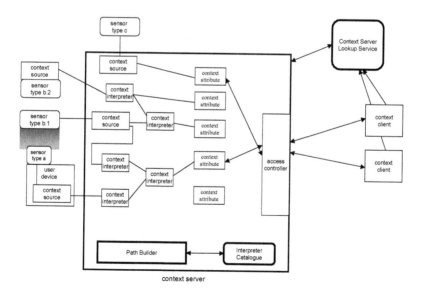

Figure 1. Context system components

4.4   Access Controller

To ensure the controllability of context information access, an *Access Controller* ensures that only authorized context clients can access context information. The access policy can be controlled by the focus entity of an attribute (or, if this entity is not a human, by the user that is allowed to manage the attribute). Although full control is possible, most users will probably not specify the complete access policy in detail, but use prefabricated policy templates.

4.5   Sensors

Sensors are either physical devices or logical entities that sample data such as the location of a device or the schedule of a human user. Sensors might be attached to the entity about which context data is collected (type a), e.g. GPS sensors that sense the position of a device. Other sensors (type b) might be part of the physical environment, thus sensing environmental data. Sensors of type b can be subdivided into type b.1 sensors that sense context when asked by a focus entity itself (e.g. a mobile device might ask an active badge [WFG91] system to track its position) and type b.2 sensors that operate when a party asks them to do so. Finally, sensors might be located elsewhere (type c), sensing context data like the schedule of the user. These sensors might be part of the mobile service platform (e.g. in the case of type c sensors), or might be located outside the platform. To insert user context data that exists in the service portal for administrative reasons (e.g. user profile data and the service usage history), normally, type c sensors are used that are connected to the corresponding platform components.

4.6   Context Sources

Normally, sensors do not issue context data in a format the context system can process. Therefore, a component is needed that translates the sensor-specific format into a format that is understood by the context system (this translation does not need to be a format conversion, but might be adding just some metadata, e.g. about the used format). Additionally this component represents the sensor in the context system. This component is called *context source*. Context sources can be located either on the same device the sensor is attached to (if this device allows to add such a component) or on a context server, thus allowing the sensor system to be used without modification.

In case that a Context Source is located on a Context Server, there might be a rather dynamic set of sensors that are connected to a Context Source. Either there are several sensors that work in parallel delivering data of the same context type and format (e.g. a GPS sensor and a GSM-based location sensor), or the sensor changes over time, e.g. because the user is moving. This latter case occurs when e.g. thermometers are used that are installed in different rooms.

Context sources deliver their data either directly to a certain context attribute or to an intermediate component, the context interpreter.

4.6.1   Finding Sensors

Although in most cases sensors simply deliver data to a Context Attribute via a Context Source, it might be the case that the Context Source is sometimes asked to deliver context data. This might happen when a user moved or when no data exists inside a Context Attribute. In this case, the Context Source has to contact a corresponding sensor to get data. In case there is a 1-to-1 connection between a sensor and a Context Source, the latter might be able to contact the sensor directly. Sometimes, the Context Source has first to find an appropriate sensor in order to contact it (especially for type b.2 sensors). If the sensors cover a certain geographic area, they can be found using the Global Area Service Directory and the current position of e.g. a mobile user. In this case, a Context Source can be also a context client, consuming location information.

4.7   Context Interpreters

Context interpreters are components that take context data from one or more context sources or other context interpreters, process the context data and issue new context data. Context sources and Interpreters offer the same interface, so they can be "plugged together" in an arbitrary manner.

Context interpreters can be used for various purposes. Format converting interpreters transform context data into a new format. The semantic of the context remains (mainly) the same. Selecting interpreters take two or more data elements and choose one of them. This can be used e.g. to issue the most exact location by considering location information from a number of sources. Combining interpreters take two or more data elements and combine them into one new data Deriving interpreters finally consider one or more data elements and derive or infer a new data element of a higher order. A classical example is an interpreter that tries to determine whether a meeting takes place in a room by considering a motion detection sensor and a microphone sensor detecting voice frequencies.

Interpreter structures are created by the Path Builder component.

4.8   Path Builder

When a Context Attribute is created, the Path Builder seeks Context Sources that are able to deliver the needed information (i.e. that claim to offer data that fits into certain context data schemes). If such a Context Source exists, i.e. is already running in the Context server, the Attribute is simply connected to the Source. This means that the source delivers future data also to the new Attribute. If not Context Source exists, another component, the Interpreter Catalogue is consulted. This component offers also descriptions of possible Context Sources that can be installed on demand. If one of these descriptions fit into the context data scheme, the corresponding Context Source is installed into the Context Server and connected to the corresponding Context Attribute. It might be the case rather often that there are no Context Sources that are able to satisfy the need of a Context Attribute. For this case, the Path Builder seeks Context Interpreters to build a path from a Context Source via a chain of Context Interpreters to the Context Attribute. For doing that, a scheme similar to the one used in Ninja (see [GWB00]) is used. In every step (trying to find the next Interpreter), it is checked whether the corresponding Context Interpreter already exists in the system or can be installed from the Interpreter Catalogue.

4.8.1   Context Data Schemes

A context data scheme consists of at least three parts: the specification of the focus entity, the context type and the format of the data. The focus entity is important because there might be sensors that deliver data only for a specific entity. This is especially true for type a sensors, as they are attached to a user device. An example for such a sensor is the GPS sensor connected to a PDA. The context type specifies the "semantic" value of a context element. Context types establish class hierarchies like in object-oriented systems (like 1D position - 2D position - 3D position). If a context type class is specified, context data qualify if they are of this class or a subclass. Additionally, multiple inheritance for context type classes is allowed as sensors e.g. might deliver data that does not relate to each other (there are e.g. digital compasses that deliver the heading, but also the temperature and the roll angle).

The context format finally specifies the structure of the context data. Typically, there are different formats for the same context type. One example is location data that can occur as WGS84- or as Gauss-Krueger-formatted data.

Context data schemes are used both to specify the need of Context Attributes and Context Interpreters as well as to define the data that can be delivered by Context Sources and Context Interpreters. Obviously, some of these components are able to offer data that fit into a whole number of context data schemes, e.g. GSM network-based location services that allow to locate a lot of mobile users. In this case, the corresponding part of the context data scheme can be specified as "any value".

4.9   Event Management

On a context server, context clients can subscribe for events, so they are informed in case the event happens. The occurrence of these events is checked if one of the participating Context Attributes changes its value. The "basic events" that occur during the operation of a context server are:

- changes in the value of a context attribute (either any changes or such that overstep a certain threshold)
- the connection/disconnection of a new sensor
- the creation/deletion of a context attribute
- the occurrence/deletion of a context interpreter or source in the Interpreter Catalogue

5   Sample Applications

In this section we will present three sample applications that illustrate the benefit of our context system.

5.1   Context-Aware Answering Machine

Often, an answering machine shall be turned on as soon as the last person leaves the house. Unfortunately, humans sometimes forget to do this. An answering machine that has a connection to the context system of the house can subscribe for being informed when the last person leaves and then turn on itself.

5.2   Shopping List Reminder

In order to remind a person to buy needed goods, a service uses the event mechanism of a context system to notify this person as soon as he/she approaches a certain shop when it offers the needed goods and is open. This notification can be sent to any device of this person, a mobile phone, a PDA, a car radio, even a video camera using a wireless connection.

5.3   Context-Aware Video Camera

Metadata for audio and video recordings is getting more and more important. A video camera that is able to access the context systems of surrounding devices via Bluetooth can store any context data along the recording, like the location and heading of the camera, the names of the persons that appear in the recording, etc.

6   Security and Privacy

Security and privacy aspects occur at different areas in the context system. The relevant questions are:

1. *Which context server is allowed to access sensor data?*

    From a sensor's point of view, context servers are information sinks (i.e. clients). If this context data relates to a human person, this person might want to control who can access this information (like he/she wants to control which application can access context information at the context server). Here, either a general trust model can be used (like the assumption that every user has to trust the platform), or the person authorizes single context servers (e.g. the one that is employed by this person). If a sensor is attached to a user device (e.g. a thermometer), this information can relate to that user implicitly ("Where have you been last night? You told me that you stay overnight at a schoolmate, but the temperature at your device was about 0 C on 3am...").

    Another aspect is that the owner of a sensor (e.g. a thermometer owner) might want to control the access to his/her sensor (e.g. for commercial reasons).

2. *Can we achieve for type b.1 sensors that the sensor does not have the knowledge about the identity of the tracked entity?*

    This can be done by using random, temporary entity identifiers. The relation of these identifiers to the global entity names is known only to the entity and the Context Server, but not to the sensor.

3. *How to protect the transport of sensor data from sensors to context servers if done via an insecure network?*

While context data are transported from sensors to context servers, sometimes insecure networks might be used. Therefore, it is necessary to protect these data from being read by an attacker, from being modified, and from being inserted. This can be achieved by means of traditional public-key cryptography.

4. *Which context client is allowed to access context data on a context server?*

Already discussed in the section about the Access Controller.

5. *How to protect the transport of context data from context servers to context clients if done via an insecure network?*

While Context Clients might be located most often on the same computer as the Context Server, sometimes the two components might want to communicate remotely being located on different machines. In this case, the same problem occurs as for sensors that have to submit context data to remote Context Servers. Therefore, the same mechanisms can be used.

6. *Do we reveal already too much information by returning the corresponding context server when queried using the name of a focus entity in the Context Server Lookup Service?*

This might be perhaps a very specific question. Nevertheless, such an information can be used to e.g. harm the Context Server containing context about a certain focus entity by using a Denial-of-Service attack.

7   Related Work

Currently, only a small number of architectures exist that aim at providing generic context support for applications. In this section, we will shortly present three of them and the relation of our context architecture to their approaches.

7.1   Telenor Context Architecture

The context architecture (see [BMU00]) proposed by the Norwegian telecom operator Telenor is based on code mobility and tuple space technologies. This approach differs from ours in the fact that this system supports applications on mobile devices whereas our architecture is focused on supporting services that run on a mobile service platform.

7.2   CHANSE

CHANSE (Context Handling Architecture for Networking Service Environment, see [NMI00]) is a general architecture that supports applications that need access to context information. Compared to our approach CHANSE offers the more detailed context model and incorporates various components to match the context data specification with the context data offered by sensors. While the distribution structure of CHANSE employs a single central server that mediates context data requests, our approach uses a single mediation point per focus entity. Finally, we employ an easier context model and an easier component structure.

7.3   Context Fabric

A recent paper ([HL01]) argues why an "infrastructure" approach of context support offers advantages over the "library" approach of the Context Toolkit and describes five challenges for building such an infrastructure. Our approach in fact is an infrastructure according to the definition in [HL01] and tackles these five challenges, e.g. by offering an automatic path creation.

7.4   Context Toolkit

The Context Toolkit (see [Dey00]) is an architecture that allows applications to access an open number of context sensors in an uniform manner. This is achieved by having a generic abstraction of a context sensor, the so-called Context Widget (see Figure below). Aggregators allow to bundle context information which relate to a particular entity, e.g. a person. Finally, interpreters allow to deduce information out of a number of context information provided by an application or Context Widget. The deduced information is returned to the component (i.e. application or widget) that called the interpreter.

Our architecture is in some aspects very similar to the Context Toolkit approach (in fact we tried to use the same terms for components that have the same functionality). The main differences of our approach to the Context Toolkit are the dynamic association of sensors to the processing infrastructure, the automatic configuration of this infrastructure, the access control component, and the access also to past context data.

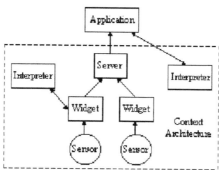

Figure 2. Components of the Context Toolkit Architecture [DA99]

8   Conclusion & Outlook

In this article, the design of a context system architecture for the mobile service platform of the Youngster project was presented. To that end, we first examined the context concept and presented a classification of context data. The requirements were listed that result from the usage of a context system in a mobile service platform. Then, the components of the context system architecture were presented. Finally, the existing work was presented and related to the presented approach.

Conceptually, the context system stores context data only, but as "context" is more an agreement than a natural attribute, the system presented in this article can be used to store also other, e.g. constant data.

The context system, of which the design was presented here, is partially implemented for the mobile service platform of the Youngster project and will be finished in early 2002. Afterwards it will be used to implement some context-aware mobile services that will be evaluated in a field test in Norway.

In a later stage, extensions of the context data schemes by more parameters of a context type will be examined and probably incorporated. These parameters (e.g. accuracy, level-of-detail and cost) will allow to select context data sources in a finer granularity.

9   References

[BMU00] Bygdås, Sigrid; Malm, Pål; Urnes, Tore: A Simple Architecture for Delivering Context Information to Mobile Users. Position Paper at [IFSD00], 2000

[DA99]   Dey, A.K. & Abowd, G.D.: Towards a better understanding of context and context-awareness. GVU Technical Report GIT-GVU-99-22, College of Computing, Georgia Institute of Technology. (ftp://ftp.cc.gatech.edu/pub/gvu/tr/1999/99-22.pdf), 1999

[Dey00] Dey, Anind: Providing Architectural Support for Building Context-Aware Applications. PhD thesis, College of Computing, Georgia Institute of Technology, December 2000. http://www.cc.gatech.edu/fce/ctk/pubs/dey-thesis.pdf

[GWB00] Gribble, Steven ; Welsh, Matt ; von Behren, Rob ; Brewer, Eric ; Culler, David ; N. Borisov, S. Czerwinski, R. Gummadi, J. Hill, A. Joseph, R.H. Katz, Z.M. Mao, S. Ross, and B. Zhao. The Ninja Architecture for Robust Internet-Scale Systems and Services. To appear in a Special Issue of Computer Networks on Pervasive Computing.

[HKL99] Hohl, Fritz; Kubach, Uwe; Leonhardi, Alexander; Rothermel, Kurt; Schwehm, Markus: "Next Century Challenges: Nexus - An Open Global Infrastructure for Spatial-Aware Applications", Proceedings of the Fifth Annual ACM/IEEE International Conference on Mobile Computing and Networking (MobiCom'99), Seattle, Washington, USA, August 15-20, 1999, T. Imielinski, M. Steenstrup, (Eds.), ACM Press, 1999, pp. 249-255.

[HL01]   Hong, Jason I.; Landay, James A.: An Infrastructure Approach to Context-Aware Computing. In Human-Computer Interaction, 2001, Vol. 16, 2001

[IFSD00] Abstracts and Slides of the "Workshop on Infrastructure for Smart Devices - How to Make Ubiquity an Actuality". Web page. http://www.inf.ethz.ch/vs/events/HUK2kW/

[LK99]   Leonhardi, Alexander; Kubach, Uwe: "An Architecture for a Universal, Distributed Location Service", Proceedings of the European Wireless '99 Conference, Munich, Germany, pp. 351-355, ITG Fachbericht, VDE Verlag, 1999.

[NMI00] Nakamura, Tetsuya; Matsuo, Nakamura; Itao, Tomoko. Context Handling Architecture for Adaptive Networking Services. Proceedings of the IST Mobile Summit 2000

[WFG91] R. Want, V. Falcao, and J. Gibbons. The active badge location system. ACM Transactions on Information Systems, 10(1):91-102, 1991.

[YOU01] The Youngster Consortium. Public web page of the project Youngster. http://www.ist-youngster.org/

Detecting Context
in Distributed Sensor Networks
by Using Smart Context-Aware Packets

Florian Michahelles[1], Michael Samulowitz[2], and Bernt Schiele[1]

[1] Perceptual Computing and Computer Vision Group, ETH Zurich
http://www.vision.ethz.ch/pccv
[2] Corporate Technology, Siemens AG
Otto-Hahn-Ring 6, 81730 Munich, Germany

Abstract. Context modeling and detection will play a major role for pervasive computing. This paper proposes an approach to reveal the user's context in a self-organized sensor network without a central point of control. A uniform communication scheme, referred to as *Smart Context-Aware Packet*'s (*sCAP*'s), allows single sensors to share sensed data and to cooperate in order to build a meaningful context model from manifold inputs. In this approach, *sCAP*'s are injected into the sensor network by the context inquirer. In particular, *sCAP*'s contain a retrieving plan specifying which types of sensors should be visited to obtain the desired context information. The paper concentrates on the routing concepts which allow to deal with breakdowns of sensor nodes and continuous changes of the network topology.

1 Introduction

Processors and sensors are becoming smaller, cheaper, less power consuming, unobtrusive, and perhaps even invisible. Consequently, computing resources and devices metamorphose to a matter of course, vanish to the background and blend one in another. Several computing paradigms can be envisioned. The notion of proactive computing for example [ ] assumes, that humans get out of the interaction loop but get serviced specifically according to their needs. Or, a shift from explicit to implicit human-computer interaction may be achieved [ ] by using the context, the task and the user situation directly as input to the system.

Often, users desire to access computing resources anytime and anywhere in an ubiquitous [ ] manner without restricting their mobility. Users want to get supported in everyday tasks by manifold services tailored to their specific needs. We argued in [ ] that services should be aligned to the user's task. In particular, the system should independently discover and execute services considering the user's context [ ]. Therefore, services should be offered in a user-centric way.

The vision of pervasive computing [ ] poses several important research issues. Challenges such as service discovery and interface description have been partly solved by various discovery protocols as JINI [ ], IETF SLP [ ], SDS [ ],

H. Schmeck, T. Ungerer, and L. Wolf (Eds.): ARCS 2002, LNCS 2299, pp. 34–17, 2002.
© Springer-Verlag Berlin Heidelberg 2002

abstract devices [ ], among others. Another challenge is context-aware service provision which goes beyond location based services. More general context detection as well as context modeling is still at an unsatisfying stage. Applying multiple distributed sensors for revealing context [ ] is still in its infancy.

Advances in wireless networking, microfabrication (e.g. MEMS [ ]) facilitate a new generation of large sensor networks [, ,]. Application of those sensors networks range from tracking and identification to sensing applications. Thus, deploying large numbers of sensors in everyday environments becomes feasible. Those sensors might be used for context detection.

Today, research in wireless sensor networks [ ] mainly focuses on power consumption and routing. In this work we want to go beyond that. We propose an approach of exploiting manifold sensors attached to everyday devices, referred to as Smart-Its [ ], for revealing the user's context. Often [ ] sets of sensors are treated as a black box. This paper describes a uniform communication scheme, by which many sensors can share sensed data among them. Context detection and routing takes place in a self-organized sensor network without requiring a central point of control. In our approach, so-called *Smart Context-- Aware Packet*'s (*sCAP*'s) are injected onto a sensor network. The packets are governed by an enclosed *retrieving plan*, specifying which sensors to visit for gaining a specific piece of context information. The underlying routing concept is capable to deal with breakdowns of individual nodes and with changes of the network topology. This paper mainly focuses on these routing issues.

The next section motivates the problem of context detection. We present our vision of pervasive computing and sensor networks, talk about benefits to humans, and describe several scenarios. Section 3 summarizes the general concept of our packet oriented *sCAP* approach. This is followed by a discussion and detailed presentation of the *Smart Stack Routing* (*SSR*). Finally, the approach is summarized and an outlook is given.

2   Problem Statement

This section gives a motivation to the problem we address with this work. For common understanding, first we present our vision of a pervasive environment. Secondly we motivate the role of users in these environments and give a short overview on scenarios.

2.1   The Envisioned Environment

We envision a pervasive environment instrumented with computing empowered sensors [ ], so-called Smart-Its [ ]. A large number of those autonomous units form a wireless sensor network [ ] with distributed processing capabilities. Due to wireless communication, the sensor network can be easily deployed. Accordingly, single sensors are close to the phenomena, which should be monitored by the network.

In particular, the Smart-Its are attached to everyday devices such as cups, tables, chairs etc.; they can be equipped with various sensors for perceiving a range of inputs as temperature, light, audio, co-location, movement and so on. The sensor units deliver defined abstractions of sensed information as simple feature values (loudness, brightness, speed...).

Further, these tiny devices are supplied with a wireless communication such as RF or Bluetooth [ ]. Accordingly, the connectivity of the network is constrained by the reach of wireless communication.. Due to the fact of mobile nodes and incremental addition and removal, the communication quality may be weak and encounter intermittent disconnection. The stability of the network is unpredictable.

An on board micro-controller provides computing power and enables simple feature calculation from the sensors inputs. These features, loudness, brightness, speed, temperature etc., are described by discrete number values. The envisioned Smart-Its operate autonomously with no central point of control, there is no directory service giving information about the sensors available in the current environment. Cooperation among sensor nodes is a general goal, as streamlining the activity of several nodes can increase performance of the entire network. Each device is self-aware, such that it knows about its own sensing capabilities and can report those, if inquired, to its neighbors.

Finally, there exist two different types of globally unique identifiers: one for distinguishing Smart-It units, the other one for distinguishing types of feature values Smart-Its are capable to deliver.

2.2   Bringing the User into the Play: Scenarios for Context-Awareness

The Smart-Its environment as described above is predestined for mobile computing [ ]. Combining the output of manifold sensors, which are deployed in the environment, can be used for revealing the user's current context [ ]. By making use of the term context, it is important for us to go beyond pure location awareness but taking more meaningful measures as the semantic proximity hierarchy [ ] into account. Context may be used as an invocation context for configuring services the user intends to access. This section gives a brief overview on how (mobile) users may benefit from our environment.

Smart Chemical Lab In today's biology laboratories information is both created and consumed at the lab bench. As workers are focused on the their task at hand, currently it is extremely tedious to interface with computer at the same time. On the other hand, biologists need to access and disseminate information in digital form, which is performed in a traditional office. The vision of a smart chemical lab, as Labscape [ ], might bridge the gap between today's laboratories and traditional offices. In the **Smart Chemical Lab** embedded technology is available in a pervasive way, such that the process of experiments can be observed, recorded, and triggered in a flexible manner. Facilities in the lab may be equipped with Smart-Its, which have the potential to assist biologists in laboratory work and promote new forms of collaboration.

Smart Warehouse Factory warehouses can become smart [ ], such that items are located automatically, tracked for location history or significant changes in inventory levels are reported. This information could be further processed in consecutive steps, such as revealing long-term correlations between workflows. In smart environment approaches as [ ] sensors are attached to infrastructure such as walls, or embedded in floors and ceilings. We rather focus on the stocking items themselves and want to make them become smart. Then, these items themselves can perceive characteristics of their stock environment, can sense their neighbors and further maintain their stocking history: the items are self-aware. Based on that information the items themselves can alert wether they are going to expire or dangerous conditions occur, such as chemicals get too close to each other or environmental conditional are getting hazardous. The full sensor network based system provides valuable data about the entire warehouse. But in contrast to common systems working with identifier tags where one central server owns the entire information, in our approach the information is distributed among the goods. The goods are self-aware.

Support-System for Individual Drivers As individual traffic is constantly raising, support systems for individual drivers are needed. Attaching smart-its to vehicles could provide different aspects of information, such as location, vehicle size and speed. State of the art systems collect and process the data in a central unit. The support system we are envisioning could calculate traffic densities, plan alternate routes, estimate trip times locally at each vehicle and warn of hazardous driving conditions. When vehicles pass each other they could exchange this information. Based on local communication the application would scale as the number of vehicles grows. In contrast to central server concepts where information would be derived in one place, we believe that collecting and processing data at the individual car would lead to more immediate feedback tailored to the driver's needs.

3   Revealing Context
Using *Smart Context-Aware Packet*'s

As this paper builds on top of the notion of *Smart Context-Aware Packet*'s (*sCAP*'s) [ ], this section summarizes the main concepts of those packets and motivates why a special routing scheme will be needed.

3.1   The Concept of *Smart Context-Aware Packet*'s

In contrast to mobile code concepts as [ ] ours is more lightweight. *sCAP*'s do not feature the mobile code concept, *sCAP*'s are passive packets. Our concept is a

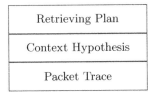

Fig. 1. Decomposition of a *Smart Context-Aware Packet*

document-based approach [ ], as *sCAP*'s act as passive containers for collecting feature values from manifold sensors.

As Figure 1 depicts, an *sCAP* document is organized into three parts: **retrieving plan**, **context hypothesis**, **packet trace**. The **retrieving plan** embodies the execution plan that determines the sensor types being involved into the context detection. It describes which types of sensors have to be queried for revealing the current context. Due to single sensor percepts this **retrieving plan** can be continuously refined at each receiving sensor unit, such that the detection process can adapt to the actual sensor inputs.

The **context hypothesis** is represented by the accumulation of feature values retrieved from several sensors. At dedicated units in the sensor network the value set of the **context hypothesis** can be shifted to another level of interpretation[1]. As yet, the **context hypothesis** is simply represented by a list of perceived features. Each feature is described by following entries: *Feature ID*, *Feature value*, *Sensor type ID*, *Smart-It ID*, *Sensor location* and *timestamp*. The **packet trace** section is organized of two stacks which have the following functions. The first stack maintains a route history of traveled units in the wireless network. The second stack directs an *sCAP* according to a given route. If the second stack is empty the packet just strays the network in order to meet meaningful sensors by random. Both stacks aim to provide a rough estimate of the current topology in the highly unstable wireless network. In fact, the **packet trace** is core for our *Smart Stack Routing* algorithm presented in section 4.

3.2   Applying *Smart Context-Aware Packet*'s

sCAP's are injected into the network in order to gather context information. The notion of *sCAP*'s fosters abstraction from the network composition and allows to focus on the types of sensor information. As soon as an *sCAP* is received by a sensor, sensed features values maybe added to it, if those are scope of the packet. Then, the sensor node forwards the packet to all of its neighbors. Accordingly, the *sCAP* accumulates meaningful sensor feature values. Combining the gained features stored in the *sCAP* allows each node to make an assumption about the current context. Based on that knowledge it can direct this *sCAP* to an appropriate sensor for further investigation of the current context. Thus, there

---

[1] We envision to have some computing empowered nodes, referred to as *Compute-Its*, in our sensor network later on.

is a permanent in network re-calculation of the context, which allows continuous refinement [ ] of the assumption and adaptation of the *sCAP* routing plan. As soon as the accumulated information is complete it is returned to the inquirer of this information. For processing *sCAP*'s we assume some computing unit at each node in the sensor network as outlined in section 2.1.

Figure 2 gives an example. The user is interest in the audio and light context. Accordingly he creates and sends out an *sCAP* to the network, the solid lines in Figure 2 illustrate the connectivity. The packet is properly received by node *A*. As *A* does neither have light or audio sensors, it cannot contribute to the packet and forwards it to its neighbors *B* and *E*. The packet splits into *P*, which continues to *F*, and *P'*, which heads to *D*. As *D* is equipped with an audio sensor, it wraps sensed data into the packet and returns it to the user. The situation at *F* is similar, it contributes light information to the packet. In this situation, one copy (*P"*) is returned to the user, another one (*P*) is forwarded to *G*. Node *G* contributes audio information, such that *P* is complete and can be returned to the user as well.

Accordingly, the user receives *P* carrying audio and light, P' carrying only audio and *P"* carrying only light information. Further, all three packets know their itinerary, such that the user may contact the nodes *D*, *F* and *G* directly at another time. The *sCAP* approach is user-centric in that way, that the user can acquire knowledge about the network's topology. He either can rely on that information or tackle dynamic changes by initiating other *sCAP*'s.

The itinerary information stored in the **packet trace** is provided by the *Smart Stack Routing* strategy described in the consecutive section.

4   Routing of *sCAP*'s: *Smart Stack Routing*

This section describes our routing strategy, referred to as *Smart Stack Routing (SSR)*, suitable for *sCAP*'s. As routing in general, *SSR* describes a process of prescribing the routing path tailored to the means of *sCAP*'s. First we will

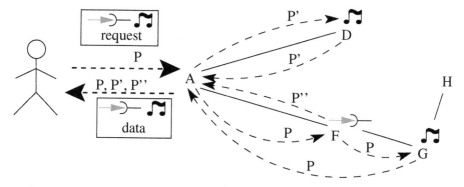

Fig. 2. Application example: A user is asking for light and sound data

classify existing routing strategies and differentiate *SSR* from those. Thereupon *SSR* will be discussed in section 4.2 in greater detail.

4.1   Classification of Routing Strategies

Instead of classifying the manifold state of the art routing protocols [22] we will just focus those affecting our *SSR* approach. In Table 4.1 these protocols are classified by their application environment they are most dedicated to. We differentiate networks due to their topology and their participating nodes. We see a network's topology either to be totally connected or neighbor connected. Totally connected means, that every node is in reach of every other node. In contrast to that, neighbor connected defines, that nodes are clustered into neighborhoods, which are defined by signal reach. Accordingly, communication between two nodes only can happen, if they are in the same neighborhood, cross neighborhood communication requires at least one intermediary node linking two neighborhoods. The participating nodes may be static, such that their location is fixed and nodes do not appear and disappear too frequently. Obviously, this results in a pretty solid network. However, for sensor networks dynamic nodes, which can appear and disappear rapidly and may change their position as well, seem to be more realistic.

Gnutella The Gnutella network [10] is a fully-distributed information-sharing technology. It enables private users to share files among each other on the internet. Each user becomes part of the network by using a Gnutella client software, each node is both a server and client. As users may enter and leave the network, Gnutella is somewhere in between our definitions of dynamic and static above. But on the other hand, the network is definitely totally connected, as building upon the internet an IP address is assigned to each user. Each user is assigned to a local cluster, which is constrained by the time-to-live of his initial requests. Each user has this local view, but by accepting and forwarding search and initiation packets of other users, connection to the entire network can be established. Accordingly, the Gnutella network can be seen a sort of wading into a sea of people. People as far as the eye can see. And further, but they disappear over the horizon. In contrast to wireless networks, the Gnutella clusters are just set up artificially because of performance reasons during search and initiation of

Table 1. Classification of routing strategies

	static nodes	dynamic nodes
neighbor connected *everybody to subset*	Stack Routing Directed Diffusion	Smart Stack Routing
totally connected *everybody to everybody*	Gnutella	Gnutella

new users. In a second step, the file sharing itself is established by peer-to-peer connection as the network is totally connected. However, the idea of local routing tables tracking the last hundred incoming requests have been adopted to *SSR*.

Stack Routing Stack Routing [ ] is another approach for distributed file-sharing. Instead of setting up local clusters, two motions for sending packets are introduced: undirected and directed. *Undirected motion* does not aim at specific individuals or entities, but at anybody fulfilling certain criteria. *Directed motion* follows one declared path. It is oriented toward specific entities. Stack Routing uses *undirected motion* for sending out requests from the network. The packet records its return path. Every node on the route pushes data onto the packet's stack. This data memorizes the previous node the packet came from. Consequently, at any residing node the return path to the inquirer is stored on the packet's node. Again, a time-to-live counter in the packet is used to limit the length of any path during *undirected motion*. Reaching the final receiver fulfilling the criteria, the packet is returned by *directed motion*. Using two stacks allows to establish bidirectional paths between nodes. One stack records the return path (*push stack*) as described, the other one (*pop stack*) is either empty (*undirected motion*) or contains a return path (*directed motion*). Thus, the direction of a packet is reversed by swapping stacks. Though Stack Routing is very reasonable for neighbor connected networks, it still assumes a more or less static network. Otherwise, packets may get lost during *directed motion* to their inquirer. However, our work was very much influenced by the Stack Routing approach. We also make use of stacks storing paths but we extended *directed motion* in order to be more reactive towards dynamic changes in the network.

Directed Diffusion Directed Diffusion [ ] belongs to the same category as Stack Routing. However, Directed Diffusion seeks to be used for large sensor networks. This approach is data-centric as each sensor node names its generated data with one or more attributes. According to those attributes, other nodes may express interests, which are propagated throughout the network. The path of interest propagation sets up a reversed path for data matching that interest. Interests establish gradients that direct the diffusion of data. Thus, a data paths from sources to sinks are computed. Though Directed Diffusion is reactive to changes in the network topology time evolves during updating the gradients localized throughout the network. Directed Diffusion could be applied to improve *undirected motion* constraining the choices by calculated gradients. In our current approach We have not taken this into account yet, but this might be reasonable for future work.

4.2 *Smart Stack Routing (SSR)*

This section gives details about *SSR* for routing *sCAP*'s in wireless sensor networks. *SSR* builds upon the routing strategies presented in the previous section, but overcoming the shortcomings of those. Accordingly, *SSR* has to be capable for neighbor connected networks with highly dynamic participating nodes. We have adopted the main ideas of Stack Routing: *undirected motion* and *directed motion*, *time to live* for controlling the reach of *sCAP*'s,and the notion of *push-* and *pop stack*. Further, we make use of unique identifiers existing in our Smart-Its environment in order to distinguish network nodes. However, tailoring our strategy to more unstable wireless networks. In the following we will introduce several enhancements and illustrate those by an example, see Figure 3.

Request ID The *Request ID* is a non-ambiguous identifier of a single request. The main purpose of this ID is to filter out same copies of packets finding there way to the final receiver on different routes in the network. The *Request ID* is the first element pushed onto the *push stack* by the data inquirer. It is assembled of the inquirer's identifier and a consecutively generated number for distinguishing between several requests from the same node. However, as the validity of packets is limited due to a *time to live* counter, the consecutive numbers may be reused after a while.

Semi-directed Motion *Semi-directed motion* is a mixture of *undirected motion* and *directed motion*. It aims at dealing with breakdowns of intermediary nodes of given paths during *directed motion*. In this case, a dedicated token is pushed on the *pop stack* indicating the packet is on *semi-directed motion*. From now on, the packet is traveling the network in an undirected manner. It aims at strolling the network for returning back to its origin return-path by skipping breakdowns on detours. Due to that, the packet's *pop stack* is continuously browsed for an entry-point in order to switch back to *directed motion* again. As soon as a visited node is part of the *pop stack*, all elements above this node entry are eliminated from the stack and the packet is back in *directed motion*.

Dead-End Detection In wireless networks the topology may create dead-ends. A packet going into a dead-end reaches a final node which has no other neighbor than the packet arrived from. In this case the final node should delete the packet: As we assume that every node is always propagating a packet to all of his neighbors, it does not make sense to route a packet from a dead-end back to the branching node. Before reaching the dead-end, the packet already has been split and a copy is already on the way. Dead-end detection is very simple. If a node is not the final receiver of a packet and it only can forward it to the node it was received from, then the node is a dead-end and has to kill the packet.

A *receiving table* resides at each node. It keeps track of previous packets this node has been final receiver.of. The size of this table also depends on the packets' *time to live*.

Example We illustrate the concepts of *SSR* with the aid of an example scenario. In the following, we assume a sample wireless network consisting of the nodes

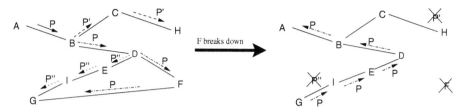

Fig. 3. Example connectivity of wireless nodes

A, B, C, D, E, F, G, H, and I. These nodes are connected to each other as the solid lines depict in Figure 3.

Further, we assume to have some dynamics in the system, such that node F breaks down after a while. Node A requests certain data which is assumed to reside at node G. For an $sCAP$ moving from A to G SSR works as follows. Initially, both *push-* and *pop stack* are empty. Starting from A, there is only one choice of connection. Before sending the packet from A to B, A indicates itself as the inquirer of the data request by pushing its identifier, shown as **A*** in Table 2, onto the *push stack*. B receives the packet from A but realizing that it cannot contribute to the packet's needs. Consequently, it pushes the return path to A, represented by Ba in this case, onto the push stacks. After that it forwards the packet to its neighbors. As there are two nodes reachable from B, C and D, the primary packet splits. One is heading to C, referred to as P', the other one is continuing to D, denoted as P in Table 3.

As packet P' reaches node H, see Table 3, a dead-end is detected and P' is removed from the network. Meanwhile, the other copy of the primary $sCAP$ is making it's way to D. D also pushes its return path to the previous node B onto the packet's *push stack*.

As depicted in Figure 3, D branches to E and F, such that packet P is forked again. P makes its way to G via F. Due to the fact that P'' still has to make two hops via E and I, we assume that it will reach G after P already has been there. As P reaches G fulfilling the inquirer's needs, the node F breaks down. G queries its *receiving table* and recognizes that this request has not been accomplished yet. Hence, G wraps the desired data into the $sCAP$'s *context hypothesis* part.

As shown in Table 2, G swaps the packet's stacks and *semi-directs* P to I as the primary return path is not valid anymore. Simultaneously[2], P'' reaches G.

Thereupon, G, queries its *receiving table*, identifies P'' as an identical copy of P and removes it, see Table 4. Meanwhile, P records its path from G to D on its *push stack*. As D was part of the original path P was arriving from, it is found on the *pop stack* and motion can be changed from *semi-directed* to *directed*. Thence, D pushes it link to E onto the *push stack* and reveals B as the node to route the packet to by popping this information from the *pop stack*.

---

[2] We assume collision-detection to be handled by lower network layers, which is out of scope of our work

Table 2. Stack trace of packet P

Node	Action	Push Stack	Pop Stack
A	push **A*** send to B	**A***	
B	push Ba send to D	Ba **A***	
D	push Db send to F	Db Ba **A***	
F	send to G	Fd Db Ba **A***	

node F breaks down

G	wrap data swap stacks push **S*** semi-direct to E		**S*** Fd Db Ba **A***
E	browse Pop Stack push Eg semi-direct to D	Eg	**S*** Fd Db Ba **A***
D	browse Pop Stack entry point found revise Pop Stack push De pop Db send to B	De Eg	Ba **A***
B	pop Ba push Bd send to A	Bd De Eg	**A***
A	push Ab pop **A*** unwrap data	Ab Bd De Eg	

Table 3. Stack trace of packet P'

Node	Action	Push Stack	Pop Stack
B	push Ba send to C	Ba **A***	
C	push Cb send to H	Cb Ba **A***	
H	kill packet	Hc Cb Ba **A***	

Table 4. Stack trace of packet P"

Node	Action	Push Stack	Pop Stack
D	push Db send to E	Db Ba **A***	
E	push Ed send to I	Ed Db Ba **A***	
I	push Ie send to G	Ie Ed Db Ba **A***	
G	packet expires kill packet	n/a	n/a

Finally *A* receives *P* from *B*, identifies itself as the creator of the packet and unwraps the data part. Further *A* can extract the return-path to *G*. It may initiate a second data request, e.g. an information update, sending another packet in by using more efficient *directed motion* following that proven path. Moreover, it seems to be reasonable to store proven paths in a trace table for late use of *directed motion*.

5   Conclusion

Envisioning pervasive computing several challenges have to be be addressed. We demand context-aware behavior of pervasive environments to service humans in an adequate manner. Therefore, we described a packet oriented approach in order to reveal the user's context from sensors available in the environment. Our work was influenced by Stack Routing [ ] and inspired by the Smart-Its project [ ] assuming interconnected everyday objects that are instrumented with embedded sensors in an unobtrusive manner. Building upon *Smart Context-Aware Packet*'s [ ] we developed a routing mechanism tailored to wireless sensor networks. Our *Smart Stack Routing* approach promotes exchange of sensor data throughout wireless sensor networks without central points of control. Embedding the entire routing intelligence into *sCAP*'s, makes our approach powerful to tackle break downs of single nodes in the sensor network.

6   Related Work and Outlook

This section gives short overview on related work and briefly reflects how it relates to our work.

Using the publish-subscribe paradigm [ ] for querying data in sensors networks is a more centralized approach than ours. The authors intend to provide simpler communication interfaces and abstractions above raw network communication to application and system programs. It will be interesting to see, how look-up service, composition service and dynamic adaptation service behave with respect to changes and break downs in the network.

MADSN [ ] is more similar to our packet approach. Mobile agents, which could be interpreted as powerful *sCAP*'s, are used to execute a refined multi-resolution integration algorithm. It aims to obtain a correct estimate of observed parameters from a homogeneous set of partly faulty sensors. The authors demonstrate in a case study, that their mobile agents reduce the network transfer compared to conventional multi-resolution integration [ ]. MADSN may serve as building block in our framework to handle homogeneous sets of faulty sensors.

Directed Diffusion [ ] constraints information flows propagating interests and setting gradients accordingly, as already mentioned in section 4.1. Currently, we envision directed diffusion as an underlying principle for optimizing flows of *sCAP*'s during *directed motion*.

Finally we will investigate the integration of our *SSR* approach into scatter networks, such as Bluetooth [ ], which provide more powerful network topologies than simple local broadcast topology.

Acknowledgements

The Smart-Its project is funded in part by the Commission of the European Union under contract IST-2000-25428, and by the Swiss Federal Office for Education and Science (BBW 00.0281).

References

1. Smart Spaces and their related areas.
   http://www.nist.gov/smartspace/smartSpaces/. 37
2. The Ultra Low Power Wireless Sensors project.
   http://www-mtl.mit.edu/~jimg/project_top.html. 35
3. G. Banavar, J. Beck, E. Gluzberg, J. Munson, J. Sussman, and D. Challenges Zukowski. An Application Model for Pervasive Computing. In *Proceddings of the 6 th Annual ACM/IEEE Intl Conf. Mobile Computing and Networking (Mobi-Com2000)*, pages 66–274, Boston, MA, August 2000. 35
4. The Bluetooth SIG. WWW. http://www.bluetooth.com/v2/document. 36, 45
5. S. Czerwinski, B. Zhao, T. Hodes, A. Joseph, and R. Katz. An Architecture for a Secure Service Discovery Service. In *In Proceedings of MobiCom '99*, Seattle, WA, August 1999. 34
6. Anind Dey and G.D. Abowd. Towards a Better Understanding of Context and Contex-Awareness. Technical Report 22, GeorgiaTech, 1999. 34, 36
7. N. Diehl. *Mobile Computing*. Thomson Publ., 1995. 36
8. D. Estrin, L. Girod, G. Pottie, and Srivastava M. Instrumenting the world with wireless sensor networks. In *In Proceedings of the International Conference on Acoustics, Speech and Signal Processing (ICASSP 2001)*, Salt Lake City, Utah, May 2001. 35
9. D. Estrin, R. Govindan, J. Heidemann, and S. Kumar. Next Century Challenges: Scalable Coordination in Sensor Networks. In *In Proceedings of the ACM/IEEE International Conference on Mobile Computing and Networking*, pages 263–270, Seattle, Washington, USA, August 1999. ACM.
   http://www.isi.edu/ johnh/PAPERS/Estrin99e.html. 37
10. Gnutella. Welcome to Gnutella. http://gnutella.wego.com/. 40
11. T. Hodes and R. Katz. A Document-based Framework for Internet Application Control. In *2nd USENIX Symposium on Internet Technologies and Systems*, October 1999. 38
12. What is Pervasive Computing. http://www-3.ibm.com/pvc/pervasive.html. 34
13. C. Intanagonwiwat, R. Govindan, and D. Estrin. Directed Diffusion: A Scalable and Robust Communication Program for Sensor Network. In *Proc. Mobicom 2000*. 41, 45
14. Jini(TM), 1998. http://java.sun.com/products/jini. 34
15. Labscape. http://csi.washington.edu/comsystec/labscape/. 36
16. A. Lim. Distributed Services for Information Dissemination in Self-Organizing Sensor Networks. *Special Issue on Distributed Sensor Networks for Real-Time Systems with Adaptive Reconfiguration, Journal of Franklin Institute*, 2001. 45
17. Micro Electro Mechanical Systems (MEMS). http://mems.isi.edu/. 35
18. Florian Michahelles and Michael Samulowitz. Smart CAPs for Smart Its - Context Detection for Mobile Users. In Mark Dunlop and Stephen Brewster, editors, *Proceedings of the Third International Workshop on Human-Computer Interaction with Mobile Devices*, Lille, France, September 2001. 37, 39, 45

19. J.G. Pottie and W.J. Kaiser. Wireless integrated network sensors. *Comm. ACM*, 3(5):51–58, May 2000. 35

20. L. Prasad, S.S. Iyengar, R.L. Rao, and R.L Kashyap. Fault-tolerant sensor integration using multiresolution decomposition. *Physical Review E*, 49, April 1994. 45

21. H. Qi, S. Iyengar, and K. Chakrabarty.   Distributed multiresolution data integration using mobile agents. In *Proc. IEEE Aerospace Conference*, 2001.   37, 45

22. E. Royer and C. Toh. A review of current routing protocols for ad hoc mobile wireless networks. *IEEE Personal Communication*, 6:46–55, April 1999. 40

23. M. Samulowitz, F. Michahelles, and C. Linnhoff-Popien. Adaptive interaction for enabling pervasive services. In *MobiDE01*, Santa Barbara, California, USA, May 2001. 34

24. B. Schiele and S. Antifakos. Beyond Position Awareness. In *Proceedings of the Workshop on Location Modeling at Ubicomp*, October 2001. 36

25. A. Schmidt. Implicit human-computer interaction through context. In *2nd Workshop on Human Computer Interaction with Mobile Devices*, Edinburgh, Scotland, August 1999. 34

26. Service Location Protocol (svrloc). http://www.IETF.org/html.charters/svrloc-charter.html. 34

27. Smart-Its. http://www.smart-its.org. 35, 45

28. TEA - Technology for Enabling Awareness. http://www.teco.edu/tea/. 35

29. David L. Tennenhouse. Proactive Computing. *Communications of the ACM*, 43:43–50, May 2000. 34

30. K. Van Laerhoven, K. Aidoo, and S. Lowette. Real-time analysis of Data from Many Sensors with Neural Networks. In *In Proceedings of the fourth International Symposium on Wearable Computers (ISWC 2001)*, Zurich, Switzerland, October 1999. 35

31. Marc Weiser. The Computer for the 21st Century. *Scientific American*, 265(3):94–104, September 1991. 34

32. The WINS project. http://www.janet.ucla.edu/WINS/. 35

33. WorldOS. Routing - Directed vs. Undirected. http://worldos.com/technology/routing.php. 41, 45

Session II

System Aspects

A Ubiquitous Control Architecture
for Low Power Systems

James "Wez" Weatherall[1] and Duncan Grisby[2]

[1] Laboratory for Communications Engineering
Cambridge, England
jnw22@eng.cam.ac.uk
[2] AT&T Laboratories Cambridge
Cambridge, England
dpg1@uk.research.att.com

Abstract. The Eucalyptus architecture aims to support ubiquitous interaction between devices ranging from tiny low power devices through to fully fledged computer systems. Low power ad hoc networking presents problems for conventional middleware protocols both in terms of performance and of network availability. The work presented here addresses the problem of efficient and interoperable communication between low power devices, and describes interfaces and structures used to manage distributed systems composed of such devices.

1   Introduction

Improvements in processor technology made in the past ten to twenty years have meant that the PDAs carried by users today and treated as little more than electronic diaries are significantly more powerful than desktop computers used to be.

Cheap processing technology not only means cheaper computing platforms but means that some degree of "intelligence" can be embedded in even very tiny and low-cost devices. Products built around cheap microprocessors are often easier to develop than systems based around custom chips and can support extra features much more easily.

By combining low-end microprocessors with low power wireless networks, devices can be built which interoperate transparently with each other to perform tasks. Such devices include sensors, home or office equipment and other consumer electronics. Using short range networks, these devices can provide context-aware features to their users, as well as cooperating to perform more conventional tasks.

Ad hoc systems of this kind, comprising often disconnected networks of roaming devices pose problems for many traditional network protocols. Low power wireless protocols tend to introduce significant latency in communications, adversely affecting RPC (Remote Procedure Call) and similar protocols. Use of short range radio networks allows context to be inferred from connectivity but poses problems for lengthy interactions between mobile nodes.

H. Schmeck, T. Ungerer, and L. Wolf (Eds.): ARCS 2002, LNCS 2299, pp. 51–66, 2002.

This paper presents a low power radio messaging layer, wide-area routing services and a distributed control architecture suitable for home and office environments.

2   The Prototype Embedded Network

PEN (Prototype Embedded Network) is a lightweight, low-power wireless radio network designed to perform introduction and low bit-rate data transfer between arbitrary devices. PEN may be embedded in devices from simple sensors, through household appliances, to full computer systems. This distinguishes PEN from more sophisticated technologies such as BlueTooth [ ] or IEEE 802.11b[1]. PEN shares similar design goals with the more recent PicoRadio [ ] project. The Smart Dust [ ] project aims to support extremely tiny sensors using free space optical links, rather than radio.

PEN's short range allows a table of nearby devices to be constructed from which context information may be inferred. The restricted radio range of PEN allows the amplification stage to use less power, as well as increasing the aggregate bandwidth available to applications by reducing the number of devices sharing the medium.

2.1   Hardware

PEN components consist of a standard 418/433MHz radio module, a PIC (Programmable Interface Controller) to manage it, and a power source. The radio module is calibrated to have a range of around 5 metres and provides a usable data rate of 24Kbps. Simple PEN devices such as sensors could conceivably be powered by either a coin-cell, or an ambient power source such as sunlight.

Prototype PEN units contain an embedded microprocessor, RAM and ROM modules and serial communication ports. All results provided in this paper are based these prototype units, used either stand-alone, connected to Psion Series 5/Compaq iPAQ 3600 PDAs or to PCs.

2.2   Software

Power consumption of active PEN prototype nodes is dominated in equal part by the radio, CPU and memory subsystems. When fully active, a node consumes 600mW of power. With these three subsystems idle, the same node can consume as little as $16\mu W$. The PEN runtime, EEK, therefore contains a democratic power management scheme, allowing applications and system components to indicate when they require other components to remain active via vote. The runtime is based around the μCOS [ ] micro-kernel and has a similar modular design to the more recent TinyOS [ ].

Rather than accessing the radio interface directly, PEN applications use the R-Layer (Rendezvous Layer) [ ] [ ], a low power rendezvous and messaging

---

[1] IEEE 802.11b is commonly referred to by the "WaveLAN" product trademark.

service. The R-Layer uses a specially designed rendezvous protocol to allow the radio hardware to remain powered down for all but a few tens of milliseconds out of every minute, while still providing useful functionality. This results for typical applications in an average power consumption of around 1mW.

Like the base radio interface, the R-Layer supports only relatively small datagrams. To support large datagrams, data streams or ad hoc multi-hop routing, specialised extensions to the protocol stack are required, such as the PEN Transport and Routing Layers [ ].

2.3 Network Topology

The IrDA [ ] and BlueTooth technologies both employ a *star* network topology. Devices using these technologies are arranged into groups, each with a single *master* device and a number of *slaves*, as shown in Fig. 2.3. All messages between slaves must first be passed to the master, to be forwarded to the destination. This doubles the bandwidth and power required to deliver messages, the brunt of which is borne by the master device.

PEN instead assumes a totally decentralised network, in which all devices communicate as peers. Since no central authority schedules communication, the PEN Media Access Control (MAC) layer must take measures to avoid collisions between transmissions. PEN uses a variant of the Singly-persistent Data Sensing for Multiple Access (1-DSMA) scheme to achieve this, resulting in a reduction in PEN's effective bandwidth. Decentralised operation allows devices to communicate directly without prior configuration, and removes the need for a well-powered device such as a PDA or laptop to manage communications.

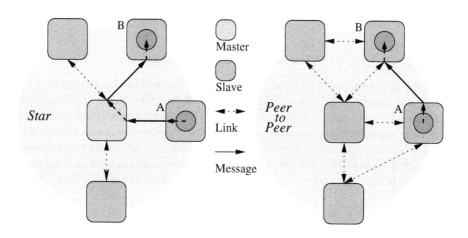

Fig. 1. Star vs Peer-to-Peer Network Topologies

3   The R2 Low Power Messaging Layer

As part of the Eucalyptus project, a second low power messaging protocol has been built, dubbed the R2-Layer [ ]. The R2-Layer is a modular system providing a superset of the functionality provided by the more monolithic R-Layer. In particular, the R2-Layer provides both *transmitter-managed* and *receiver-managed* rendezvous implementations.

3.1   Transmitter-Managed Rendezvous

The original R-Layer provides a transmitter-managed rendezvous scheme for messaging between nodes. Because PEN nodes spend most of their time "sleeping", unable to send or receive data, they must first arrange to wake simultaneously before they can communicate. Transmitter-managed schemes place the responsibility for rendezvous with the sender. R-Layer nodes wishing to receive data must wake to transmit broadcast *beacon* datagrams at regular intervals. After each datagram the node must remain awake, listening for incoming data. To send data, the transmitter first listens for a beacon from the target device, then delivers the payload in the subsequent *listen window*

3.2   Receiver-Managed Mode

In addition to the transmitter-managed rendezvous scheme provided by the original R-Layer, the R2-Layer provides a receiver-managed scheme designed to support extremely low power embedded sensors. Receiver-managed schemes require devices wishing to obtain data from transmitters to arrange rendezvous with them. The R2-Layer implements a simple receiver-managed scheme in which nodes add a small payload to their regular beacons. Nearby recipients may then synchronise with these beacons to receive their payloads.

3.3   Local Area vs Wide Area Communication

Both the R-Layer and R2-Layer provide ad hoc low power rendezvous and messaging services directly between pairs of nodes. While the short range of the PEN radio provides valuable context information for many applications, it severely limits the number of services and other devices a node may communicate with. Devices in otherwise isolated clusters of PEN nodes may use multi-hop routing to extend their sphere of influence. Devices in environments with pre-configured infrastructure may instead use backbone routing services to perform long-distance communication.

The APIDgate and R-Link services [ ] provide wireless-to-wired and wireless-through-wired routing for PEN. Both services use the Predator Location Service [ ] to track potentially very large numbers of devices on a world-wide scale. Although PEN devices may communicate directly whether or not such infrastructure is present, it may also be used to provide further power savings over direct communication.

4   The Koala Object Request and Event Broker

The PEN protocols previously described solve problems of rendezvous and messaging between low power devices. In an ad hoc distributed system, it is not sufficient to provide basic messaging services and expect appliances to cooperate seamlessly.

Standards such as CORBA [ ] specify standard programming models and interoperability requirements suitable for conventional computer systems. The Koala Object Request and Event Broker [ ] builds on the core CORBA object model but aims to support embedded low power devices. This presents problems both of efficiency in use of storage and CPU cycles and of managing the high latencies inherent in the operation of the underlying PEN protocols.

4.1   Object Model

The Koala object model closely matches that specified by the OMG's CORBA standard. Interfaces are defined in Interface Definition Language (IDL) [ ], specifying sets of types, constant values, methods and attributes. The stub compiler uses these interfaces to build *servant* skeleton code, on which interface implementations are based, and client *stub* code, through which remote methods are invoked by clients. Objects are addressed by the device hosting them, the Application Identifier (APID) through which they are contacted, and a per-object *key*.

Most control interactions between objects and their clients occurs using Remote Procedure Calls (RPC). RPC provides a convenient and familiar model upon which to build distributed applications but has characteristics which limit its applicability in high latency environments. The Koala ORB provides two main additions to the CORBA object model to tackle this.

4.2   Asynchronous Remote Procedure Calls

Standard remote procedure calls cause the caller to "block" until the call has been sent across the network, dispatched, and a result received. Each invocation therefore incurs a single round-trip delay, equivalent in a deterministic network to twice the network latency. Figure 4.2, shows the raw datagram *fundamental latency*, the *hard latency* resulting from PEN's plea/offer/beacon protocol, and the *soft latency* incurred by low power operation. The soft latency in this case is three orders of magnitude greater than that of a raw transmission. Since PEN is already a relatively high latency network, this poses a considerable problem for latency dependent protocols.

Many applications dispatch batches of logically independent invocations sequentially. This avoids the overhead of dispatching each in a separate thread, and the complexities of existing asynchronous invocation mechanisms such as the *dispatch-and-callback* and *dispatch-and-poll* schemes provided by the CORBA Messaging Service, for example. However, it introduces artificial and unnecessary dependencies between invocations, resulting in excessive numbers of round-trip delays.

Table 1. Fundamental, hard and soft latencies of the PEN protocols

Type	Average Latency (ms)
Fundamental	7
Hard	21
Soft	5000

Dispatch-and-Callback Dispatch-and-callback RPC mechanisms allow clients to pass a callback function to asynchronous invocations. When the invocation has completed and its results are received, they are passed to the callback function for processing.

Dispatch-and-Poll Dispatch-and-poll RPC mechanisms immediately return a pollable object to clients calling asynchronous methods. The client then polls the object periodically, until it indicates that the invocation has completed and a result is available.

Block-by-Need The Koala ORB supports both dispatch-and-callback and dispatch-and-poll methods of asynchronous invocation, in addition to its own *block-by-need* scheme. Asynchronous Koala RPC immediately returns a result object when an asynchronous method is invoked. The caller then stores this object in the same way as it would any normal result from an invocation. When the result must be used, the client *dereferences* it, perhaps using "*" in C++ or "()" in Python, to obtain the actual value it contains. If the result has not been received by the time the object is first dereferenced then the calling thread is blocked until it becomes available. This avoids much of the complication of callbacks or polling while providing similar performance benefits. Results objects nonetheless provide for applications suited to use of callbacks or polling.

4.3   Lazy Lists

In environments with multiple similar objects, it is often the case that a particular request is to be made to several objects, and the results collated. Using sequential RPC, each object would be contacted in turn, resulting in latency proportional to the number of objects contacted[2]. Using asynchronous RPC, all invocations would first be dispatched and their results then collected using the block-by-need mechanism. This reduces the latency of the operation to the that of the slowest object to respond. As the number of objects contacted increases, this will tend towards twice the beacon interval.

If such results require CPU-intensive post-processing then the caller could benefit if each result were to be delivered as soon as it became available, rather

---

[2] This assumes all devices hosting similar objects to share a common beacon interval

than waiting for all results before returning any. Even if no post-processing is required, it may be beneficial to provide feedback through a user interface, for example, as data is received. The Koala ORB provides the *lazy list* primitive for this purpose. Lazy lists consist of a value and a successor function and may have either immediately available data or block-by-need result objects appended to them.

When the successor function is called, the next item in the list is returned. If this is immediate data then a value, successor pair is returned. If it is a result object then it is first polled for availability. If the result is not ready then it is moved to the back of the list and the next value in the list is considered. If no items in the list are currently available then the successor blocks until one becomes available.

Using lazy lists, distributed operations touching many objects may be dispatched asynchronously and their results processed as they become available via a convenient and intuitive interface. If a lazy list containing pending result objects is destroyed by the recipient then Koala will notify host devices to indicate that the corresponding replies are no longer required.

4.4   Attribute State Events

Distributed applications for wireless systems often take advantage of their inherent context aware features. Context-aware applications typically involve a degree of monitoring of state of nearby devices, to which conventional RPC is not ideally suited.

Although CORBA IDL has the syntactic notion of object "attributes", their semantics are described by the object model in terms of methods to set and retrieve their value — CORBA attributes therefore have no real semantic significance.

Koala extends the CORBA notion of attributes to give them more semantic significance, in a similar manner to the Omni Object Services [ ]. Interface definitions may inherit from the special "Watchable" interface, if they wish their attributes to be "watchable". Whenever an action occurs inside an object which causes a watchable attribute to change, the implementation calls a notification function supplied by the Koala skeleton code. The notification function dispatches an update event containing the current state of the object's watchable attributes to all interested event sinks.

Exactly how events reach clients depends upon the supported event transport. Very simple sensor devices will typically use receiver-managed rendezvous and embed event data in their beacon payload, while more complex devices might use a counting-event scheme instead, to provide greater reliability. In order to interoperate with event-based architectures such as SPIRIT [ ] or LocALE [ ] running on conventional systems, events might be transfered using the standard CORBA Event or Notification services [ ] [ ].

5   The Eucalyptus Control Architecture

5.1   Overview

Eucalyptus assumes a world of roaming and static *appliances*, physical devices hosting one or more *components*, as illustrated in Fig. 2 for a simple sensor application. Components are objects derived from the `Component` interface, which correspond to some functional capability of the appliance. The architecture builds on the Koala object model and defines the syntax and semantics of a number of standard interfaces designed to support efficient interoperability between appliances.

5.2   Object Interfaces

Because Eucalyptus uses an object model with well defined semantics and which employs static interfaces and typing, components need not provide complex reflexive functionality. The simplest Eucalyptus sensor might broadcast a preformed beacon datagram at regular intervals. The datagram would include the sensor's supported interface types. The only dynamic component would be an event containing the current sensor value. We assume that to use the sensor, clients must be aware of the sensor's interface. This is reasonable since, even with dynamic interface information, clients must understand the semantics of the interface in order to use it.

Although static typing is preferable to dynamic typing when linking components together into a distributed system, dynamic typing provides benefits when component browsers or gateways between object models are required. The CORBA Dynamic Invocation Interface (DII) [ ] is provided for just this purpose. Better-equipped Eucalyptus devices may therefore make their interface details available if they wish, via a standard Eucalyptus interface. When a browser or gateway cannot obtain such information from a component directly, it may fall back to fetching interface details from an interface repository.

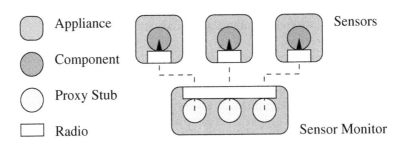

Fig. 2. A simple sensor system using Eucalyptus

5.3   Discovery

Eucalyptus is primarily designed for low power platforms such as PEN. Since PEN devices spend most of their time inactive and unable to receive data, they will usually hear beacons from other nodes only when explicitly listening for them. The R2-Layer therefore provides modules to aid ad hoc discovery of nearby devices. To discover components hosted by such devices, the Koala ORB assumes that discovered devices which advertise the well-known Koala APID must host a *primary component* with a well-known object key.

Locating Components The Koala ORB provides *import traders* for each supported network transport. These traders support queries for objects based on the interfaces they support. Traders are partitioned into hierarchical name-spaces, and queries may be made against all or part of a trader, as required. The PEN import trader uses the R2-Layer's discovery features to listen for local appliances arriving and departing and populates itself with the primary components of those which are currently local. Applications may watch the trader for changes in order to be notified when new components become available.

Publishing Components Eucalyptus allows one or more components hosted by an appliance to be *published*. If an appliance publishes only a single component then that component is made the appliances primary component and is thus implicitly advertised by the Koala ORB. If two or more components are published then Eucalyptus instead creates an *export trader* as the primary component and registers the published components with it. Figure 3 shows a single appliance publishing multiple components via an advertised export trader.

Queries made to Koala traders which contain links to other traders will propagate into them. Queries to import traders will therefore propagate into any export traders discovered locally. This allows clients to search amongst all components published by nearby devices. Koala traders return their results using the ORB's lazy list primitive, considerably reducing the effects of network latency.

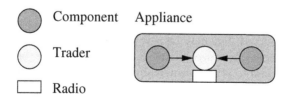

Fig. 3. An appliance advertising components through a trader

5.4 Specialist Traders

In contrast to the ANSA Trader [ ] and those employed by Jini [ ] and Blue-Tooth [ ], Eucalyptus traders do not provide attribute-matching trader facilities. General attribute-matching presents to heavy a burden to impose on very simple devices.

Suitably powerful devices may instead choose to support *specialist* traders. These traders maintain up-to-date lists of objects supporting a particular interface, and allow interface-specific attribute-based queries to be made by clients. Specialist traders operating on different devices can cooperate to satisfy queries efficiently, or may instead use the standard trader interface to index remote objects.

5.5 Access Control

By default, any component may be monitored and controlled by any number of clients. This allows components such as clocks and sensors to be treated as freely available resources. More complex components, particularly configurable *devices*, must arbitrate between conflicting requests in some way. Eucalyptus assumes that conflict resolution is a sufficiently complex and personal task that no appliance should provide it as an implicit function. Instead, Eucalyptus defines the `Device` interface. This interface provides `Reserve` and `Release` methods.

The Device Interface The Koala ORB provides low level authentication of incoming requests, assigning clients unique identifiers internally which may be queried by method implementations. The standard `Reserve` implementation verifies that the object is not already reserved and, if successful, stores the unique identifier of the caller. Subsequent invocations to other methods of the object may check the caller's ID against that stored, if required, to enforce access control. The standard device implementation therefore allows only one client to reserve the device at any one time.

Delegated Ownership An extension to the base device implementation allows delegated ownership. The device is first reserved by its administrative owner, who indicates that they wish to allow the device to be re-reserved. When a second client reserves the device, the reservation succeeds as if the device were not previously reserved, but may be revoked at any time by the administrative owner. While reserved by a second client, the device cannot be manipulated by the owner, other than to revoke ownership, whereupon all sensitive internal state must be destroyed [ ].

Shared Devices When multiple clients must access a device, a proxy is added to the system which assumes ownership of the original device and provides a shared interface to it. The shared interface provides the same interface as the device itself, but allows multiple clients to reserve it simultaneously and stores internal state for each. Manufacturers can thus provide multiple conflict resolution schemes and allow users to select one.

A home multimedia system may have a single speaker interface to which multiple audio sources must be "connected". Depending upon their preference, the user might choose between an intermediary component which switches between audio sources, and one which mixes them into a single stream.

A personal data storage device might use a transactional model to allow multiple pieces of information to be updated atomically. When reserved, the store would maintain a separate copy of any data changed by the client, committing it when the `Commit` method was invoked, and discarding it when the object was released.

5.6 Domains

Infra-red systems can use the line-of-sight properties of the media as a heuristic for the proximity and relevance of an appliance to the user. Short range radio systems can use the availability of a connection between devices as a proximity heuristic but this is not generally sufficient to indicate relevance. Because radio waves can propagate through walls and other materials, a device which is "nearby" may in fact be hidden or even inaccessible to the user.

Eucalyptus allows devices to be grouped into *domains*. A domain might be an office, building or company. Domains contain a pre-configured trader which clients may query, to avoid the ambiguities of the radio proximity heuristic. Domains will usually retain administrative ownership of the devices they contain, allowing them to be revoked from use by malicious clients if required.

Each domain has a unique hierarchical name. A typical structure for the name might be *organisation, building, room, appliance*. When a client discovers multiple domains, it compares their names in order to establish the longest common prefix. Subsequent queries to the import trader are then passed to all domains matching the prefix. The current domain prefix may be overridden or ignored entirely, in order to revert to normal ad hoc operation.

Automated configuration services also benefit from the domain mechanism. In an ad hoc environment, such services activate configuration operations based on which appliances are available locally. Using the domain mechanism devices may be reconfigured dependent upon the current domain, reducing the scope for conflicts between automated configuration changes.

5.7 Connections

A simple but nonetheless powerful abstraction in configuring Eucalyptus devices is the notion of a *connection* between two components. Connections consist of a *source* which produces data and a *sink* which accepts it. Multiple sinks may be connected to a single source, in which case they will all receive the same data. Each sink may be connected to only one source.

The Eucalyptus `Source` and `Sink` interfaces are used to connect data streams, for example audio or video streams. High data rate connections will require a separate wireless or wired network between the source and sink in addition to PEN. In this case, PEN is used only to configure the stream, allowing the controlled devices to switch off their more power hungry data connection when not connected.

The connection mechanism is also used to cause one Eucalyptus component to "watch" another. This is mainly used to cause the sink devices to reconfigure itself based the state of the source. We have, for example, built a PEN "clicker", which provides a monotonically increasing count of the number of times the user has clicked it. Software running on a meeting-room PC can be connected to the clicker so that each click causes the next slide in a presentation to be displayed. The same clicker may instead be used to control the lighting in the room or to power the meeting room equipment on or off, depending upon what is connected to it.

Although we wish to provide generic connection interfaces to allow general-purpose user interfaces to connect components without prior knowledge of their types, we also wish to suppress connections between incompatible components from being available to the user. It makes little sense, for example, to allow users to attempt to connect a light switch to a speaker. We therefore provide the `const` pragma which may be applied to any interface attribute. This pragma specifies that the associated attribute is immutable and may therefore be passed to clients as part of the object reference and cached for later use. The `Source` and `Sink` interfaces may then have an immutable `ConnectionType` attribute which clients can use to avoid attempting to connect incompatible components. ORBs which do not implement the const pragma will implement immutable attributes in the same way as mutable attributes, requiring clients to query their value via RPC.

6   Evaluation

To evaluate the performance of the Eucalyptus system, we have considered a number of remote control and automation tasks. The simplest of these tasks is to control a lamp based on the present light level. In our example we assume an environment containing ten source devices and ten sinks, all using ten second beacon intervals.

6.1   Configuration

Our PEN lamp and sensor both support Eucalyptus' connection-oriented configuration method. As well as providing the `Sink` interface, however, our lamp also implements the `Device` interface, to provide access control. A wireless remote controller is used to connect the two components. The controller contains sufficient code to make connections between arbitrary sources and sinks.

Locating a Lamp The user interface application makes a query to the controller's import trader for all locally available components providing the `Sink` interface. The list of components is then presented to the user to select from.

The trader query requires that each available component is contacted to establish whether or not it provides the Sink interface. Using sequential RPC, this task incurs 5s latency for each of twenty components. The user must wait for over a minute before receiving any response.

Assuming that device's beacons are evenly spread within each beacon interval, performing the trader query using asynchronous RPC will take 9.5s, the query latency being determined by the last component to respond.

Finally, using the lazy list mechanism, a new result will be returned every 1s on average, since one component will respond roughly every 0.5s to the trader and only half the components match the query. The lazy list mechanism provides the obvious benefit of feedback to the user, who can see the list of available sinks being populated, and may select a lamp from the list without waiting for the query to complete.

Locating a Light Sensor Once a sink has been selected, the controller repeats the query to locate suitable source components. Depending upon the amount of memory available to the controller device, interface details may already be cached for many local components, speeding up the operation. Only source components whose ConnectionType matches that of the selected sink are presented to the user. If immutable attributes are supported then this check is practically instantaneous. If not then a delay of 5s is incurred while contacting the sensor.

Connecting a Lamp to a Sensor Once a lamp and sensor are selected, the controller invokes the lamp's Connect method to connect them. To do so, the controller must first have reserved the lamp, an operation taking 5s. The effect of this latency may be reduced by dispatching the reserve request asynchronously as soon as the lamp has been selected, so that it occurs in parallel to selection of a sensor.

6.2   Operation

After connecting the lamp and sensor, the controller may release the lamp component and need take no further action. Upon receiving the Connect request from the controller, the lamp arranges receiver-managed receipt of sensor data. The R2-Layer will wake the lamp device at suitable intervals to hear the sensor's beacons, containing the sensor data. This increases the lamp's power consumption but does not affect the sensor. Since sensors will typically be smaller and less well powered than other devices, this is a reasonable division of labour.

Using PEN's raw radio interface and our prototype hardware platform, a sensor can operate for only 18 hours on a 9V battery. Using transmitter-managed messaging to deliver event data, the same sensor can operate for around four months. Using the R2-Layer's receiver-managed messaging for event distribution, the sensor can operate for between one and two years. Enhancements to the PEN hardware could improve this by an order of magnitude.

7   Conclusions

The work presented here has been conducted as part of the Eucalyptus project. The project aims to explore the potential applications of short range wireless networks, and their requirements. To this end the project takes a vertical approach, ranging from power management issues at the messaging level up to interoperability issues at the programming level.

Eucalyptus has been implemented natively for PEN devices, as well as for PDA and PC platforms communicating via slaved PEN nodes. At the base of the system, the R2-Layer provides a flexible low power messaging service suitable for a variety of devices, including simple sensors, LCD display units and actuators such as lamps and hi-fi equipment. The Koala ORB has been implemented natively in C for use on PEN, and also in Python for use on PCs and PDAs, both via PEN and TCP/IP. It provides both RPC and event-oriented interfaces, as well as supporting several asynchronous invocation mechanisms which greatly reduce the practical effects of latency for many applications.

By using an object-oriented programming model similar to the CORBA object model, the Eucalyptus system makes management of large numbers of PEN sensors, interfaces and actuators straightforward. Koala objects may be manipulated directly from Python scripts in our prototype system, or may be accessed by CORBA applications via a Koala-to-CORBA bridge. Equally, devices may communicate directly without intervention from or reliance on infrastructural services. Several lights in a room, for example, may be configured by a remote controller or backbone services to monitor a light sensor in the room. The lights will then operate based upon the sensor's reading even when the remote controller or backbone network are no longer available, if required.

Use of an object-oriented abstraction supporting multiple communications mechanisms, in our implementation RPC and state-change events, allows network-specific Koala mappings to make better use of available network primitives. Our PEN mapping, for example, implements events both using receiver-managed messaging and over RPC. The IP equivalent delivers events over standard TCP/IP streams but can also deliver them to hosts on the same subnet via UDP, decreasing latency.

One issue we have not dealt with directly is that of disconnected operation. The Eucalyptus system is designed to provide efficient communications between diverse devices in a peer-to-peer fashion. In addition, existing backbone networks can be employed by even the simplest nodes to support wide-area communication. The applications we have considered can be divided into those for which disconnected operation is simply not possible e.g. remote control applications, and those in which disconnection is used by the application itself to provide context. We take the view that disconnected operation is best handled by applications themselves. Algorithms to support commonly-used forms of disconnected operation merit attention in future research in this area.

Acknowledgements

The author wishes to acknowledge the support received from the members of the Laboratory for Communications Engineering at Cambridge University, and of AT&T Laboratories Cambridge. Particular thanks are due to Professor Andy Hopper, Dr. Sai-Lai Lo and Dr. Alan Jones, who have provided invaluable input to the project.

References

1. Architecture Project Management Ltd. *The ANSA Model for Trading and Federation*, February 1993. AR.005.00. 60
2. BlueTooth Consortium. *Specification of the Bluetooth System Version 1.0A*, July 1999. 52
3. BlueTooth Consortium. Service discovery protocol. In *BlueTooth Core Specification, Version 1.0A*, chapter 3. BlueTooth Consortium, July 1999. 60
4. Diego Lopez de Ipina and Sai-Lai Lo. Locale: a location-aware lifecycle environment for ubiquitous computing. In *15th IEEE International Conference on Information Networking*, February 2001. 57
5. David Evers *(AT&T Laboratories Cambridge)*. Omni Object Services. 2000. 57
6. Gray Girling, Jennifer Li Kam Wa, Paul Osborn, and Radina Stefanova. The design and implementation of a low power ad hoc protocol stack. In *IEEE Wireless Communications and Networking*, September 2000. 53
7. Gray Girling, Jennifer Li Kam Wa, Paul Osborn, and Radina Stefanova. The pen low power protocol stack. In *IEEE International Conference on Communications and Networks*, October 2000. 52
8. Object Management Group. *The Common Object Request Broker: Architecture and Specification*, 2.4.2 edition, 2001. 55
9. Object Management Group. Dynamic Invocation Interface. In *The Common Object Request Broker : Architecture and Specification, Revision 2.4.2*, chapter 7. OMG, February 2001. 58
10. Object Management Group. Event Service Specification, version 1.1, February 2001. 57
11. Object Management Group. Notification Service Specification, Version 1.0, February 2001. 57
12. Object Management Group. *OMG IDL Syntax and Semantics*, February 2001. 55
13. Andy Harter, Andy Hopper, Pete Steggles, Andy Ward, and Paul Webster. The anatomy of a context-aware application. In *5th Annual ACM/IEEE International Conference on Mobile Computing and Networking*, August 1999. 57
14. Jason Hill. A Software Architecture Supporting Networked Sensors. Master's thesis, University of California at Berkeley, September 2000. 52
15. Infrared Data Association. *IrDA SIR Data Specification*, February 1999. 53
16. J. M. Kahn, R. H. Katz, and K. S. J. Pister. Next Century Challenges: Mobile Networking for "Smart Dust". *ACM/IEEE Intl. Conf. on Mobile Computing and Networking (MobiCom 99)*, August 1999. 52
17. Jean J. Labrosse. *MicroC/OS, The Real-Time Kernel*. R & D Publications, Inc., 1992. 52
18. Sun Microsystems. Service architecture. In *Jini Architecture and Specification, Version 1.0.1*, chapter 2.3. Sun Microsystems, November 1999. 60

19. Jan M. Rabaey, M. Josie Ammer, Julio L. da Silva Jr., Danny Patel, and Shad Roundy. PicoRadio Supports Ad Hoc Ultra-Low Power Wireless Networking. *Wireless Computing - p42-48*, July 2000. 52
20. Frank Stajano and Ross Anderson. The Ressurrecting Duckling: Security Issues for Ad-hoc Wireless Networks. In B. Christianson, B.Crispo, and M.Roe, editors, *Security Protocols. 7th International Workshop Proceedings*, Lecture Notes in Computer Science. Springer-Verlag Berlin Heidelberg, 1999. 60
21. Terry Todd, , and Fraser Bennett Alan Jones. Low Power Rendezvous in Embedded Wireless Networks. In *1st International Workshop on Mobile Ad Hoc Networking and Computing*, August 2000. 52
22. James Weatherall and Andy Hopper. Predator: A Distributed Location Service and Example Applications. In *Cooperative Buildings*, October 1999. 54
23. James Weatherall and Alan Jones. Ubiquitous Networks and their Applications. *IEEE Personal Communications Magazine, Wireless Applications Special Issue*, February 2002. 54
24. James "Wez" Weatherall and David Scott. Mobile Computing with Python. In *The Ninth International Python Conference*, pages 87–96, March 2001. 55
25. J. N. Weatherall. The R2 Low-Power Messaging and Rendezvous Layer. In *SIGOPS European Workshop*, September 2000. 54

Software Architecture-Based Adaptation
for Pervasive Systems

Shang-Wen Cheng, David Garlan, Bradley Schmerl, João Pedro Sousa,
Bridget Spitznagel, Peter Steenkiste, and Ningning Hu

School of Computer Science, Carnegie Mellon University
5000 Forbes Ave, Pittsburgh PA 15213 USA
Phone: 1 412 268 5056
{zensoul,garlan,schmerl,jpsousa,sprite,prs,hnn}@cs.cmu.edu

Abstract. An important requirement for pervasive computing systems is the ability to adapt at runtime to handle varying resources, user mobility, changing user needs, and system faults. In this paper we describe an approach in which dynamic adaptation is supported by the use of software architectural models to monitor an application and guide dynamic changes to it. The use of externalized models permits one to make reconfiguration decisions based on a global perspective of the running system, apply analytic models to determine correct repair strategies, and gauge the effectiveness of repair through continuous system monitoring. We illustrate the application of this idea to pervasive computing systems, focusing on the need to adapt based on performance-related criteria and models.

1   Introduction

An important requirement for pervasive computing systems is the ability to adapt themselves at runtime to handle such things as user mobility, resource variability, changing user needs, and system faults. In the past, systems that supported self-adaptation were rare, confined mostly to domains like telecommunications switches or deep space control software, where taking a system down for upgrades was not an option, and where human intervention was not always feasible. However, in a pervasive computing world more and more systems have this requirement, because they must continue to run with only minimal human oversight, and cope with variable resources as a user moves from one environment to another (bandwidth, server availability, etc.), system faults (servers and networks going down, failure of external components, etc.), and changing user priorities (high-fidelity video streams at one moment, low fidelity at another, etc.).

Traditionally system self-repair has been handled within the application, and at the code level. For example, applications typically use generic mechanisms such as exception handling or timeouts to trigger application-specific responses to an observed fault or system anomaly. Such mechanisms have the attraction that they can trap an

H. Schmeck, T. Ungerer, and L. Wolf (Eds.): ARCS 2002, LNCS 2299, pp. 67-82, 2002.
© Springer-Verlag Berlin Heidelberg 2002

error at the moment of detection, and are well-supported by modern programming languages (e.g., Java exceptions) and runtime libraries (e.g., timeouts for RPC). However, they suffer from the problem that it can be difficult to determine the true source of the problem, and hence the kind of remedial action required. Moreover, while they can trap errors, they are not well-suited to recognizing "softer" system anomalies, such as gradual degradation of performance over some communication path.

Recently several researchers have proposed an alternative approach in which system models – and in particular, software architectural models – are maintained at runtime and used as a basis for system reconfiguration and repair [25]. An architectural model of a system is one in which the overall structure of a running system is captured as a composition of coarse-grained interacting components [28]. As a basis for self-repair the use of architectural models has a number of nice properties: An architectural model can provide a global perspective on the system allowing one to determine non-local changes to achieve some property. Architectural models can make "integrity" constraints explicit, helping to ensure the validity of any change. By "externalizing" the monitoring and adaptation of a system using architectural models, it is possible to engineer adaptation mechanisms, infrastructure and policies independent of any particular application, thereby reducing the cost and improving the effectiveness of adding self-adaptation to new systems.

In this paper we illustrate how architecture-based adaptation can be applied to pervasive computing systems. Specifically, we show how to use the approach to support adaptation of applications in a pervasive computing environment. This pervasive environment consists of a set of mobile users accessing shared information through a variety of devices. These devices communicate over a heterogeneous communications infrastructure.

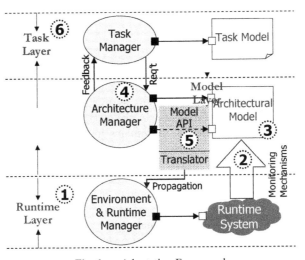

Fig. 1.   Adaptation Framework

2   Overview of Approach

Our approach is based on the 3-layer view illustrated in Figure 1. The *Runtime Layer* is responsible for observing a system's runtime properties and performing low-level operations to adapt the system. It consists of the system itself, together with its operating environment (networks, processors, I/O devices, communications links, etc.) (1). Observed runtime information is propagated upwards using a monitoring infrastructure that condenses, filters, and abstracts those observations in order to render that information in architecture-relevant terms (2).

The *Model Layer* is responsible for interpreting observed system behavior in terms of higher-level, and more easily analyzed, properties. It forms the centerpiece of the approach, consisting of one or more architectural models of the system (3), together with respective architecture managers (4) that determine whether a system's runtime behavior is within the envelope of acceptable ranges. An architecture manager includes a constraint checker and a repair handler. The former determines when architectural constraints are violated; the latter determines how to adapt the system. Repairs are propagated down to the running system (5).

The *Task Layer* is responsible for determining the quality of service requirements for the task(s). A task is a high-level representation of a user's computational needs, and indicates the services required, as well as the desired performance profile for those services. These profiles in turn determine the range of behavior permissible at an architectural level.

To illustrate how the approach works, consider a set of mobile users interacting with a pervasive environment, each user currently performing one or more tasks that require access to shared information. We will assume that this shared information is provided by a set of server groups distributed over a pervasive network, as illustrated in Figure 2(a). Each server group consists of a set of replicated servers (Figure 2(b)), and maintains a queue of requests, which are handled in FIFO order by the servers in the server group. Individual servers send their results back directly to the requesting user.

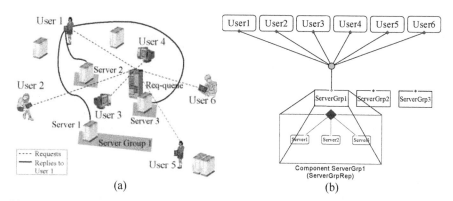

Fig. 2.   Deployment Architecture (a) and Software Architecture (b) of the Example System

The pervasive computing environment that manages this overall infrastructure needs to make sure that two inter-related system qualities are maintained. First, to guarantee the quality of service for each user, the request-response latency for users must be under a certain threshold, which may vary depending on the task and user. Second, to keep costs down, the set of currently active servers should be kept to a minimum, subject to the first constraint.

Achieving these goals requires cooperation from three levels. The *Task Layer* has knowledge of the kind of information a user requires and the quality of service requirements for retrieving this information. This knowledge feeds into the *Model Layer*, so that relevant analyses can be performed to determine the appropriate configuration when a new task is created. The *Model Layer* then makes changes through the *Runtime Layer*, to the executing system to fulfill those requirements.

Establishing the correct configuration for the system only when a task is created, however, is not sufficient in a pervasive computing environment, since resources and requirements change dynamically. For example, suppose that some user's task requires her to review a set of images and select some of them to be included in a report. Suppose that initially this user is carrying out the task on a PDA, which communicates over a wireless network, and which can only display low-resolution grayscale images. As the user moves through the environment, her PDA may move from a wireless cell that has an access point getting good bandwidth to a server group to a cell that is not. In this case, the environment may need to locate another server group with a better bandwidth and move her requests to that server group. This change of resources should be sensed automatically and the reconfiguration done transparently, so that the user is not unnecessarily distracted. Furthermore, this same user might later move into a resource-rich environment that contains a high-resolution color display. The task layer may then want to change the user's bandwidth requirements so that she can view larger images on this screen. These new bandwidth requirements may force a change in the *Model Layer*, which will invoke a concomitant change in the implementation.

The approach outlined above has a number of distinct advantages for the systems builder over current approaches that hardwire adaptation mechanisms into the components of the application. First, the use of architectural models permits non-local properties to be observed, and non-local adaptations to be effected. For example, suitable monitoring mechanisms can keep track of aggregate average behavior of a set of components. Second, formal architectural models permit the application of analytical methods for deriving sound repair strategies. For example, a queuing-theoretic analysis of performance can indicate possible points of adaptation for a performance-driven application. Third, externalized adaptation (via architectural models) has several important engineering benefits: adaptation mechanisms can be more easily extended; they can be studied and reasoned about independently of the monitored applications; they can exploit shared monitoring and adaptation infrastructure.

3   Architecture-Based Adaptation

The centerpiece of our approach is the use of stylized architectural models [26,28]. Although there are many proposed modeling languages and representation schemes for architectures, we adopt a simple scheme in which an architectural model is represented as a graph of interacting components. This is the core architectural representation scheme adopted by a number of architecture description languages, including

Acme [11], xADL [8], and SADL [23]. Nodes in the graph are termed components. They represent the principal computational elements and data stores of the system: clients, servers, databases, user interfaces, etc. Arcs are termed connectors, and represent the pathways of interaction between the components. A given connector may in general be realized in a running system by a complex base of middleware and distributed systems support. For example, in the software architecture illustrated in Figure 2(b), the server group, servers, and users are components. The connector includes the request queue and the network connections between users and servers.

To account for various behavioral properties of a system we allow elements in the graph to be annotated with extensible property lists. Properties associated with a connector might define its protocol of interaction, or performance attributes (e.g., delay, bandwidth). Properties associated with a component might define its core functionality, performance attributes (e.g., average time to process a request, load, etc.) or reliability. In addition we associate with each architecture a set of constraints defined in a first-order predicate logic augmented with a set of primitives appropriate for architectural specification [22]. These constraints can be attached to components or connectors to express things like the fact that some property value must always lie between a given range of values.

In our system each architecture is identified with a particular architectural style. An architectural style defines a set of types for components, connectors, interfaces, and properties together with a set of rules that govern how elements of those types may be composed. Requiring a system to conform to a style has many benefits, including support for analysis, reuse, code generation, and system evolution [10,31,32]. Moreover, the notion of style often maps well to widely-used component integration infrastructures (such as EJB, HLA, CORBA), which prescribe the kinds of components allowed and the kinds of interactions that may take place between them.

One of the significant advantages of architectural descriptions is that they provide opportunities for analysis, including system consistency checking [3], conformance to architectural style constraints [1], conformance to quality attributes [7], and dependence analysis [30].

We can model our example using a client-server architectural style. The architectural style provides definitions for client, server, and server group components and the connections between them. Properties include those required for queuing-theoretic performance analysis, and integrity constraints include the necessity for each client to be connected to one and only one server group.

As mentioned in our example, the *Task Layer* sets the performance profile for the architecture. These profiles can be expressed as threshold constraints in the architecture. These constraints can then be checked dynamically to see if the system is functioning within bounds. In the context of our example, we desire each user to receive no more than some maximum latency. This can be expressed in the architecture as a constraint on each of the client's connections to the server group. In the architecture of our example, the constraint is of the form:

averageLatency < maxLatency.

This constraint appears on each client's connection, and needs to be evaluated dynamically. In our approach, the *Task Layer* sets the value for *maxLatency*; the *averageLatency* value is an observed value determined by monitoring.

3.1   Using Architectural Analysis to Guide System (Re)Configuration

As we argued above, one of the main benefits of using software architecture is that the level of abstraction gives us the ability to use analytical methods to evaluate properties of a system's architectural design. To illustrate how this works, consider our example, where we have modeled the application in a style amenable to M/M/m performance analysis [29]. The M/M indicates that the probability of a request arriving at component s, and the probability of component s finishing a request it is currently servicing, are assumed to be exponential distributions (also called "memoryless," independent of past events); requests are further assumed to be, at any point in time, either waiting in one component's queue, receiving service from one component, or traveling on one connector. The m indicates the replication of component s; that is, component s is not limited to representing a single server, but rather can represent a server group of m servers that are fed from a single queue. Given estimates for clients' request generation rates and servers' service times (the time that it takes to service one request), we can derive performance estimates for components.

Applying this M/M/m theory to the style used in our example tells us that with respect to the average latency for servicing user requests, the key design parameters in our style are (a) the replication factor m of servers within a server group, (b) the communication delay between clients and servers, (c) the arrival rate of client requests, and (d) the service time of servers within a server group. We can use performance analysis to decide (1) the number of replicated servers that must exist in a server group so that it is properly utilized, and (2) where server groups should be placed so that the bandwidth is sufficient to achieve the desired latency.

Given a particular service time and arrival rate, performance analysis of this model gives a range of possible values for server utilization, replication, latencies, and system response time. Say that the task layer for each user informs us that the arrival rate is 180 requests/sec, the average request size is 0.5KB, and the average response size is 20KB. Assume also that the server service time is between 10ms and 20ms. Given these values, then the performance analysis gives us the following bounds:

Initial server replication count= 3-5
Average Bandwidth = 10.5KB/sec

This analysis gives us parameters for a configuration of the architecture of the software that satisfies the above requirements. We use this information to configure the system to locate appropriate server groups, monitor the application to make sure it is in conformance with these requirements, and attempt to adapt the system transparently as the user moves about the environment.

If the *Task Layer* changes the requirements, for example when the user begins using a large display, the analysis is performed again to determine a satisfactory reconfiguration of the system. Again, this can be done transparently.

3.2   Using Architecture to Assist Adaptation

The representation schemes for architectures and analyses outlined above were originally created to support design-time development tools. As suggested above, these schemes and analyses need to be made available at runtime. This section discusses an augmentation to architectures that allows them to function as runtime adaptation mechanisms. This includes *adaptation operations*, based on the style of the architecture, to change an architectural model, and *repair strategies* that apply these operations to adapt the architecture. These operations need to be translated into operations on the runtime system. We consider the supporting runtime infrastructure needed to make this work in practice in Section 3.3.

3.2.1   Architecture Adaptation Operators

The first extension is to augment an architectural style description with a set of operators that define the ways in which one can change systems in that style. Such operators determine a "virtual machine" that can be used at runtime to adapt an architectural design.

Given a particular architectural style, there will typically be a set of natural operators for changing an architectural configuration and querying for additional information. In the most generic case, architectures can provide primitive operators for adding and removing components and connections [24]. However, specific styles can often provide higher-level operators that exploit the restrictions in that style and the intended implementation base.

In terms of our example, we define the following operators:

addServer(): This operation is applied to a server group component and adds a new replicated server component to its representation, ensuring that the architecture is structurally valid.

move(*to:ServerGroupT*): This operation is applied to a client and deletes the role currently connecting the client to the connector that connects it to a server group and performs the necessary attachment to a connector that will connect it to the server group passed in as a parameter.

remove(): This operation is applied to a server and deletes the server from its containing server group. Furthermore, it changes the replication count on the server group and deletes the binding.

The above operations all effect changes to the architectural model. The next operation queries the state of the running system:

findGoodSGroup(*cl:ClientT,bw:float*):*ServerGroupT*;   finds the server group with the best bandwidth (above *bw*) to the client *cli*, and returns a reference to the server group.

These operators reflect the style in question and the implementation base. First, from the nature of a server group, we get the operations for activating or deactivating a server within a group. Also, from the nature of the asynchronous request connectors, we get the operations for adapting the communication path between particular clients and server groups. Second, based on the knowledge of supported system change operations, outlined in Section 3.3.2, we have some confidence that the architectural operations are actually achievable in the executing system.

3.2.2   Architecture Repair Strategies

The second extension is the specification of repair strategies that correspond to selected constraints of the architecture. The key idea is that when an architectural constraint violation is detected, the appropriate repair strategy will be triggered.

A repair strategy has two main functions: first to determine the cause of the problem, second to determine how to fix it. Thus the general form of a repair strategy is a sequence of repair tactics. Each repair tactic is guarded by a precondition that determines whether that tactic is applicable. The evaluation of a tactic's precondition will usually involve the examination of various properties of the architecture in order to pinpoint the problem and determine applicability. If it is applicable, the tactic executes a repair script that is written as an imperative program using the style-specific operators described above.

To handle the situation where several tactics may be applicable, the enclosing repair strategy decides on the policy for executing repair tactics. It might apply the first tactic that succeeds. Alternatively, it might sequence through all of the tactics, or use some other style-specific policy.

One of the principal advantages of allowing the system designer to pick an appropriate style is the ability to exploit style-specific analyses to determine whether repair tactics are sound. By sound, we mean that if executed the changes will help reestablish the violated constraint.

In general an analytical method for an architecture will provide a compositional method for calculating some system property in terms of the properties of its parts. By looking at the constraint to be satisfied, the analysis can often point the repair strategy writer both to the set of possible causes for constraint violation, and for each possible cause, to an appropriate repair.

Illustrating this idea for our example, we can show how the repair strategy developed from the theoretical analysis. The equations for calculating latency for a service request, derived from [4], indicate that there are four contributing factors: 1) the connector delay, 2) the server replication count, 3) the average client request rate, and 4) the average server service time. Of these we have control over the first two. When the latency is high, we can decrease the connector delay or increase the server replication count to decrease the latency. Determining which tactic depends on whether the connector has a low bandwidth (inversely proportional to connector delay) or if the server group is heavily loaded (inversely proportional to replication). These two system properties form the preconditions to the tactics; we have thus developed a repair strategy with two tactics.

Figure 3 illustrates the repair strategy and tactics associated with a latency threshold constraint. Line 1 defines the constraint that the average latency must not be below the maximum latency set by the task requirements. Line 2 calls the repair strategy to be invoked if the constraint fails. The repair strategy in lines 4-14, *fixLatency*, consists of two tactics. The first tactic, defined in lines 16-26, handles the situation in which a server group is overloaded, identified by the precondition in lines 22-23. Its main action in lines 24-25 is to create a new server in any of the overloaded server groups. The second tactic, defined in lines 28-42, handles the situation in which high latency is due to communication delay, identified by the precondition in lines 30-31. It queries the architecture to find a server group that will yield a higher bandwidth connection in lines 35-36. In lines 37-39, if such a group exists it moves the client-server connector to use the new group. The repair strategy uses a policy in which it executes these two tactics sequentially: if the first tactic succeeds it commits the repair strategy; otherwise it executes the second. The strategy will abort if neither tactic succeeds, or if the second tactic finds that it cannot proceed since there are no suitable server groups to move the connection to.

```
1   invariant r : averageLatency <= maxLatency
2   !→ fixLatency(r);
3
4   strategy fixLatency (badRole : ClientRoleT)={
5     let badClient : ClientT =
6       select one cli : ClientT in self.Components |
7         exists p : RequestT in cli.Ports |
8           attached(badRole, r);
9     if (fixServerLoad(badClient)) {
10      commit repair; }
11    else if (fixBandwidth(badClient,badRole) {
12      commit repair; }
13    else {abort ModelError;}
14  }
15
16  tactic fixServerLoad (client :ClientT) :boolean={
17    let loadedServerGroups :set{ServerGroupT}=
18      select sgrp:ServerGroupT in
19        self.Components |
20          connected(sgrp,client) and
21          sgrp.load > maxServerLoad;
22  if (size(loadedServerGroups) == 0)
23    return false;
24  foreach sGrp in loadedServerGroups {
25    sgrp.addServer(); }
26  return (size(loadedServerGroups)>0);
27
28  tactic fixBandwidth(client:ClientT
29                      role:ClientRoleT):boolean={
30    if (role.bandwidth>=minBandwidth) {
31      return false;}
32    let oldSGrp: ServerGroupT =
33      select one sGrp:ServerGroupT in
34        self.Components | connected (client,sGrp);
35    let goodSGrp : ServerGroupT =
36      findGoodSGrp(client,minBandwidth);
37    if (goodSGrp != nil) {
38      client.move (oldSGrp,goodSGrp);
39      return true;
40    } else {
41      abort NoServerGroupFound;
42  }}
```

Fig. 3. Repair Strategy for High Latency

3.3   Bridging the Gap to Implementation

While the use of architectural models allows us to provide automated support for adaptation at an architectural level, through use of constraints, operators, and analytical methods, we must furthermore relate model changes to the real world. There are two aspects to this. The first is getting information out of the executing system so we can determine when architectural constraints are violated. The second is propagating architectural repairs into the system itself.

3.3.1   Monitoring

In order to provide a bridge from system level behavior to architecturally-relevant observations, we have defined a three-level approach illustrated in Figure 4. This monitoring infrastructure is described in more detail elsewhere [12]: here we summarize the main features.

The lowest level is a set of *probes*, which are "deployed" in the target system or physical environment. Probes monitor the system and announce observations via a "probe bus." We can use off-the-shelf monitoring components (such as Remos [19]) and write wrappers to turn them into probes, or write custom probes. At the second level a set of *gauges* consume and interpret lower-level probe measurements in terms of higher-level model properties. Like probes, gauges disseminate information via a "gauge reporting bus." The top-level entities in Figure 4 are *gauge consumers*, which consume information disseminated by gauges. Such information can be used, for example, to update an abstraction/model, to make system repair decisions, to display warnings and alerts to system users, or to show the current status of the running system.

In the context of architectural repair, we use the architectural style to inform us where to place gauges. Specifically, for each constraint that we wish to monitor, we must place gauges that dynamically update the properties over which the constraint is defined. In addition, our repair strategies may require additional monitored information to pinpoint sources of problems and execute repair operations.

For instance, in the example above we are concerned with the average latency of client requests. To monitor this property, we must associate a gauge with the *averageLatency* property of each client role. Each latency gauge in turn deploys a probe into the implementation that monitors the timing of reply-request pairs. When it receives such monitored values it averages them over some window, updating the latency property in the architecture model when it changes. In addition to this gauge, we are also guided by the repair tactics to place gauges that measure the bandwidth between the client and the server group and also to measure the load on the server group. The gauge for measuring bandwidth uses the same probe used by the latency gauge for measuring the time it takes to receive a reply. An additional probe measures the size of the reply and calculates the bandwidth based on these values. A probe measuring the size of the request queue indicates whether a server group is overloaded.

3.3.2   Repair Execution

The final component of our adaptation framework is a translator that interprets repair scripts as operations on the actual system (Figure 1, item 5). The nature of these operations will depend heavily on the implementation platform. In general, a given architectural operation will be realized by some number of lower level system reconfiguration operations. Each such operator can raise exceptions to signal a failure. These are then propagated to the *Model Layer*.

To illustrate, the specific operators and queries supported by the runtime system in our example are listed in Table 1. These operators include low-level routines for creating new request queues, activating and deactivating servers, and moving client communications to a new queue. The operations at the *Model Layer*, describe in Section 3.2.1, are translated into calls on the operations in the *Runtime Layer* (Table 1) to effect the actual change in the system.

4   Implementation

Previously, the work on tools software architecture has mostly focused on design-time support. We have adapted these tools so that they can be used as runtime facilities. Specifically, AcmeStudio, an architecture design environment, can now make available an architectural description at runtime. This description can be analyzed by runtime versions of our Armani constraint checking and performance analysis tools, as well as be manipulated by our repair engine. Collectively, these tools implement the *Model Layer* elements in Figure 1.

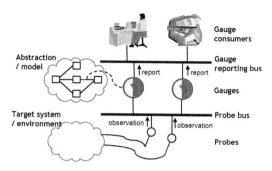

Fig. 4. Gauge Infrastructure

Table 1. Environment Manager Operators and Queries

CreateReqQueue()	Adds a logical request queue to *Req-queue* machine in Figure 2.
findServer([string cli_ip, float bw_thresh])	Finds a spare server that has at least *bw_thresh* bandwidth between it and the client.
moveClient(ReqQ newQ)	Moves a client to the new request queue.
connectServer(Server srv, ReqQ to)	Configures a server so that it pulls client requests out of the *to* request queue.
activateServer ()	Signals that the server should begin pull requests from the request queue.
DeactivateServer()	Signals that a server should stop pulling requests from the request queue.
remos_get_flow (string clIP, string svIP)	This is a Remos API call that returns the predicted bandwidth between two IP addresses.

In terms of monitoring, we have developed prototype probes for gathering information about networks, based on the Remos system [19]. Remos has two parts: (1) an API, that allows applications to issue queries about bandwidth and latency between groups of hosts; and (2) a set of *collectors* that gather information about different parts of the network [21]. A probe uses Remos to collect the information required for the probe and distributes it as events using the Siena wide area event bus [6]; gauges listen to this information and perform calculations and transformations to relate it to the software architecture of the system.

Currently, we have hand-tailored support for translating APIs in the *Model Layer* to ones in the *Runtime Layer* that need to be changed for each implementation. Our work in this area will concentrate on providing more general mechanisms where appropriate, and perhaps using off-the-shelf reconfiguration commands for commercial systems.

With respect to the *Task Layer*, we are actively investigating effective means for specifying user tasks, as part of our broader research in the Aura project at Carnegie Mellon University [27,33].

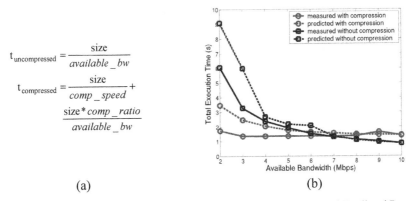

$$t_{uncompressed} = \frac{size}{available\_bw}$$

$$t_{compressed} = \frac{size}{comp\_speed} + \frac{size * comp\_ratio}{available\_bw}$$

(a)   (b)

Fig. 5. (a) The Analytical Compression Model; (b) Comparing Measured and Predicted Performance

For our modeling and analysis approach to be feasible, we need to have some confidence that the analysis at the *Model Layer* is relevant at the *Runtime Layer*. To explore specific data points of this, we have conducted some initial experimentation with comparing predicted performance and measured performance. Our simple experimental testbed was a client-server application where the repair tactic was to use compression to make more effective use of the available bandwidth [17]. In this case, we used simple analytical models instead of queuing models – shown in Figure 5(a).

The model variables in italics have to be determined at runtime. For our prototype (where compression uses gzip), the compression ratio (*comp_ratio*) depends on the data type (text, JPEG, etc.) and is simply determined through look up in a predefined table. The compression speed (*comp_speed*) is machine dependent. It is estimated based on benchmarks. Finally, the estimated network throughput (*available_bw*) is obtained using the Remos system.

Figure 5(b) shows the result of a set of experiments performed on a dedicated testbed. The testbed allows us to vary the available bandwidth (x-axis) by generating a variable competing UDP stream. The y-axis shows execution, both estimated (dashed lines) and measured (full lines). The experiments show two interesting results. First, the crossover point for the estimated execution time with and without compression happens at about the same point as the crossover point for the measured execution times with and without compression (indicated by the arrows in Figure 5(b)). This shows that the choice of tactics based on an analytical model will have the desired effect in the implementation. Second, around the crossover point, the execution times for the different tactics are very similar, suggesting that even if the client would pick the wrong tactic (for example because of a probe value with an unusually large error), the impact on performance would be minimal.

5   Related Work

Considerable research has been done in the area of dynamic adaptation at an implementation level. There are a multitude of programming languages and libraries that provide dynamic linking and binding mechanisms (e.g., [15,16]), as well as exception handling capabilities and distributed debugging [14]. Systems of this kind allow self-repair to be programmed on a per-system basis, but do not provide external, reusable mechanisms that can be added to systems in a disciplined manner, as with an architecture-driven approach.

There is a large body of research in the area of pervasive computing (e.g., [2]) and many companies are exploring support for this area. This research primarily focuses on user interface issues and the provision of low-level services and infrastructure in the environment. The notion of adaptation is hardwired into particular applications or services [5,9,18]. Again, our architecture-based approach provides a general solution that supports adaptation of applications and systems for which it is not explicitly supported.

The BBN QuO system [20] extends CORBA to support applications that adapt to resource availability. One aspect of the system is that users can define operating regions. The runtime system monitors the application and execution environment, and invokes application specific handlers when the application changes operating region. QuO is a specific example of an adaptive and reflective middleware system, which in general do not have an explicit architectural model of the application.

There has been some related research on architecture-based adaptation. However, this research relies on specific architectural styles, and implementations that match these styles [13,24]. In this paper, we have concentrated on how architectural models can be used to guide adaptation in a pervasive system, and the extensions need to software architectures to make them useful in a dynamic setting. In our broader approach we decouple the style from the system infrastructure so that developers have the flexibility to pair an appropriate style to a system based on its implementation and the system attributes that should drive adaptation. To accomplish this we have introduced some new mechanisms to allow "runtime" styles to be treated as a design parameter in the runtime adaptation infrastructure. Specifically, we have shown how styles can be used to detect problems and trigger repairs. We have also provided mechanisms that bridge the gap between an architectural model and an implementation – both for monitoring and for effecting system changes.

6   Conclusions and Future Work

In this paper we have presented a technique for using software architectural models to automate dynamic repair of systems. In particular, architectures and their associated analyses:

- make explicit the constraints that must be maintained in the face of evolution;
- direct us to the set of properties that must be monitored to achieve system quality attributes and maintain constraints;
- define a set of abstract architectural operators for repairing a system; and
- allow us to select appropriate repair strategies, based on analytical methods.

We illustrated how the technique can be applied to performance-oriented adaptation in a pervasive computing environment with mobile users, time-varying resources, and heterogeneous devices.

For future research we need to be able to develop mechanisms that provide richer adaptability for executing systems. We also need new monitoring capabilities, and reusable infrastructure for relating monitored values to architectures. Finally, we need new analytical methods for architecture that will permit the specification of principled adaptation policies. Additionally we see a number of other key future research areas. First is the investigation of more intelligent repair policy mechanisms. For example, one might like a system to dynamically adjust its repair tactic selection policy so that it takes into consideration the history of tactic effectiveness: effective tactics would be favored over those that sometimes fail to produce system improvements. Second is the link between architectures and tasks. We need to further explore both how to specify user tasks and the precise interaction between them and the architectural parameters and constraints.

Acknowledgements

DARPA, under Grants N66001-99-2-8918 and F30602-00-2-0616, supports this work. Views and conclusions contained in this document are those of the authors and should not be interpreted as representing the official policies, either expressed or implied, of DARPA.

References

1. Abowd, G., Allen,R., and Garlan, D. Using Style to Understand Descriptions of Software Architectures. In Proceedings of SIGSOFT'93: Foundations of Software Engineering, December 1993.
2. Abowd, G., Burmitt, B., and Shafer, S. (Eds). Ubicomp 2001: Ubiquitous Computing - Third International Conference Atlanta, Georgia, USA, September 30 - October 2, 2001 Proceedings. Lecture Notes in Computer Science **2201**, Springer, October 2001.
3. Allen, R. and Garlan, D. A Formal Basis for Architectural Connection. *ACM Transactions on Software Engineering and Methodology*, June 1997.
4. Bertsekas, D. and Gallager, R. Data Networks, Second Edition. Prentice Hall, 1992. ISBN 0-13-200916-1.
5. Bollinger, J., and Gross, T. A Framework-Based Approach to the Development of Network-Aware Applications. *IEEE Transacations on Software Engineering (Special Issue on Mobility and Network Aware Computing)* **24**(5):367-390, May 1998.
6. Carzaniga, A., Rosenblum, D.S., and Wolf, A.L. Achieving Expressiveness and Scalability in an Internet-Scale Event Notification Service. Proceedings of the Nineteenth ACM Symposium on Principles of Distributed Computing (PODC2000), Portland OR, July, 2000.
7. Clements, P., Bass, L., Kazman, R., Abowd, G. Predicting Software Quality by Architecture-Level Evaluation. In Proceedings of the Fifth International Conference on Software Quality, Austin, TX, October 1995.

8. Dashofy, E., van der Hoek, A., and Taylor, R.N. A Highly-Extensible, XML-Based Architecture Description Language. Proceedings of the Working IEEE/IFIP Conference on Software Architecture, Amsterdam, The Netherlands, August 2001.
9. Flinn, J., Narayanan, D., Satyanarayanan, M. Self-Tuned Remote Execution for Pervasive Computing. In Proceedings of the 8th Workshop on Hot Topics in Operating Systems (HotOS-VIII), Oberbayen, Germany, May 2001.
10. Garlan, D., Allen, R.J., and Ockerbloom, J. Exploiting Style in Architectural Design. Proceedings of SIGSOFT '94 Symposium on the Foundations of Software Engineerng, , New Orleans, LA, December 1994.
11. Garlan, D., Monroe, R.T., and Wile, D. Acme: Architectural Description of Component-Based Systems. Foundations of Component-Based Systems. Leavens, G.T., and Sitaraman, M. (eds). Cambridge University Press, 2000 pp. 47-68.
12. Garlan, D., Schmerl, B.R., and Chang, J. Using Gauges for Architecture-Based Monitoring and Adaptation. The Working Conference on Complex and Dynamic System Architecture. Brisbane, Australia, December 2001.
13. Gorlick, M.M., and Razouk, R.R. Using Weaves for Software Construction and Analysis. Proceedings of the 13th International Conference on Software Engineering, IEEE Computer Society Press, May 1991.
14. Gorlick, M.M. Distributed Debugging on $5 a day. Proceedings of the California Software Symposium, University of California, Irvine, CA, 1997 pp. 31-39. Magee, J., Dulay, N., Eisenbach, S., and Kramer, J. Specifying Distributed Software Architectures. Proceedings of 5th European Software Engineering Conference (ESEC '95), Sitges, September 1995. Also published as Lecture Notes in Computer Science 989, (Springer-Verlag), 1995, pp. 137-153.
15. Gosling, J. and McGilton, H. The Java Language Environment: A White Paper. Sun Microsystems Computer Company, Mountain View, California, May 1996. Available at http://java.sun.com/docs/white/langenv/.
16. Ho, W.W. and Olsson, R.A. An Approach to Genuine Dynamic Linking. Software – Practice and Experience 21(4):375—390, 1991.
17. Hu, N. Network Aware Data Transmission with Compression. In Selected Papers from the Proceedings of the Fourth Student Symposium on Computer Systems (SOCS-4) Carnegie Mellon University School of Computer Science Technical Report, CMU-CS-01-164, October 2001.
18. Krintz, C., and Calder, B. Reducing Delay with Dynamic Selection of Compression Formats. Proceedings of the Tenth IEEE International Symposium on High Performance Distributed Computing, California, USA, August 2001.
19. Lowekamp, B., Miller, N., Sutherland, D., Gross, T., Steenkiste, P., and Subhlok, J. A Resource Query Interface for Network-aware Applications. Cluster Computing, 2:139-151, Baltzer, 1999.
20. Loyall, J.P., Schantz, R.E., Zinky, J.A., and Bakken, D.E. Specifying and Measuring Quality of Service in Distributed Object Systems. In Proceedings of the 1st IEEE Symposium on Object-oriented Real-time Distributed Computing, Kyoto, Japan, April 1998.
21. Miller, N., and Steenkiste, P. Collecting Network Status Information for Network-Aware Applications. IEEE INFOCOM 2000, Tel Aviv, Israel, March 2000.

22. Monroe, R.T. Capturing Software Architecture Design Expertise with Armani. Carnegie Mellon University School of Computer Science Technical Report CMU-CS-98-163.
23. Moriconi, M. and Reimenschneider, R.A. Introduction to SADL 1.0: A Language for Specifying Software Architecture Hierarchies. Technical Report SRI-CSL-97-01, SRI International, March 1997.
24. Oreizy, P., Medvidovic, N., and Taylor, R.N. Architecture-Based Runtime Software Evolution in the Proceedings of the International Conference on Software Engineering 1998 (ICSE'98). Kyoto, Japan, April 1998, pp. 11—15.
25. Oreizy, P., Gorlick, M.M., Taylor, R.N., Johnson, G., Medvidovic, N., Quilici, A., Rosenblum, D., and Wolf, A. An Architecture-Based Approach to Self-Adaptive Software. IEEE Intelligent Systems 14(3):54-62, May/June 1999.
26. Perry, D.E., and Wolf, A. Foundations for the Study of Software Architecture. *ACM SIGSOFT Software Engineering Notes* 17(4):40-52, October 1992.
27. Satyanarayanan, M. Pervasive Computing: Vision and Challenges. IEEE Personal Communications, pp. 10-17, August 2001.
28. Shaw, M., and Garlan, D. Software Architectures: Perspectives on an Emerging Discipline. Prentice Hall, 1996.
29. Spitznagel, B. and Garlan, D. Architecture-Based Performance Analysis. Proceedings of the 1998 Conference on Software Engineering and Knowledge Engineering, June, 1998.
30. Stafford, J., Richardson, D.J., and Wolf, A.L. Alladin: A Tool for Architecture-Level Dependence Analysis of Software. University of Colorado at Boulder, Technical Report CU-CS-858-98, April 1998.
31. Taylor, R.N., Medvidovic, N., Anderson, K.M., Whitehead, E.J., Robbins, J.E., Nies, K.A., Oreizy, P., and Dubrow, D.L. A Component- and Message-Based Architectural Style for GUI Software. IEEE Transactions on Software Engineering 22(6):390-406, 1996.
32. Vestel, S. MetaH Programmer's Manual, Version 1.09. Technical Report, Honeywell Technology Center, April 1996.
33. Wang, Z., and Garlan, D. Task-Driven Computing. Carnegie Mellon University School of Computer Science Technical Report CMU-CS-00-154, May 2000.

KECho - Event Communication
for Distributed Kernel Services

Christian Poellabauer, Karsten Schwan, Greg Eisenhauer, and Jiantao Kong

College of Computing, Georgia Institute of Technology
Atlanta, GA 30332, USA
{chris,schwan,eisen,jiantao}@cc.gatech.edu

Abstract. Event services have received increased attention as scalable tools for the composition of large-scale, distributed systems, as evidenced by their successful deployment in interactive multimedia applications and scientific collaborative tools. This paper introduces KECho, a kernel-based event service aimed at supporting the coordination among multiple kernel services in distributed systems, typically to provide applications using these services with certain levels of Quality of Service (QoS). The publish/subscribe communication supported by KECho permits components of remote kernels as well as applications to coordinate their operation. The target group of such a kernel-based event service is the rapidly increasing number of extensions that are being added to existing operating systems and are intended to support the Quality of Service and real-time requirements of distributed and embedded applications.

1   Introduction

Kernel-level services and their run-time coordination. The need to offer high or predictable levels of performance, especially in distributed and embedded systems, has resulted in the kernel-level implementation of certain applications and services. Examples include the in-kernel web servers khttpd and tux on Linux, kernel-level QoS management and resource management mechanisms [ ], and load balancing algorithms [ ]. To attain desired gains in predictable performance, distributed kernel-level extensions must coordinate their operation. For example, for load balancing, multiple machines in a web server cluster must not only exchange information about their respective CPU and device loads (e.g., disks), but must also be able to forward requests to each other without undue involvement of clients and forwarding engines [ ]. Similarly, to ensure the timely execution of pipelined sensor or display processing applications in embedded systems, hosts must not only share detailed information on their respective CPU schedules and the operation of the communication links they share [,], but they must also coordinate the ways in which they allocate resources to pipelined tasks. Finally, the run-time coordination among kernel-level services illustrated above is highly dynamic, involving only those kernel services and machines that currently conduct a shared application-level task. In addition, the

H. Schmeck, T. Ungerer, and L. Wolf (Eds.): ARCS 2002, LNCS 2299, pp. 83–97, 2002.
© Springer-Verlag Berlin Heidelberg 2002

extent of such cooperation strongly depends on the application-level quality criteria being sought, ranging from simply 'better performance' to strong properties like 'deadline guarantees.'

Run-time kernel coordination with KECho. This paper presents KECho, a kernel-level publish/subscribe mechanism for run-time coordination among distributed kernel services. Using KECho, any number of kernel-level services on multiple hosts can dynamically join and leave a group of information-sharing, cooperating hosts. Using KECho, services can exchange resource information, share resources (e.g., via request forwarding), and coordinate their operation to meet desired QoS guarantees. KECho uses anonymous event-based notification and data exchange, thereby contrasting it to lower-level mechanisms like kernel-to-kernel socket communications, RPC [ ], or the RPC-like active messaging developed in previous work [ ]. Furthermore, compared to object-based kernel interactions [ ] or to the way in which distributed CORBA, DCOM, or Java objects interact at the user level [, ,], KECho's model of communication provides improved flexibility, since its use of anonymous event notification permits services to interact without explicit knowledge of each others identities.

The *KECho* kernel-level publish/subscribe mechanism shares several important attributes with its user-level counterparts. First, KECho events may be used to notify interested subscribers of internal changes of system state or of external changes captured by the system [ ]. Second, it may be used to implement kernel-level coordination among distributed services, perhaps even to complement the application-level coordination implemented with user-level event notification architectures [, , ,]. Applications constructed with event-based architectures include peer-to-peer applications like distributed virtual environments, collaborative tools, multiplayer games, and certain real-time control systems. Third, KECho's functionality is in part identical to that of known user-level event systems, which means that we describe it using interchangeable terms like *event notification mechanism*, *event service*, and *publish/subscribe mechanism*. Further, KECho's event services faithfully implement the publish/subscribe paradigm, where events are sent by publishers (or *sources*) directly to all subscribers (or *sinks*). Channel members are anonymous, which implies that members are freed from the necessity to *learn* about dynamically joining and leaving members.

KECho is implemented as an extension to the Linux operating system (using kernel-loadable modules) and offers a lightweight high-performance event service that allows Linux kernel-level services (which could themselves be extensions) to coordinate their actions. The intent is to ensure that distributed applications achieve high/predictable performance and good system utilization. By using the resulting distributed kernel services, distributed applications can improve their use of shared underlying machine resources like processing power and disk space, without having to explicitly interact at the application level. Application-level counterparts to such functionality typically require additional kernel calls and inter-machine communications, and they may even require the implementation of extensions to existing user/kernel interfaces, so that applications can gather the resource information they need from their respective operating system kernels. In contrast, the kernel-level solutions to distributed resource management enabled by KECho can access any kernel or network service and any kernel data structures without restrictions, which is particularly important for fine-grained resource monitoring or control. Finally, KECho can also be used directly by applications, thereby permitting them to directly interact with their distributed components.

Contributions. (1) KECho is an in-kernel event-based group communication mechanism that supports the anonymous and asynchronous cooperation of distributed kernel-based services and user-level applications. (2) KECho (i) achieves high event responsiveness by using a kernel extension that monitors socket activity and (ii) reduces processing and networking overhead by filtering events based on information supplied by the event publisher and by all event sinks. (3) The advantages of the KECho kernel-based communication tool are explained by means of two extensions to the Linux kernel's functionality: (i) a novel resource management system and (ii) a load balancing mechanism for cluster-based web services.

2   Kernel Event Channels

Event notification systems have been used in applications including virtual environments, scientific computing, and real-time control. Compared to user-level implementations of event services, the advantages of a kernel-level implementation include:

- *Performance:* each call to a user-level function of the event system (e.g., residing in statically or dynamically linked libraries associated with the application) can internally result in a high number of system calls. These calls can block, thereby delaying an application and causing unpredictable application behavior. By using a kernel-based service, we can significantly reduce both the number of system calls used in its implementation and the effects on predictability of its execution. Furthermore, if the application components using event services are implemented entirely within the kernel, then no system calls are required at all, and performance is improved further by minimized blocking delays within the kernel. Specifically, a kernel-thread waiting for an event can be invoked immediately after the event occurs, while a user-level application may suffer further delays by waiting in the CPU scheduler's run queue for a time period dependent on its scheduling priority and the current system load.
- *Functionality:* an increasing number of services is being implemented inside of an operating system's kernel, mainly for performance reasons. Only a direct, kernel-to-kernel connection of such services without the additional overheads of user/kernel crossings allows for fine-grained and direct communication and coordination among remote kernel services.

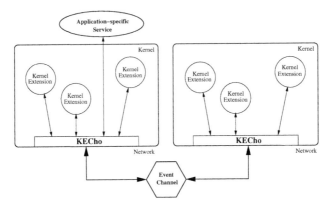

Fig. 1. Event channels in KECho

- *Accessibility of resources:* typical user/kernel interfaces restrict the number and type of kernel resources that can be accessed. Kernel-based implementations have no restrictions regarding the access to such resources, that is, resources and kernel data structures (e.g., task structures, file structures) can be accessed and used directly. This allows kernel solutions to make 'smarter' decisions compared to user-level solutions.

2.1   Architecture of KECho

The goal of a kernel-based event service is to support the coordination and communication among distributed operating system services.

Figure 1 shows the architecture of KECho, using which both kernel- and user-level OS services and user-level applications can dynamically create and open event channels, subscribe to these channels as publishers and subscribers, and then submit and receive events. Although the event channel in Figure 1 is depicted as a logically centralized element, it is a distributed entity in practice, where channel members are connected via direct communication links. The channel creator has a prominent role in these communications only in that it serves as the contact point for anyone wishing to join or leave a group. Any number of kernel services can subscribe to an event channel, and events can be typed, the latter meaning that only events that fit a certain description will be forwarded to subscribers.

The implementation of KECho is based on its user-level counterpart, called *ECho* [ ], the libraries of which have been ported to six kernel-loadable modules for Linux 2.4.0, each with a certain task:

- *KECho Module:* the main interface to kernel services for channel management and event submission/handling.
- *ECalls Module:* a richer interface to user-level applications that implements a lightweight version of system calls and shared memory segments. In addi-

tion, this module can influence CPU scheduling decisions to maximize event responsiveness [ ].

- *Group Manager Module:* a user-level *group server*, running on a publicized host, serves as channel registry, where channel creators store their contact information and channel subscribers can retrieve this information. This module supports the communication among subscribers and the group server.
- *Communication Manager Module (CM):* this module is responsible for the connection management, including creating and operating the connections between remote and local channel members. It currently supports TCP connections as well as a reliable version of UDP to which we are planning to add real-time communication properties.
- *Attribute List Module:* this module implements attributes, which are name-value pairs with which performance or QoS information may be piggybacked onto events.
- *Network Monitoring Module (NW-MON):* this module monitors socket activity and notifies the CM module of newly arrived data at any of the sockets associated with an event channel.

2.2   Event Delivery

The lowest module in the KECho module stack, the network monitoring module (NW-MON), allows KECho to register *interest* in certain sockets. Specifically, KECho registers interest in all sockets associated to event channels. NW-MON then will be notified by the network interrupt handler once data arrives at one of these sockets. In return, this module then notifies the CM module of this event.

As an example, a subscriber waits for a new event (step 1 in Figure 2) by sleeping or blocking. Activity of a socket related to an event channel (step 2) prompts the network monitoring module to send a *wake-up* call to the CM module (step 3). CM then reads the data from the socket (step 4) and identifies and notifies (step 5) the thread owning this socket. Finally, the thread can now copy the received data from the CM module (step 6) and act upon this event.

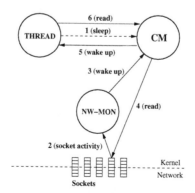

Fig. 2. Event Delivery in KECho

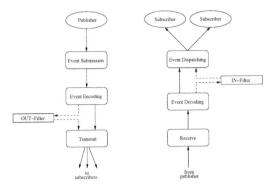

Fig. 3. Channel filters in KECho

While CM awakens and notifies waiting threads about the arrival of events, it can also *accelerate* event responsiveness by increasing the CPU scheduling priority of the process receiving an event. This is part of the ECalls module and is described in more detail in two other papers [,].

2.3   Filtering

Most event systems offer the possibility to limit the number of events received through *event filters*. Filters can be placed at either the event sink or the event source and can significantly reduce event processing and network overheads. The most basic filters ensure that events are delivered only if they are of certain *types*. Typical event systems allow those filters to base their decisions only on a per-connection basis, where a filter makes its decision without considering the overall channel condition. In addition to event filters, KECho offers so-called *channel filters*, which (1) can be dynamically inserted by the event source and (2) can decide on a per-channel basis which sinks will receive an event, that is, filtering decisions are based on information collected from the publishers and subscribers via separate event channels or via attributes piggybacked onto events. As an example consider the task of load balancing. Here, a service request from a machine in a web server cluster is forwarded to an event channel if the local server is not able to service this request. A filtering function can collect load information from all other servers and then decide which other server will receive the event carrying the forwarded request. Alternatively, if load information is outdated and requests are idempotent, then the quality of load balancing can be improved by simultaneously forwarding the request to n servers, where n is chosen by the event source. Upon delivery of the event to the n best servers (e.g, the servers with the lightest loads) and completed event handling, duplicate responses can be discarded by the load balancing mechanism. In this example, the event source supplies the number of desired recipients of a forwarded request and all event sinks supply their current load information.

A filter can also be applied to incoming events, in which case it is simply invoked once each time an event arrives at the channel. For example, such a filter can decide – based on information from the event source and from all sinks – to which sinks the event will be dispatched. In the load balancing example mentioned above, this kind of filter could make sure that the response to a request is being returned to only the one sink that issued the original request, or it could block multiple responses to the same request. A kernel service can register two filter functions with an event channel, an IN-filter and an OUT-filter (Figure 3). An IN-filter is invoked each time an event is being received by KECho. The IN-filter is able to investigate the event before it is being dispatched to the event sinks. On the other hand, an OUT-filter is being invoked each time an event is being submitted by a local event source. Again, the filter inspects the event and can decide which remote sinks will ultimately receive the event.

3   Example 1: Resource Management

Applications rely on the availability of certain *system resources* in order to perform their tasks successfully. System resources can include processing power, network bandwidth, disk bandwidth, RAM, and input/output devices such as cameras or printers. Resource management systems [13,14] have the task to allow applications to discover, allocate, and monitor such distributed resources. This task is made difficult by (i) the dynamic behavior of resources (i.e., resources can join and leave at any time), (ii) the dynamic arrival and departure of application components requiring resources (e.g., through process migration), and (iii) run-time variations in the current resources required by an application.

Figure 4 shows how KECho connects resource managers to facilitate the task of locating and acquiring resources for applications. Kernels I and II have 3 resp. 2 resources that are shared with other hosts, e.g., CPU, disk, and network resources. As an alternative, a kernel could have only one resource manager, which assumes the task of managing all available resources at a host, as shown in kernel III. In both cases, resource managers can forward requests for resource allocations from applications to other, remote resource managers by submitting an

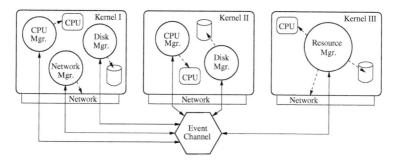

Fig. 4. Resource management with KECho

event. If a remote resource manager can fulfill the request, it responds accordingly to the manager that forwarded the original request. If there are several positive responses, a resource manager can use certain criteria (e.g., response times, location of the resource) to decide which response to accept or discard. Resource managers can dynamically join or leave resource-sharing groups, by joining a group it makes its resources publicly available to all other members in the group. However, all managers are unaware of the number or the location of other group members and resource requests are submitted and accepted/denied via events.

4   Example 2: Load Balancing

Load balancers in web server clusters [,] have the task to forward requests that can not be handled locally to other servers in the cluster. Figure 5 shows the architecture of a simple load balancing mechanism for a web server cluster.

When using KECho to implement load balancing, each server in the cluster subscribes to the shared *data channel*, which is used to forward requests to other servers if the load on the host is too high to successfully handle a request. Further, servers send responses to such requests in form of events over the same event channel. All servers also register two filters, which are supplied by the load balancing mechanism in the kernel: (i) an OUT-filter, which intercepts service requests and decides which remote server(s) will receive a forwarded request, and (ii) an IN-filter, which discards multiple responses from different servers if the request has been forwarded to more than one server. The load balancing decision is based on *load information* exchanged between all servers via a separate event channel, called *monitoring channel*. In addition, the server forwarding a request determines how many remote servers will receive this request. This can improve the server utilization even more if the load information is not updated frequently enough, that is, the n servers with the lowest utilization receive a request and only the first response from these servers will be used, all other responses are discarded.

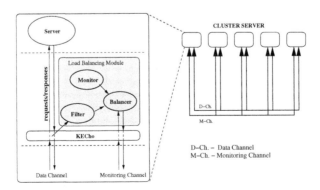

Fig. 5. Load balancing with KECho

5   Simulation Results

The following microbenchmarks have been performed on a dual-Pentium III with 2x800MHz, 1GB RAM, running Linux 2.4.0. The intent is to investigate the overheads associated with event submission and delivery, channel management, and filtering.

5.1   Event Submission

The first measurement compares the event submission overheads of the user-level implementation of event channels (ECho), the kernel-level event channels used by a user-level application (KECho-UL), and the kernel-level event channels used by a kernel-thread (KECho-KL).

The graphs in Figure 6 compare the event submission overheads of these three scenarios for 100b and 1Kbyte, where the overheads of ECho and KECho-UL differ only minimally. This can be explained by the fact that ECho uses only two system calls per sink for the submission of an event, where KECho requires also two system calls, but that number is independent from the number of sinks. Event submissions with KECho-KL show up to 15% (for 100b) and up to 20% (for 1Kb) less overhead compared to ECho.

Table 1 compares the performance of some of the functionality of KECho (KECho-UL/KECho-KL) with the performance of the user-level implementation ECho. Channel creation requires $850\mu s$ in ECho, compared to $182\mu s$ in KECho-UL and $170\mu s$ in KECho-KL. The large difference between kernel-level and user-level approach can be explained by the number of system calls required for the creation of a channel in ECho, which is 56, compared to 5 in KECho-UL. The

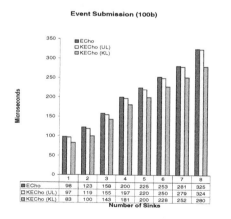

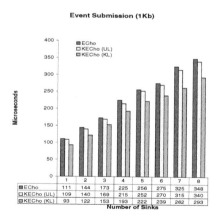

Fig. 6. Event submission overheads for data sizes of 100 bytes and 1 Kbyte

Table 1. Overheads and number of system calls

	ECho	KECho-UL	KECho-KL
Channel Creation	850μs (56)	182μs (5)	170μs (-)
Channel Opening	approx. 1.5s (117)	approx. 1.5s (5)	approx. 1.5s (-)
Event Submission	100μs (2 per sink)	95μs (2)	85μs (-)
Event Polling	32μs (4)	40μs (2)	5μs (-)

opening of a channel depends on the current number of subscribers, the network transmission delays and other factors, however, typical values for this operation are approximately 1.5s in all three cases. Event submission takes about 100μs per event subscriber for ECho, compared to 95μs and 85μs for KECho-UL and KECho-UL, respectively. In ECho, the overhead for polling for new events is 32μs (4 system calls) compared to 40μs (2 system calls) in KECho-UL. The reason for this increase are some inefficiencies in the implementation which will be addressed in our future work. However, the overhead for event polling in KECho-KL decreases to only 5μs. Note that while typical applications using ECho have to periodically poll for new events, KECho is able to notify kernel threads almost immediately of the arrival of a new event. This ability is investigated in the following section.

5.2 Event Delivery

Events in KECho are pushed from event sources to event sinks. The network monitoring module of KECho is able to immediately notify a waiting thread of the arrival of such an event. Typical latencies measured from the arrival of an event at a socket to the invocation of a handler function are in the range of 250-300μs. In the case of ECho and KECho-UL, these latencies depend heavily on the polling frequency, the systems load, and the scheduling priority of the application receiving the event. However, ECalls ability to *boost* the scheduling priority of an application that receives a newly arrived event can significantly reduce these latencies. This cooperation between ECalls and the CPU scheduler is described in detail in [ ].

5.3 Filtering Overhead

The following measurements have been performed on a cluster of 4x200MHz Pentium Pros, with 512MB RAM, connected via 100Mbps Ethernet, running Linux 2.4.0.

The filtering functions (IN- and OUT-filter) serve to reduce processing and network overhead depending on application-specific attributes, supplied by the event producer and the event subscribers.

The left graph in Figure 7 compares the advantages of event filtering with IN- and OUT-filters. The left bars show the event handling overhead for a host with 8 sinks, i.e., an incoming event is dispatched to all 8 sinks and the overhead

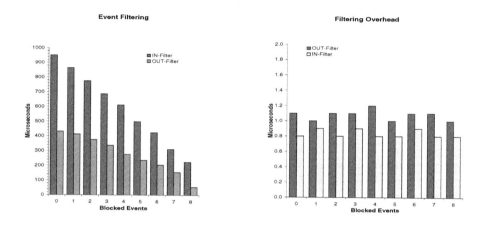

Fig. 7. Filtering of events can reduce event submission and event handling over-heads (a), while the filtering overhead is only in the microsecond range (b)

is approximately 950μs (event handling in this example means copying of the incoming event into a buffer and printing a time-stamp into a file). This overhead can be reduced significantly when we use an IN-filter to block the event from being dispatched to all 8 sinks, e.g., if only one sink receives the event, the overhead is reduced to 312μs. If the filter blocks the event completely (i.e., the event is discarded), the overhead is a little more than 200μs. The right bars in the same graph compare a similar scenario, however, the overhead shown in the graph is the overhead associated with event submission, when the number of remote sinks is 8. The overhead in this example is 430μs. However, when an OUT-filter is being used to block the submission of the event to some servers, this overhead can be reduced, e.g., if the event is submitted to only one sink, the overhead is 156μs. If the event is discarded (i.e., no sink will receive the event), the overhead is 56μs. The second graph in Figure 7 compares the overhead of the IN- and OUT-filters that have been used for the results in the left graph. Both the IN-filter and the OUT-filter use a number of simple if-else statements to decide if an event has to be submitted/dispatched to a certain sink or not. The overheads are independent of the number of events submitted or blocked and are very low in the example shown here, e.g., approximately 1μs for the OUT-filter and 0.9μs for the IN-filter.

5.4   Simulated Web Server Results

In this section we investigate the load balancing mechanism introduced in Section 4 in more detail. Measurements have been performed on a cluster of 8 nodes, acting as a web server cluster. Web servers receive requests at rates ranging from

20 to 50 requests per second. Each request requires a simulated web server to perform processing for approximately 38ms. The first graph in Figure 8 shows the response times (in milliseconds) without any load balancing compared to the scenario where load balancing is being used. Requests in this experiment have a time-out of 5s, leading to the leveling off at 5s of the first line in the graph, i.e., requests are either being handled within 5s after request receipt or discarded otherwise. In the second scenario, we modify the server such that requests that have been waiting for more than 2.5s are being forwarded to other servers in the cluster. In these experiments, we assume that there is at least one server in the cluster with utilization less than 10%.

The second line in the graph (w/ load balancing - local requests) shows the response times of all requests which are handled on the local node. This time, the response times level off at 2.5 at request rates of approximately 33 per second. The third line shows the response time of the requests being handled on remote servers, which is slightly higher than the times measured at the local server due to the overhead of two events being submitted and received (forwarded request and request response). The second graph in Figure 8 analyzes the overhead for the load balancing mechanism, which makes sure that only one other server (dependent on load information collected from these servers) will receive the forwarded request. The graph compares the overhead of three actions performed by the load balancing mechanism: (i) the monitoring of CPU utilization and the submission of events carrying this information, (ii) the handling of incoming CPU information from other servers in the cluster, and (iii) the filtering necessary to ensure the delivery of the forwarded request to the server with the lowest utilization. The graph shows that all these overheads vary only minimally with

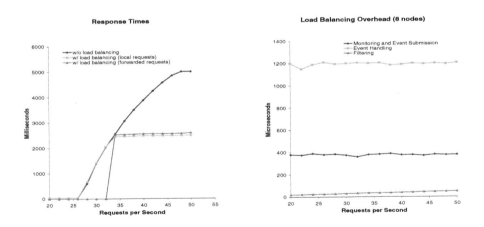

Fig. 8. (a) Response times for a simulated web server cluster and (b) overheads of the load balancing mechanism used in this experiment

the number of requests, where the task of event handling is the most expensive (approximately 70% of the total load balancing overhead).

The final experiment investigates the advantage of event filtering in more detail. The OUT-filter introduced above forwards requests to the servers with low load to ensure small response times. However, the frequency of load information exchange among the nodes in a server cluster has an obvious influence on the load balancing quality, i.e., if load information is not exchanged frequently enough, the forwarding decision can be based on outdated information, which reduces the effectiveness of load balancing.

The left graph in Figure 9 compares the overhead of load balancing dependent on the frequency of load information events. The overhead is mainly due to the event handling process, followed by the load monitoring and event submission process. Smaller overheads are caused by the actual forwarding of the requests and the filtering functions. The overhead increases rapidly with the number of events exchanged per second, e.g., more than 8ms with a frequency of 5 events per second. The right graph in Figure 9 compares the approach, where the frequency of load events is kept constantly at 1 per second, however, the filter forwards the request to up to 5 different servers. In other words, multiple servers in the cluster respond to the event and only the first response is being used by the server that issued the event carrying the forwarded request. Again, the event handling and the load monitoring and event submission contribute most to the overheads, however, the overhead increases only minimally with the number of event sinks. The biggest increase in overhead is caused by the IN-filter, which has the task of discarding duplicate responses. This experiment ignores the increased total utilization in the whole cluster due to the request handling by multiple servers.

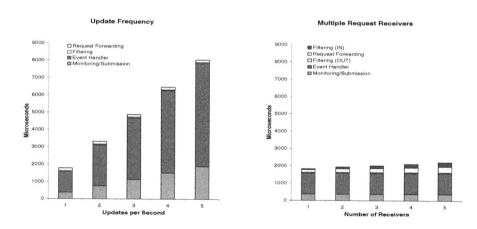

Fig. 9. Comparison of update frequency of load information (a) and forwarding of events to more than 1 server in the cluster (b)

As an alternative to the solution suggested above, a server could issue a *cancel event* to all other servers, that makes sure that only one server handles a request. If several servers issue a cancel event, a time-stamp or some other criterion can decide which server wins. This approach reduces the unnecessary processing on the servers, however it increases the event communication by up to n cancel events per forwarded request.

6   Conclusions

The need for globally managing system services is exemplified by previous work on distributed resource management, on load balancing, and QoS mechanisms. This paper addresses dynamic service management by providing a novel facility for inter-service cooperation in distributed systems. KECho is a kernel-based publish/subscribe communication tool that supports anonymous and asynchronous group communication. KECho's main components are its lightweight interface to user-level service realizations, a network monitor that minimizes the latency of event delivery, and channel filters that allow kernel services and applications to intercept event submissions with the goal of minimizing network traffic and optimizing system performance.

Our future work will investigate the two examples introduced in this paper in more depth and analyze their performance compared to user-level solutions. Further, we will extend KECho to support real-time events, thereby addressing the substantial set of applications requiring real-time guarantees. In addition, we will deploy KECho in the embedded, wireless system domains for which its ability to access and use power, load, and network information is critical to the success of this class of ubiquitous applications. Finally, while protection issues have been ignored to this point, we are already investigating and implementing protection mechanisms that will ensure the proper system operation in face of misbehaving kernel extensions.

References

1. A. Rowstron, A-M. Kermarrec, P. Druschel, M. Castro: SCRIBE: The Design of a Large-scale Event Notification Structure. Proc. of the 3rd Intl. Workshop on Networked Group Communications, London, UK, 2001. 84
2. G. Eisenhauer, F. Bustamente, K. Schwan: Event Services for High Performance Computing. Proc. of High Performance Distributed Computing, 2000. 84, 86
3. T. H. Harrison, D. L. Levine, D. C. Schmidt: The Design and Performance of a Real-time CORBA Object Event Service. Proc. of the OOPSLA '97 Conference, Atlanta, Georgia, October 1997 . 84
4. C. Ma, J. Bacon: COBEA: A CORBA-Based Event Architecture. Proc. of the Fourth USENIX Conf. on Object-Oriented Technologies, Santa Fe, New Mexico, April 1998. 84
5. C. Poellabauer, K. Schwan, R. West: Coordinated CPU and Event Scheduling for Distributed Multimedia Applications. Proc. of the 9th ACM Multimedia Conference, Ottawa, Canada, October 2001. 87, 88, 92

6. C. Poellabauer, K. Schwan, R. West: Lightweight Kernel/User Communication for Real-Time and Multimedia Applications. Proc. of the 11th International Workshop on Network and Operating Systems Support for Digital Audio and Video (NOSSDAV 2001), Port Jefferson, NY, June 2001. 88
7. T. Plagemann, V. Goebel, P. Halvorsen, O. Anshus: Operating System Support for Multimedia Systems. The Computer Communications Journal, Elsevier, Vol. 23, No. 3, February 2000, pp. 267-289. 83
8. A. Bestavros, M. Crovella, J. Liu, D. Martin: Distributed Packet Rewriting and its Application to Scalable Web Server Architectures. Proc. of the 6th IEEE International Conference on Network Protocols, Austin, TX, October 1998. 83, 90
9. A. D. Birrell, B. J. Nelson: Implementing Remote Procedure Calls. ACM Transactions on Computer Systems, 2(1), February 1984. 84
10. Object Management Group: CORBAservices: Common Object Services Specification, July 1997, (http://www.omg.org/). 84
11. D. Box: Understanding COM. Addison-Wesley, Reading, MA, 1997. 84
12. A. Wollrath, R. Riggs, J. Waldo: A Distributed Object Model for the Java System. USENIX Computing Systems, vol. 9, November/December 1996. 84
13. F. Kon, T. Yamane, C. K. Hess, R. H. Campbell, M. D. Mickunas: Dynamic Resource Management and Automatic Configuration of Distributed Component Systems. Proc. of USENIX COOTS 2001. 89
14. I. Foster, C. Kesselman, C. Lee, R. Lindell, K. Nahrstedt, A. Roy: A Distributed Resource Management Architecture that Supports Advance Reservations and Co-Allocation. In International Workshop on Quality of Service, 1999. 89
15. V. Cardellini, M. Colajanni, P. S. Yu: Dynamic Load Balancing on Web-server Systems. IEEE Internet Computing, Vol. 3, No. 3, May/June 1999. 90
16. M. Aron, D. Sanders, P. Druschel, W. Zwaenepoel: Scalable Content-aware Request Distribution in Cluster-based Network Servers. Proc. of the USENIX 2000 Annual Technical Conference, San Diego, CA, June 2000. 83
17. D. Ivan-Rosu, K. Schwan: FARA– A Framework for Adaptive Resource Allocation in Complex Real-Time Systems. Proc. of the IEEE Real-Time Technology and Applications Symposium, June 1998. 83
18. D. Steere, A. Goel, J. Gruenberg, D. McNamee, C. Pu, J. Walpole: A Feedback-Driven Proportion Allocator for Real-Rate Scheduling. Proc. of the Third Symposium on Operating System Design and Implementation, New Orleans, February 1999. 83
19. T. von Eicken, D. Culler, S. Goldstein, K. Schauser: Active Messages: A Mechanism for Integrated Communication and Computation. Proc. of the 19th International Symposium on Computer Architecture, pages 256–266, May 1992. 84
20. G. Hamilton and P. Kougiouris: The Spring Nucleus: A Microkernel for Objects. Report Number: TR-93-14, April 1993. 84

Session III

Networking 1

A Fine-Grained Addressing Concept for GeoCast

Peter Coschurba, Kurt Rothermel, and Frank Dürr

Institute of Parallel and Distributed High-Performance Systems (IPVR)
University of Stuttgart
Breitwiesenstraße 20–22, 70565 Stuttgart, Germany
{Peter.Coschurba,Kurt.Rothermel,Frank.Duerr}@informatik.uni-stuttgart.de

Abstract. GeoCast provides the functionality of sending messages to everyone in a specific area. So far, only the addressing of larger two-dimensional areas was possible. For the use in an urban environment it is crucial that small and three-dimensional areas can be addressed. For example, GeoCast can then be used to send lecture notes to all in a classroom. In this paper we describe a fine-grained addressing concept for GeoCast that supports such areas. In addition we present an architecture that allows the use of that addressing concept together with the GeoRouting-approach developed by Navas and Imielinski [ ]. We also present some modifications necessary to enhance the scalability of Geo-Cast.

1 Introduction

If we look at the means of communication that human beings use, we find that there are different categories of how we determine the receiver of a message. If we speak, everyone who is at the same location will get the message. We can adjust the area in which the message is perceived by changing the tone of our voice. If we shout, the area gets larger and if we whisper the area becomes smaller. If we write a letter, we address someone specific and only that person will get the message. Finally, if we publish something, then everyone who is interested in it can get that information. These ways of communication are also reflected in the Internet. We can send messages to a specific receiver using unicast. If we use multicast, everyone who is interested in the information can tune into the group and receive the messages. Finally, as an equivalent to speech, which is a location specific way of communication we find GeoCast [,].

GeoCast is a relatively new means of communication. A sender specifies the area in which the message should be received by everyone. The receivers do not need to be known and do not have to decide that they want to receive the messages. They get the message when they are in the area that the sender specified and they do not get it if they are outside that area. Because many messages are not only interesting for users who are currently in the area, but also for those who arrive some time later, the concept of lifetime was introduced to GeoCast. The lifetime of a message determines how long this message will be available in the target area. It can be compared to a poster. While the poster is

H. Schmeck, T. Ungerer, and L. Wolf (Eds.): ARCS 2002, LNCS 2299, pp. 101–113, 2002.
© Springer-Verlag Berlin Heidelberg 2002

up, the message can be read by everyone close enough. Messages with a lifetime can be used to warn people of danger, to announce new services or for many other purposes.

In order to use such means of communication we find that the receivers have to have devices that are capable of determining their current position, maintaining a connection to the Internet and doing the necessary computation. Devices, such as future mobile phones or PDA's will become artefacts of our daily life. GeoCast is still a fairly new concept, so it is at the very beginning of its evolution. One of the main issues in GeoCast is how the area, that defines the receivers of the message, can be specified. GeoCast has been mainly driven by the work of Julio Navas and Thomasz Imielinski. Their protocols are optimized for larger two-dimensional areas [ ]. Therefore we call this kind of addressing coarse-grained. Coarse-grained addresses can be used to send a message to all people in a wood, where a wildfire is happening or send a message to a part of a city announcing that a new restaurant has opened. Considering the needs that arise if GeoCast is to be used in an urban environment we find that having coarse-grained addressing is not sufficient [ ].

Scenarios that show possible usages of what we call fine-grained addressing are to send lecture notes or subtitles for the hearing impaired to everyone listening to a talk, to distribute some information on a floor (e.g. broken lift) or to send a message to everyone on a bridge (e.g. warning of a traffic jam). Common to these scenarios is that they rely on the third dimension and that the addressed areas are small.

An important aspect of addressing a geographic area is how location information can be expressed. There are two fundamental possibilities. One can express the location of a person by stating his coordinates in a predefined coordinate system like WGS84 [ ]. Or the position information can be expressed using a symbolic identifier that states in what area a person is. Whereas coordinates are dominant in the outdoor use (e.g. used by GPS [ ]) symbolic identifiers are dominant in the indoor use (e.g. used by Active Badge System [ ]). To make GeoCast available in all kind of areas, it has to work together with both kinds of position information and therefore with all kinds of positioning systems.

In this paper we will look at the technology that is used for GeoCast. We will extract the requirements that GeoCast has to meet in order to be usable in urban as well as in rural areas. A fine-grained addressing concept will be presented that meets the requirements and finally we will show how this addressing concept can be implemented using the GeoRouting presented by Navas and Imielinski. The local dissemination of GeoCast messages imposes scalabilty problems. We will introduce a notify-pull mechanism, the so-called message announcements, in order to make GeoCast more scalable.

This paper is organized as follows: In the next section we will look at the related work. Section three deals with the requirements for a more sophisticated fine-grained addressing concept. In the following section we will present an addressing concept that meets these requirements. In section five we will look at the realisation and implementation of the addressing concept. And finally, we will conclude our paper with an outlook on future work.

2 System Model

In this section we will have a closer look at the technology that forms the foundation of this paper. We will look at the current state of GeoCast, at the way how addresses can be constructed today and define some terms that are used throughout this paper.

The focus of Navas and Imielinski is the message forwarding. They have looked at different means for transporting the message towards the target area and have defined a protocol called GeoRouting that is able to route geographic messages with acceptable performance [7,]. Such a GeoCast using GeoRouting is shown in Fig. 1. The sender S sends a message to the grey area. The node E is inside the area and therefore should receive the message. To develop an addressing concept was not their primary concern and thus their concept of defining target areas is fairly simple. The *target area* of a message is the geographic area in which the message is to be distributed. In other words, the target area is the area that the sender specifies and in which every participating node will receive the message.The target area can be described using a polygon of the area-boundary, specified through the coordinates of the edges in WGS84 coordinates [ ]. Because only two-dimensional coordinates have been chosen, it is not possible to address a three-dimensional area. The whole protocol is optimized for larger target areas, which normally span several networks.

In order to perform GeoCast several software components are needed: The *GeoHost* is the software running on the client. It is responsible for sending and receiving the messages on the device. In order to send a message, the GeoHost builds packets and forwards them to the next GeoRouter. Messages that are to be received are broadcasted by the GeoNodes on the networks in the target area. Because there might be devices connected to the network that lie outside the target area, it is necessary that the client itself checks whether it is actually supposed to receive the message or not. If the GeoHost is inside the target area, the message is forwarded to the appropriate application. Therefore, in Fig. 1 $GH1$ accepts the message and $GH2$ discards it.

The *GeoNode* is a special node that is responsible for distributing the message in the target area. In addition, it stores messages which have a lifetime. The messages are distributed by the GeoNode until the lifetime expires. There should be one GeoNode for each IP-subnetwork. A GeoNode services the network that it is directly connected to. The geographic area that is covered by that network is called the service area of the appropriate GeoNode.

Another component is the *GeoRouter*. Each GeoRouter knows its service area. The service area of a GeoRouter is the aggregate of the service areas of the GeoNodes that are assigned to it. Normally these GeoNodes are directly connected to the GeoRouter, but there is also the possibility to connect a GeoNode using tunnelling. The GeoRouters use the GeoRIP protocol to exchange the

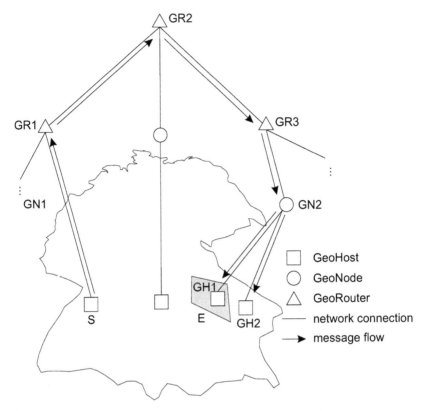

Fig. 1. GeoCast using GeoRouting

information about their service areas. This results in every GeoRouter knowing the service areas of all other GeoRouters. If a GeoCast message arrives at a GeoRouter it checks which service areas of the other GeoRouters overlap with the target area of the message and forwards the message towards them. If the target area overlaps with its own service area, then the message is forwarded to the appropriate GeoNodes.

3   Requirements on Fine-Grained Addresses

The main requirement for the fine-grained addressing concept is the ability to address small target areas. Additionally, three-dimensional target areas should be addressable in order to allow target areas like rooms. The lack of such a concept is the major flaw of existing GeoCast systems that prevents the use in an urban environment.

For GeoCast to become a success it must be efficient and scalable. So the addressing concept should not only take into account what the user might want to address, but also if addressed areas can be processed efficiently. As we have seen, there are two kinds of operations necessary in order to deliver a message. The GeoRouters check whether the target area overlaps with some service areas of other GeoRouters and the GeoHosts calculate if their position is within the target area. Especially the first check is important, because for routers it is critical to reach the forwarding decision fast, in order to prevent congestion. But also the check on the client can be critical if we want computationally "weak" devices to participate. Another issue is bandwidth consumption. As the specification of a three-dimensional body can use a large amount of space, it is an important requirement that the space used by the address stays small, in order to increase the amount of payload that can be transported in each packet.

The major strength of the existing protocol is the message forwarding itself. GeoRouting offers a good means to transport messages to two-dimensional areas. If possible, the fine grained-addressing concept should work together with the GeoRouting of Navas and Imielinski.

Hence the requirements are:

− Support for efficient handling of small target areas
− Ability to address three-dimensional target areas
− Efficient overlap calculation (for the GeoRouters)
− Efficient include operation (for the GeoHost)
− Compact addresses
− Interoperability with GeoRouting

4   Fine-Grained Addressing Concept

In this section we will present our addressing concept. As stated above, two addressing methods have to be considered. On the one hand there are coordinates and on the other hand there are symbolic identifiers. Both describe location using different concepts. The first denotes a position whereas the latter states in what area somebody is. It is important to note that there is normally only one kind of position information available in an area. Either the sensor systems in the infrastructure delivers coordinates or symbolic identifiers. To have both (expensive) infrastructures in the same building is only a rare case restricted to a few research institutions. So we can assume that inside such an area there is only one kind of position information available. Our fine-grained addressing scheme consists of two kinds of addresses. One kind is based on coordinates and the other is based on symbolic identifiers. Depending on the technology used in the target area the appropriate address can be used.

4.1   Geographic Coordinate-Based Addresses

For coordinate-based addresses we have to differentiate between two-dimensional and three-dimensional target areas. Two-dimensional ones can be specified using the concepts of the existing protocols. They allow to address polygons and

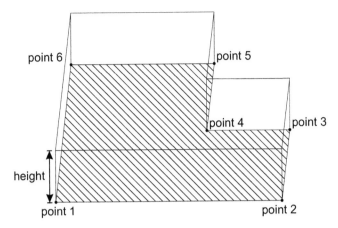

Fig. 2. 2.5-dimensional target area

circles. If 8 Bytes represent an element of a coordinate then the accuracy of the coordinates is below a millimetre, which should be enough for all kinds of applications. In the case of the polygon, one specifies all the edges using two-dimensional WGS84 coordinates. For the circle the centre and the radius have to be specified.

For three-dimensional addresses the situation is more complex. On the one hand we want to have small addresses that can be processed efficiently and on the other hand we want to give the user the possibility to address all target areas that he might need or want to address. If we look at what that target areas might be, we find that they can be modelled by using so called 2.5-dimensional bodies. Targets like a room, a floor or a house have in common that they can be defined by specifying the base and adding a fix height (see Fig. 2). An example is shown in picture where a room is addressed.

Such addresses have the advantage that they are compact, using only slightly more space then two-dimensional ones (8 Bytes for each coordinate dimension and another 8 Bytes for the height) and all the overlap and inclusion calculations can be done using the same algorithms used for two-dimensional figures adding only a check for the height. In order to address all kind of targets we provide two base figures. One is a polygon with height and the other is a cylinder. An example for such and address would be the first floor of the computer science building of the university of Stuttgart:

```
3D_Polygon((48.431782N; 9.7410E; 508) (48.43169N; 9.7398E; 508)
           (48.431815N; 9.7398E; 508) (48.43195N; 9.7363E, 508)
           2.6)
```

The coordinates of the edges are listed counter-clockwise and the height is given in metres. The third parameter of the coordinates is the height over sea level.

4.2   Symbolic Identifier-Based Addresses

Symbolic identifiers describe an area in which the object is located. Such an area is in most cases a room or an open area with a distinct extension. One could think that providing that identifier would be enough to address the room. But unfortunately these identifiers are only unique within a limited area. The addressing scheme used by company A can also be used by the neighbouring company B. So there could be two rooms with exactly the same identifier. But in order to use the symbolic identifiers as an address they have to be globally unique. To achieve that, we add to each symbolic identifier the area in which the ID is unique, that is, the area that is covered by the organisation to which the room belongs. This area can be a large two-dimensional area, in case of a large company or it can be only the floor of a large building when we look at a small company or a local branch of some company. So an address that is based on symbolic identifiers consists of two parts, the geographic address denoting the area in which the identifier scheme is valid and then the identifier itself.

Many symbolic identifier schemes are built hierarchically, thus implementing the "inside" relationship. The identifier reflects in what building and in what floor the room is. So, for example the symbolic identifier "22.2.018" in the Computer Science Dept. of Stuttgart implicitly states that the room denoted by this symbolic identifier is located in building 22 on the second floor. For GeoCast this is – of course – a nice feature. Besides single rooms, it allows to address all rooms on a specific floor or even in a building. In order to use the knowledge inside the identifiers, there must be a understanding of the semantics of the symbolic identifier. Therefore it is necessary to have a common format, how these identifiers are built. We use a scheme that will be met by most local schemes:

```
BUILDING.FLOOR.ROOM.
```

If another scheme is used, there has to be a mapping to this scheme. This mapping function has to be provided to the clients in order to make use of the knowledge embedded into the identifier.

To make things more clear we will look at our example. We want to address room 18 on the second floor of building 20 at the Computer Science Dept. of Stuttgart. The appropriate address looks as follows:

```
ID((2D_Polygon((48,431782N; 9,7410E) (48,43169N; 9,7398E)
           (48,431815N; 9,7398E) (48,43195N; 9,7363E))
   (20.2.18))
```

The first part describes the area in which the identifier scheme is valid, or in other words which is encompassed by the model. The second part is the identifier itself. If we wanted to address the whole floor we would just omit the 18 at the end of the identifier.

5   Realisation

5.1   Architecture

To integrate fine-grained addresses with the GeoRouting of Navas and Imielinski is the main focus of this paper. In order to achieve that, at least the GeoHost has to be modified. But in order to achieve a good performance and to get a scalable solution changes at the GeoNode are also needed. The basic architecture remains the same. GeoHosts have to be present on every node that wants to send or receive messages. A GeoNode is needed for each participating subnetwork and there are GeoRouters, which do not have to be modified.

However, the interface between the application and the GeoHost and between the GeoNode and the GeoHost have to be changed. The interface of the GeoHost that an application can use to send a message is modified to support the new types for target areas. The function is `sendGeoMessage(Area, Port, Lifetime, MessageID)`. Thus, the application can specify the following parameters:

- Area: The area information consists of an area type and the parameters (points and height or radius information) that specify the target area. Each point is provided using 8 bytes for longitude, latitude and, in case of a three-dimensional area, for the height information. For areas whose addresses are built using an area and a symbolic identifier, this can be specified too. The type and parameters are:
    - 2D_Polygon: For a polygon all points that specify the edges are listed counter clockwise.
    - 2D_Circle: For the 2D_Circle the centre point is specified and then the radius is provided in metres.
    - 3D_Polygon: A list of three-dimensional points and the height of the figure is specified. The height is given in metres above the base of the figure.
    - 3D_Circle: A cylinder is specified by specifying the point that is the centre of the circle that forms the base. The radius and the height are also provided in metres.
    - ID: An identifier-based address always consists of two parts. First an area is provided and then the identifier. (see Sect. 4.2)
        * Area: Any of the areas described above
        * ID: A string that contains the identifier. Points are used as delimiters.
- Port: The port specifies which applications will receive the message.
- Lifetime: The lifetime specifies for how many seconds the message will be distributed by the GeoNodes. The time starts when the GeoNode receives the message.
- Message ID: The sender creates a unique message identifier for each message.

As stated above, GeoRouting is used to forward the messages. It offers an acceptable performance and has already been implemented by Navas and Imielinski. But GeoRouting operates only on two-dimensional target areas. So it seems that the GeoRouter have to be modified to route on three-dimensional target areas. But if we look at the requirements, we see that the efficiency at the forwarding decision is one of the key requirements. The routing on three-dimensional target areas would make the forwarding decision more complex. Therefore we have chosen another alternative. We will do the forwarding decision based on two-dimensional areas. For this we introduce the concept of the *scope* of a message.

We distinguish between the address of a message, which denotes the target area and the scope, which is a simplified target area used only for routing. In order to allow an efficient routing, we use the scope, a two-dimensional area, to forward the message. All GeoNodes, that are inside that scope will get the message. They will then look inside the message and evaluate the address. If their service area overlaps with the target area, the message will be processed like normal, if not it will be discarded. So messages are only distributed in networks that service the target area. This modification in the GeoNodes makes it possible to have an efficient routing and to save the bandwidth in the networks that overlap with the scope but not with the target area.

But how is the scope generated? In case of a two-dimensional target area, the scope is just identical to the target area. If a three-dimensional target area is specified, then the third-dimension is omitted. For addresses based on symbolic identifiers, the geographical part is used to generate the scope. The result of all these operations is a two-dimensional area that can be used by GeoRouting. This is used to build a header conforming to the GeoRouting. As a result we have two headers, the outer header is conform to the GeoRouting and specifies the coarse-grained scope of the message and an inner header, that specifies the fine-grained target area.

To clarify the architecture, we will look at what happens when a GeoCast message is sent:

1. The sender specifies a target area. This is done using the fine-grained addressing concept. The message is then transferred by the sending application to the GeoHost.
2. The GeoHost calculates the scope. It then creates a message as it can be used by the GeoRouting and encapsulates the original message with the original header in it. The header for such a fine grained GeoCast message is shown in Fig. 3. This message is then processed as before the modification. It is forwarded to the next GeoRouter and from there to all the GeoNodes in the scope. The GeoNode checks whether its service area overlaps with the target area and forwards the message to the network if it does.
3. The GeoHost on the receiving device checks whether the device is actually in the target area. This is done by comparing the position information with the address information in the message header. In case of an identifier-based address, the device checks first if the area of the address equals the validation area of its identifier-based scheme. In a second step it checks whether the identifier that describes its location is either equal or enclosed in the identifier

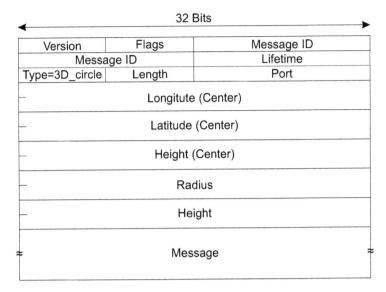

Fig. 3. Message header for coordinate-based target area

of the address. If the position is inside the area, the message is accepted and forwarded to the appropriate application, if not it is discarded.

5.2   Message Announcements

So far we have shown how to send messages using the fine-grained addressing concept. But if we look at the lifetime of a message a new problem arises. Originally, the target areas were rather large, spanning several networks. In addition it was assumed that only few messages are sent using GeoCast. With the new fine-grained addresses a different situation arises. First of all, the target areas get smaller. The average target size will probably be a room. Because most networks span more then only one room, there might be several target areas overlapping with the service area of the network.

So far, the lifetime was realized, by just re-sending the messages during the lifetime. Clearly, this is not scalable if we have lots of messages. Many of these messages would be sent without anyone being interested in it. Ideally, the messages would only be re-sent when someone enters the target area. Because the receivers do not have to announce their position and presence, this is not possible. The idea is to send only short messages that include the address of the message and the message identifier. The GeoHost on the mobile device checks, if it is in the target area and if it has already received the message. If it determines that it is inside the target area, but has not received the message so far, it issues a message request, requesting the message to be re-sent. Upon receiving such a request the GeoNode will re-send the whole message.

Whereas previously the whole messages had to be resent during the lifetime, now only short announcements are sent. This results in a large decrease of bandwidth that is used for the local dissemination of the GeoCast messages and thus makes GeoCast more scalable. Especially, if we take into account that the smaller areas will lead to an increase in message size. There is rarely a usage scenario for large areas where one wants to send, for example, a power point presentation. But to send the slides during a presentation to all people in room makes sense.

Such a message announcement consists of two parts:

- The unique message ID: Every message gets a unique message identifier. This identifier is constructed by the sender.
- The target area: Each message announcement contains the target area that forms the address of the message. The format is exactly the same as in the message header.
- The port: This allows the potential receiver to determine if there is an application registered for that port, which is interested in such messages. Only those messages are requested for which receiving applications are registered which eliminates unneccessary transmissions.

Since the size that is needed to store the target area is not fixed, we can not state how large such an message announcement will be. But if we assume that the standard case will be to address a room, then such a message announcement will use 140 Bytes. So even in the unlikely case that 500 messages have a target area that overlaps with the service area and have a valid lifetime, that is a lifetime that has not yet been expired, only about 6% of the bandwidth of a 802.11b network would be used to send the announcements every second. If we assume that the average message is about 10 kilobyte, it would take about 6 seconds while using up all the bandwidth to resend the messages. So clearly we enhance the scalability of GeoCast by using message announcements.

The rate at which the messages are repeated is subject to parametrization. If the announcements are sent more frequently, they use up more of the bandwidth but people entering a target area will get the message earlier. If the messages are sent less frequently, bandwidth is saved, but the receivers will get the message later.

We think that four seconds between announcements is a good value for networks that have a bandwidth of about 10 megabit per second (like 802.11b). Four seconds is a rather small time for human beings, so the user will not notice a large delay. On the other hand, the consumed bandwidth is quite low. In the above example, we could send 500 message announcements by using only about 1.5% of the available bandwidth. Again, if we sent the whole messages all the time, we would use about the whole bandwidth in order to resend the messages all four seconds. Clearly this is not possible. Of course the frequency parameter is subject to local optimization. It has to be adjusted to the local needs and depends on the average number of messages and the bandwidth of the network.

In order to understand how this protocol works we will look at what happens when a message with a valid lifetime arrives at the GeoNode:

1. Upon reception of a new message the GeoNode checks if its service area overlaps with the target area. If it does the message is sent.
2. If the message has a valid lifetime then the message is stored, and the target area is used to build a message announcement. Every four seconds the announcement is sent (together with the other announcements) until its lifetime expires. Before the announcements are sent, the GeoNode checks if the lifetime has not expired. If it has expired, then the message is just discarded.
3. A GeoHost that receives the announcement uses the message ID to check whether the message has already been received earlier. If not, it checks if its position is inside the target area. If it is inside the target area and has not received the message yet, it sends a message request to the GeoNode. Such a message request is represented by the message ID.
4. When the GeoNode receives a message request, it re-sends the message on a broadcast channel, so that other devices that have just entered the area do also get the message.

6   Conclusion

The advent of location-aware applications and ubiquitous computing has created a need for geographic communication. The existing approach for GeoCast, however, has some disadvantages that have prevented a widespread use. So far, one of this disadvantages is the lack of a sophisticated addressing concept that allows the addressing of the intended areas. Another problem has been the scalability issue, i.e. if lot's of messages arrive for several closely connected areas. For both problems we have presented an solution.

Still more problems remain that need to be solved before GeoCast will become part of our everyday communication. So far, there are no real applications that make use of GeoCast. Without such applications, which provide a clear benefit to the user, GeoCast will not be used. We have shown several usage areas where GeoCast makes sense, so we assume that these applications will arrive soon. Actually, we have developed an application that allows the sending and receiving of geographic e-mails and messages. GeoRouting is relatively efficient, but still several magnitudes worse then all other routing methods for unicast or multicast. This remains an area of research. If GeoCast is to become popular, the message forwarding mechanism has to become more scalable and more efficient.

However, the foundations are laid, and GeoCast will become more and more popular. It's use will grow together with the number of location-aware applications. And therefore we think that it is worthwhile to do research in order to solve the above problems and create a means of communication that is beneficial to it's users.

References

1. Peter H. Dana. Global Positioning System Overview.
   `http://www.colorado.edu/geography/gcraft/notes/gps/gps_f.html`, Sep 1994.
   102
2. Department of Defense. WGS84 Military Standard.
   `http://164.214.2.59/publications/specs/printed/WGS84/wgs84.html`
   Jan 1994. 102
3. Tomasz Imielinski and Julio C. Navas. *RFC 2009 – GPS-Based Addressing and Routing.* IETF, Nov 1996. 101, 103
4. Tomasz Imielinski and Julio C. Navas. GPS-Based Geographic Addressing, Routing, and Resource Discovery. *Communications of the ACM*, 42(4):86–92, 1999.
   102
5. Young-Bae Ko and Nitin H. Vaidya. Geocasting in Mobile Ad Hoc Networks: Location-Based Multicast Algorithms. In *Proceedings of the 2nd Workshop on Mobile Computing Systems and Applications (WMCSA'99)*, 1999. 101
6. Julio C. Navas. *Geographic Routing in a Datagram Internetwork.* Ph.D. Thesis, Rutgers University – Computer Science, May 2001. 102
7. Julio C. Navas and Tomasz Imielinski. Multi-Hop Dynamic Geographic Routing. Technical Report DCS-TR-364, Rutgers University – Computer Science, May 1998.
   101, 103
8. Julio C. Navas and Tomasz Imielinski. On Reducing the Computational Cost of Geographic Routing. Technical Report DCS-TR-408, Rutgers University – Computer Science, Jan 2000. 103
9. R. Want, A. Hopper, V. Falcao, and J. Gibbons. The Active Badge Location System. *ACM Transactions on Information Systems*, 10(1):91–102, Jan 1992. 102

Data Paths in Wearable Communication Networks

Christian Decker and Michael Beigl

TecO, University of Karlsruhe
Vincenz-Priessnitz-Str.1, 76131 Karlsruhe, Germany
{cdecker,michael}@teco.edu

Abstract. Wearable communication networks are a new type of networks where communication wires are embedded into textiles. It allows the connection between sensors and devices embedded into the material. Data from such devices can be sent over various pieces of clothing to other devices in the network. A special characteristic of such a network is the unreliable connection between different pieces of clothing. This paper presents a prototype system and investigates routing methods using simulations of a fabric area network. Input data for simulations are derived from the operation of a first working prototype. Among the investigated routing methods are various Flooding, Hot- Potato and Simple Hot-Potato protocols. Throughput, way lengths and delay times were used as metrics. Results indicate that routing can optimize the performance of the FAN for each metric, but not for all metrics.

1   Introduction

We are in the maturing phase of an explosion in private devices that we can carry around with us or that are even attached to our body or clothing. Today these devices work standalone and are not interconnected. But with upcoming Ubiquitous Communication (Ubicomp) and Computing [W91] technology new applications will arise and existing applications will profit from enhanced knowledge transferred from other devices attached to us. Interconnection of such small devices is the goal of several novel technologies, especially RF based pico-networks like Bluetooth [S99] and body-networks. These systems have the disadvantage that they broadcast the information into the nearby environment [PAB00] and are therefore vulnerable for possible intruders. They also consume substantial quantities of energy compared to wire-based solutions.

This paper concentrates on one special kind of network used for interconnecting devices that are worn or near the body. The Fabric Area Network (FAN) [H01] is a wire-based network embedded into textiles that allows secure and private transfer of data between all devices that have a connection through clothes that are being worn. Possible application areas of such networks are communication of sensors incorporated into clothing with a central computer, health applications with various independent devices (pacemaker, life-care watch etc.) or blue color workers with pagers, scanners and special-purpose devices.

H. Schmeck, T. Unger, and L. Wolf (Eds.): ARCS 2002, LNCS 2299, pp. 114-130, 2002.
© Springer-Verlag Berlin Heidelberg 2002

This paper presents a system and its first outcome and finally simulations of a network implemented into the fibers of clothing. The paper concentrates on the problem of routing of packets in the network. For clothing, the intersection points can provide the connection between parts of the network and are therefore the places where routing and filtering of packets should be implemented. Various algorithms for routing are introduced and analyzed in this paper. The use of routing gives the possibility to control the workload and the power consumption of the stations and therewith the control over the workload of the entire network. The opportunity to decide which way data packets should go makes the network more powerful and more adaptable in the dynamic environment in which it resides. Characteristics of the network (e.g. packet loss, delay etc.) are derived from experimental prototypes that we had integrated into clothing and had them worn.

In the next section, we go more into detail about the FAN. This is followed by the description of the FAN simulation architecture that we designed and implemented to test the network under different conditions and to test different routing strategies. We obtained reasonable parameters for link failures by measurements, which we describe in the following section. These parameters are used in a simulation of a wearable sensor network with some user interaction. We simulate different routing strategies while focusing on certain metrics like data loss, hop counts and delay times. Our results are presented in the last section.

FAN – A Wearable Network

The Fabric Area Network (FAN) introduces a concept of coupling of different pieces of clothing to make them interconnected for data transport. The prototype developed by Starlab [H01] is based on coils creating a strong limited electromagnetic field, which is modulated with data packets. A pair of two coils forms a simple sender/receiver system and is used as a FAN link (Fig. 1).

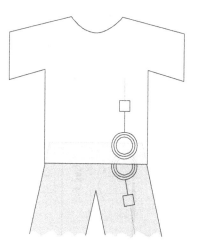

Fig. 1. FAN Link

Over these links, data is transported in packets of maximum 18 bytes with a transfer rate of 1000 bits/s. Before a data packet is transported, the hardware which drives the link has to power up the electromagnetic field and the sender performs a handshake procedure to detect the receiver. This causes a latency of 100 ms for each data packet.

FAN links reside in very dynamic areas where the parts they try to connect are loosely coupled. They are not wired links so it can be impossible to transport data for an undetermined timeframe or if a connection is reestablished it is not sure whether it will run over the same link.

The driver hardware has to be very small because it is mounted within the clothes and like the links it is distributed all over the clothing. They have only small amounts of resources for computing power, memory and available energy whereas most of the energy is used for powering the links.

The entire Fabric-Area-Network resides in a very dynamic area where data is transported over slow and unreliable links and hardware has strongly limited resources.

2   Simulation

In order to understand the behavior of networks based on the FAN system, we developed a simulator. For it to be as flexible as possible regarding the property changes, we designed an architecture that embedded the simulator. This architecture is a test bed, which enables us to design, debug and evaluate various routing protocols.

2.1   Overview: The FAN Simulation Architecture

The FAN simulation architecture consists of two distinct modules - the simulator kernel and the data processing module (see Fig. 2).

The simulator kernel is a discrete event simulator, so we have an exact trace of what happened at any time step. It is deterministic, so each simulation is reproducible. The Data Processing module is independent of the kernel's implementation and takes the Log Files as input to compute in respect of them the output we want (e.g. statistic data, plots, text,...).

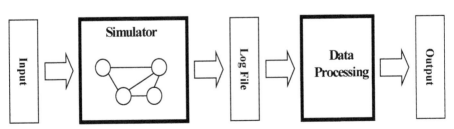

Fig. 2. FAN Simulation Architecture

Table 1. Behavior of Components

Component	Behavior	Character
Station	Router behavior	Dynamic
	Producer behavior	Dynamic
	Consumer behavior	Dynamic
Buffer	Size	Static
	Policy	Dynamic
Link	Bandwidth	Static
	Latency	Static
	half/full duplex	Dynamic
Network	size (number of stations)	Static
	number of links owned by a station	Static
	Connectivity matrix (symmetric)	Dynamic

Every FAN simulation model, given as input to the kernel, is built upon 4 different components, which are identified as station, buffer, link, and network. The way each component acts during a time step is described by the component's behaviors. We differentiate between dynamic and static behavior. A dynamic behavior can change during the run of the simulator. This is implemented by calling functions. On the other side the static behavior is fixed for the whole duration of the simulation and is implemented through parameter values. Tab. 1 lists the components and their behaviors.

The described architecture was implemented in Ptolemy II [DHK01] and tests showed that a network with the FAN properties (see section 1) could be simulated and ended up with the expected results.

2.2   Input Data

The simulation architecture requires setting up the input behavior of all components. While this is easy for all static behaviors, it becomes a concatenation of assumptions for the dynamic behaviors. Especially, the network dynamic should be described as close as possible to reality, because it strongly influences routing decisions and therewith station performance and also network performance. But, the process of network dynamic is hard to describe appropriately by assumptions. The concept of functions as input behaviors for the simulator let us supply the simulator with measured data for the network behavior.

Measurement of the Network Dynamic

We chose the T-shirt-trousers region as a typical place where data has to pass through a FAN link (see Fig. 1) and where the network behavior is important. The FAN prototype with the coil-based links was not available. To measure the link reliability in this region we mounted two electrodes (size 10.5cm x 5cm) in this region. One is located on the T-shirt and the other one is located on the trousers in such a way, that they can close an electric circuit when the T-shirt touches the trousers. Whether the circuit is closed or opened is registered by the Beck IPC [B01], a small computer system powered by a camcorder battery and mounted on the belt on the other side of the measurement region. Electrodes and the IPC can be seen in Fig. 3, and Fig. 4 shows how the T-shirt's electrode overlaps the electrode on the trousers. For the measurement we had a 4 minutes walk outside. During that time the IPC tested the circuit every 10 ms for the opened or closed state and saved it internally. At the end we had more than 24500 measured values.

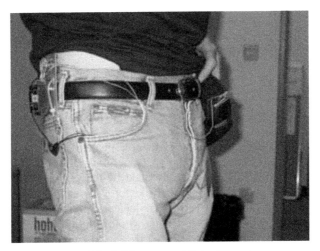

Fig. 3. Measurement Setup(1)

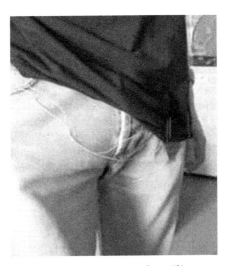

Fig. 4. Measurement Setup(2)

Interpretation

After the measurement, the next step was the interpretation, because these measured values were not obtained by the FAN prototype. The interpretation step converts them to the behavior of a FAN link. However, although this interpretation is based on assumptions, we are convinced that it describes the behavior of the network much more accurately than with a mathematical function.

One or more values indicating the same state of the circuit form a sequence. We then count how many measurement cycles the circuit was opened and closed. This is called a sequence length. These are signed to indicate the open or the closed state of the circuit. A short-time shift of the circuit's state does not mean a connection state change of a FAN link, because the electromagnetic field can transport data over a small distance. That's why we apply a high-pass filter, which kills all sequences smaller than 10, which is equivalent to a measurement timeframe of 100ms. This threshold was chosen according to the latency of 100 ms for every FAN link (see section 1). Fig. 5 shows the distribution of the relative frequency of occurrence of all measured sequences after applying the high-pass filter. Positive sequence lengths indicate a closed electric circuit, while negative lengths indicate an opened electric circuit.

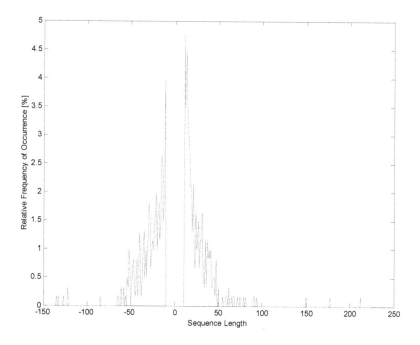

Fig. 5. Distribution of Sequence Lengths

The measurement of network dynamic gave us a set of data, which was then supplied to the simulator as a part of the network behavior for FAN links in the T-shirt-trousers region.

2.3   Output Results: Sensor Network Simulation

The aim of building a simulator (see section 2) and setting it up with input behaviors as close as possible to the reality (see section 2.2), is to get an experimental idea of how routing can improve the FAN. For this purpose we evaluate different routing protocols working in a model of a sensor network, which is distributed over different parts of our clothing. A sensor network is seen as an application, where effects on performance are easily traceable. Thereby we map a set of routing protocols to router stations. This mapping is called routing strategy. Our goal is to optimize the message distribution in respect to metrics like way lengths (hops), delay times, and message loss only by changing the routing strategy.

Topology and Simulation Parameter

Our sensor network consists of 3 sensors boards connected to a network of routers. Furthermore we have one source for user input. The topology can be seen in Fig. 6.

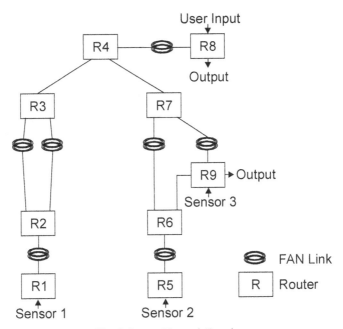

Fig. 6. Sensor Network Topology

Sensors boards are located on both shoes (R1, R5) and on the femoral (R9), which is a good place according to [LAL01]. Every 500 ms the sensor boards send a data packet of 8 bytes to their attached station, which adds a 6-byte header with source and destination address, message type number, and a maximum hop count (default value is 16). All messages are addressed to station R8, the user interface station, as the destination. The user itself can send commands as 3-bytes data packets to an attached device at R9. This is done via a random generator to simulate a user's behavior. Stations between the source and destination stations only have a routing behavior and build up a transit network. The FAN links between R1, R2 and R5, R6 are located in the shoes-trousers region while the FAN links between R2, R3 and R6, R7 respective R9, R7 are located in the T-shirt-trousers region. In the latter case the measured data for network behavior (see section 2.2) are used to describe the behavior of these links. A random generator determines the behavior of the FAN links for the shoes-trousers region. However, they are connected for 95% of the runtime. The user interface is coupled by a FAN link over R8 to station R4, but its reliability is 100%. All FAN links are half-duplex links and have a bandwidth of 1000 bits/s and a latency of 100 ms. All other links which are not indicated as FAN links are half-duplex serial links with a bandwidth of 9600 bits/s. Each link has a send buffer organized in a FIFO policy with a size of 160 bytes. Previous simulations showed that this a good buffer size for data producers like our sensors. Each station is customized with a routing protocol, which we discuss in the section below. The simulation time is 30 hours to produce enough data packets to build stable statistics.

Routing Protocols

Router stations reside in a very dynamic environment, where data is transported over slow and unreliable links and hardware has strongly limited resources. These conditions affected our choice of proper routing protocols. Protocols building up routing tables are unsuitable, because of limited memory resources. A further problem is represented by protocols, which try to get a survey of the network. Because the network is too dynamic and bandwidth is very limited, it is hard for the protocol to converge in case of link state changes and routing tables must be often updated, which stress the entire network.

We chose three routing protocols, which are simple to implement, rapidly come to a decision and do not use many resources. They do not build routing tables, nor do they use information about link states to come to a routing decision. The first protocol is Flooding Routing, which is often used because it always finds the shortest path, apart from the overhead it produces. Shoubridge [S96] made some detailed considerations about flooding. The second is the Hot-Potato protocol [B64] making its routing decision according to buffer fillings. The third one is a Hot-Potato Protocol, which comes to a routing decision according to a random generator, which decides to which link of the station the messages will be forwarded. This is called Simple Hot-Potato.

While implementing these routing protocols, we discovered that the maximum hop count for every message plays a crucial role. Previous simulations showed that lots of resources were used by messages running in loops. We decided to extend all routing protocols for stations with consumer behavior by an announcement mechanism, which generates only a small overhead. These stations announce themselves with a special message. These announcement messages have a high maximum hop count, so that they can be transported over many stations. Stations with a producer behavior can evaluate such announcement messages and initialize the maximum hop count of their messages on the basis of the number of hops it took the announcement message to reach them. There is no fixed timeslot for a consumer station to send these announcement messages. This depends on the average hops it takes for messages to reach this station. If the average number of hops becomes too bad, then a new announcement message will be sent and producer stations will align the maximum hop count for their messages. The path that the message followed is not recorded because stations are not aware of the name of their neighbor stations. Recording the traveled links is also not suitable because the states of the links are too dynamic and links are not reconnected to their same counterpart. Routing decision should be made within each station. The announcement mechanism optimizes very fast the setting of the maximum hop count in the messages. It is stable and also adaptable if the destination station moves.

Routing Strategies

To apply the previous introduced routing protocols to the sensor network (Fig. 6), we developed different routing strategies (Tab. 2), which map the protocol to every station with a routing behavior. The mapping bases on the knowledge of the domain and the task of the router stations. The routing behavior is changed for certain stations to investigate the performance of a certain routing protocol on critical junction points.

Table 2. Routing Strategies

Routing Strategy	Router Station	Routing Behavior
0	R2, R3, R4, R6, R7	Flooding Routing
	R9	Simple Hot-Potato
	R1, R5	Drop messages sent from the transit network
	R8	Takes off message from the transit network
1	R2, R3, R4, R6, R7	Flooding Routing
	R9	Simple Hot-Potato
	R1, R5	Reflect messages back into the transit network
	R8	Takes off message from the transit network
2	R2, R4, R6	Flooding Routing
	R3, R7	Hot-Potato
	R9	Simple Hot-Potato
	R1, R5	Drop messages sent from the transit network
	R8	Takes off message from the transit network
3	R2, R3, R6, R7	Flooding Routing
	R4	Simple Hot-Potato
	R9	Simple Hot-Potato
	R1, R5	Drop messages sent from the transit network
	R8	Takes off message from the transit network
4		Strategy 1 + 2
5		Strategy 2 + 3
6		Strategy 1 + 2 + 3

The strategy 0 uses the flooding algorithm for almost all router stations. Router stations R1 and R5 drop all messages from the transit network because they mark sources of packets. R8 takes all messages off the network because it is connected with only one link to the transit network.

In strategy 1 we change the behavior of R1 and R5. They send the received messages back into the transit network. What we want to achieve is that the message drop rate at these stations decreases and that wrongly routed messages are sent back into the network while trying to reach their destination.

The strategy 2 changes the routing behavior in R3 and R7 into the Hot-Potato routing. Two links are connected to each of these stations with a focus on redundancy. Changing the routing protocol into something else than Flooding will decrease the number of messages, which are sent back to R2 and R6. Here we are trying to support the forwarding to the destination station.

And strategy 3 bases on the same idea but for R4. In this case we do not use Hot-Potato because not all links are equal in their behavior. Hot-Potato would prefer the links to R3 and R7 because they are faster than FAN links. So, we set R4 to Simple Hot-Potato.

Strategies 4, 5, and 6 are combinations of the previous three cases. They will show whether a combination could increase the performance explicitly. In each combination the peculiarity of the participated strategies is taken. For instance strategy 4 combines the reflection capability of R1 and R5 from strategy 1 with the use of Hot-Potato in R3 and R7 from strategy 2. The combination of strategy 1 and strategy 3 is only used in connection with strategy 2, because in our opinion the influence on the result is not noticeable without the strategy 2.

R2 and R6 are all the time set up with the Flooding Protocol. That provides redundancy on the way to R3, R7. The router station R9 uses in all strategies the Simple Hot-Potato routing protocol. Flooding would discriminate the other sensor sources and Hot-Potato would prefer the link to R8. But, the injection of data packets should be fair for all sensor sources.

Fig. 7, Fig. 8, and Fig. 9 show the results of the simulator runs referring to the metrics average delay times, average hops, and relative amount of received messages. In the upper plot of each figure these metrics are plotted for each strategy, which uses the routing protocols implementing the announcement mechanism. The lower plot of each figure shows the plot of the metrics, which is based on the routing protocols but without implementing the announcement mechanism.

Evaluation of Routing Strategies

The first point we state is that the announcement mechanism works in the way it was designed for. For all strategies, it reduced delay times and optimized the number of hops for the messages according to their destination. This can be seen in Fig. 7 and Fig. 8. The effects of different strategies can also be seen in each metric. The strategy 0 is the so-called reference strategy. It shows how the network behaves when simply every message is sent to every station. Especially junction points like R3, R4, and R7 were sometimes heavily loaded and overloaded which result in higher delay times for instance. The strategies were developed to have a positive effect on all metrics. This only partially worked. In strategy 1, R1 and R5 should reflect misrouted messages

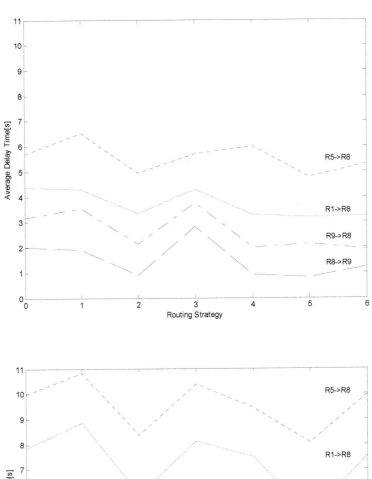

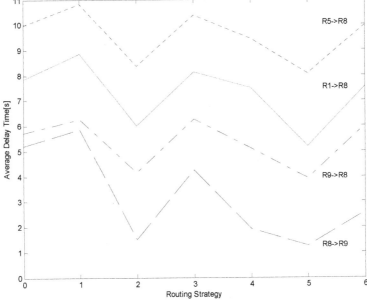

Fig. 7. Average Delay Time

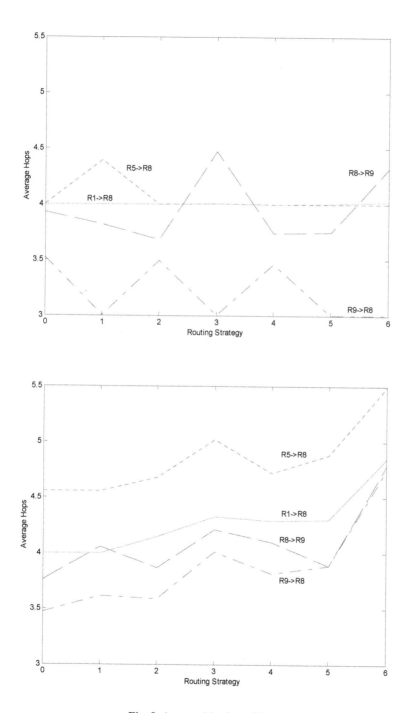

Fig. 8. Average Number of Hops

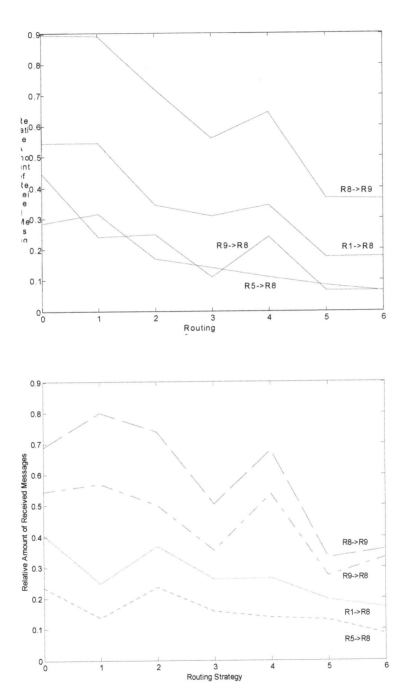

Fig. 9. Relative Amount of Received Messages

back into the transit network. While R5 could benefit from that and more messages from Sensor2 reached their destination, the throughput from Sensor3 broke down (Fig. 9, upper plot). The delay times increases as expected, but send buffer fillings in the same way. So, router stations, especially R2 and R6, were sometimes heavily overloaded and had to drop messages, for instance messages from R9. With strategy 2, we wanted to decrease the production of more duplicated messages than already produced by the use of Flooding in R2 and R6. But, with Hot-Potato for R3 and R7 in this strategy there are misrouted messages, but no duplicates anymore, which might be on the shorter way to the destination. Because of the hop counter optimization caused by the announcement mechanism, misrouted messages where dropped quickly and fewer messages reach their destination (Fig. 9, upper plot). When the mechanism was not active some messages could benefit from a longer lifetime and got the chance of being sent back on the right way (Fig. 9, lower plot). In general, delay times and number of hops could be reduced (Fig. 7 and Fig. 8). In strategy 3 we tried to decrease the number of duplicated messages at router R4 - a central point every message has to pass to reach its destination. The routing behavior was set to Simple Hot-Potato to reduce number of duplicates in the send buffers of R4. But we achieved a poor performance. Many messages were misrouted, delay times and hops increased and fewer messages reached their destination. The combinations of routing strategies also performed only partly well. While strategy 4 and 5 performed much better for delay times and number of hops (Fig. 7 and Fig. 8), they performed even worse than the single strategies referred to throughput in Fig. 9. Finally, we consider the trend of the curve for the R9-R8 route in Fig. 9. The throughput for this route in the upper plot of Fig. 9 achieves around half of the one in the lower plot. The reason for that is the announcement mechanism. It optimized the hop counter for the route over R7 to the destination R8, because it is shorter than the route over R6 (see Fig. 6). But, the R9 station works with Simple Hot-Potato protocol, which distributes messages uniformly over both routes. So, for half of the messages the hop counter exceeded its maximum value and they were dropped when routed over R6.

For all simulated strategies, there is no one method or combination of methods, which can be declared as an overall winner. It mainly depends on the focus. If the focus is on the messages reaching their destination, then strategy 0 (the flooding strategy) with the announcement mechanism performs best. However, with the focus on the delay times and way length (hops), the combination in strategy 5 (see Tab. 2) performs best. But it has a poor performance when considering the throughput.

3   Application Area and Related Work

The network is part of our ongoing research in supporting Ubiquitous Computing applications with local communication. Although applications are in the center of this research, several types of networks (wired and wireless) are developed, tested and enhanced for the use in applications. Protocols supporting these applications include the RAUM protocol [HB00]. This protocol is used for interconnecting (existing) devices equipped with computer and communication technology. In the MediaCup [BGS01] prototype RAUM is used for ISO/OSI layer 3 communication while infrared based IrDA, proprietary radio-frequency and Controller Area Network (CAN) provide functionality of layer 2 and 1. A similar research project is Roy Want's ParcTab network and application at XeroxParc [WSA97], the first prototype in Ubicomp generally.

So-called pico-networks may also be useful in this application area. Such networks allow devices to communicate to other devices nearby mainly in range of 2 to 10 meters. Bluetooth [S99] for example provides a standardized communication platform for nearby electronic devices, e.g. mobile phones and personal digital assistants. Because of the all-purpose communication stack Bluetooth adds some complexity to a device. AT&T Cambridge Research Lab has developed a very low power network (Pen, [BCE97]). Power management is a key issue in Ubiquitous Computing and this network is specially dedicated to applications with small devices that have to save as much power as possible. Research on Mobile Ad-Hoc networks (e.g. MANET of the IETF) focuses on the transmission of information over a larger distance through routing with a changing and unknown topology of the participating network nodes.

A way to interconnect devices attached to the body is provided by body networks. [PAB00] presents a system prototype with data rates up to 56 kbaud per second. Radiation to the outside and effects on vital devices (e.g. pacemakers) are still subject to research here. Other ways to interconnect devices on the body are Fiber fabrics, where communication lines, sensors and computing units are embedded into the fiber or constructed by interweaving the fibers. Examples are the FICOM research in the Disappearing Computer call of the European Union (www.disappearing-computer.org) or work at the MIT on Washable Computing (e.g. [PO97]).

4   Conclusion and Future Work

This paper presented a prototype system and investigates routing methods in the Fabric Area Network. For this purpose we developed a simulator supplied by measured data to design, debug, and evaluate different routing protocols. We chose Flooding, Hot-Potato and Simple Hot-Potato as routing protocols, which met the requirements in sense of simplicity, robustness and speed. To optimize the maximum hop counter we added an announcement mechanism for consumer stations. Simulations showed that the performance is improved by the use of routing protocols. But, the choice of an appropriate routing protocol depends on the metric that the focus is on. Throughput, way lengths and delay times were used as metrics. Results showed that routing can optimize the performance of the FAN for each metric, but not for all metrics.

Our simulations and tests have indicated that the introduction of domain specific knowledge enhances the overall performance of the system. The topology of the system is known to some extent and also the needed quality of service can be obtained from some nodes. So, sophisticated routing algorithms may be an option to the current more simple protocols. Although it is not clear if the overhead generated by such a protocol relates to the performance gain. One goal for the future is to simulate these more complex networks where links can be reconnected on routers that were not connected beforehand.

Furthermore the whole concept of coil-based communication should be replaced by contact oriented links as they were used in section 2.2. The higher rate of breaks of links can maybe be compensated by the bandwidth that is many times higher. Then protocols with more overhead and higher complexity become also more interesting. In addition, extensive application testing will provide us with more data to be fed into the simulator. It also allows us to evaluate the usefulness of the network in real settings.

Acknowledgements

We would like to thank the people from the i-Wear team at the former Starlab for supporting our work by their great cooperation. A special thank goes to Kristof Van Laerhoven, Ozan Cakmakci and Francois Galilee.

References

[B64]   Baran, P., 1964. On Distributed Communications Networks. *IEEE Transactions on Communications.* pp.1-9

[B01]   Beck IPC GmbH 2001. *Single Chip Embedded WEB-Server.* Available from: http://www.bcl-online.de/ [Accessed 09/14/01]

[BGS01] Beigl M., Gellersen H., Schmidt A. MediaCups: Experience with Design and Use of Computer-Augmented Everyday Objects, *Computer Networks, Special Issue on Pervasive Computing*, Elsevier, Vol. 35, No. 4, March 2001, Elsevier, pp 401-409

[BCE97] Bennett F., Clarke D., Evans J.B., Hopper A., Jones A., Leask D. *Piconet: Embedded Mobile Networking*, IEEE Personal Communications, Vol. 4, No. 5, October 1997, pp 8-15

[DHK01] Davis J. II, Hylands C., Kienhuis B., Lee E.A., Liu J., Liu X., Muliadi L., Neuendorffer S., Tsay J., Vogel B., Xiong Y. 2001. *Heterogeneous Concurrent Modeling and Design in Java.* [Online]. University of California, Berkeley, CA USA. Available from: http://ptolemy.eecs.berkeley.edu/ptolemyII/ [Accessed 09/14/01].

[H01]   Hum, A.P.J. 2001. Fabric area network - a new wireless communications infrastructure to enable ubiquitous networking and sensing on intelligent clothing. *Computer Networks.* 35, pp.391-399

[HB00]   Hupfeld F., Beigl M. Spatially aware local communication in the RAUM system. *Proceedings of the IDMS*, Enschede, Niederlande, October 17-20, 2000, pp 285-296

[LAL01] Laerhoven, K. Van, Aidoo K., Lowette S., 2001. Real-time analysis of Data from Many Sensors with Neural Networks. *Proceedings of the fourth International Symposium on Wearable Computers (ISWC) Zurich, 7-9 October 2001.* IEEE Press.

[PAB00] Padridge K., Arnstein L., Boriello G., Whitted T. Fast Intrabody Signaling, 3rd IEEE Workshop on Mobile Computing Systems and Applications (WMCSA) Monterey, 7-8 December, 2000

[PO97]   Post E., Orth M., Smart Fabric, or Washable Computing. *1st IEEE International Symposium on Wearable Computing*, Cambridge Massachusetts, 13-14 October 1997, pp. 167-168

[S96]   Shoubridge, P.J. 1996. *Adaptive Strategies For Routing in Dynamic Networks.* PhD thesis, University of South Australia.

[S99]   D. Sonnerstam (Hrsg.) *Specification of the Bluetooth System Version 1.0 B*, Bluetooth SIG; Dezember 1999

[WSA97] Want R., Schilit B., Adams N., Gold R., Goldberg D., Petersen K., Ellis J., Weiser M. *Mobile Computing* , Kluwer Publishing, Edited by Tomasz Imielinski, Book Chapter 2, pp 45-101, ISBN 0-7923-9697-9, February 1997.

[W91]   Weiser M. *The Computer for the 21st Century*, Scientific American, September 1991 Vol. 265 No. 3, pp 94-104

Location and Network Quality Issues in Local Area Wireless Networks

Georgi Tonev[1], Vaidy Sunderam[1], Roger Loader[1,2], and James Pascoe[1,2]

[1] Math & Computer Science, Emory University
Atlanta, GA 30322, USA
{gtonev,vss}@emory.edu
http://www.mathcs.emory.edu/janus/
[2] Department of Computer Science
The University of Reading
Reading RG6 6AY, United Kingdom
{r.j.loader,j.s.pascoe}@reading.ac.uk

Abstract. Wireless networks intrinsically contain pockets of lowered quality within the coverage area, where environmental factors cause packet loss, lowered bandwidth, or intermittent connectivity. Early detection of such regions can be extremely valuable; in order to facilitate preemptive or corrective action by protocols and applications, we propose a software framework that detects and predicts impending "trouble spots" when a mobile device moves through a wireless network. Based on measurements of signal strength, network latency and packet loss, we postulate that mobile devices (and their landline communication partners) can be forewarned with a high degree of accuracy when approaching trouble spots. In this paper we describe a lightweight software framework that assists in monitoring network quality within a coverage area, based on several parameters in isolation and in combination. The effectiveness of using these metrics was measured, and experimental results indicate that accuracies of the order of 95% with very low false positives can be obtained. We conclude with an exemplary outline of how applications may use this software to detect regions of degraded network quality and take compensatory action, resulting in enhanced effectiveness.

1 Introduction

Wireless networks are increasing in popularity and use, and trends suggest very widespread deployment in the near future. In particular, local area wireless networks based on the 802.11b standard are becoming ubiquitous, not only in business and commercial settings, but also in public places and in private homes. With this increasing adoption, quality of network service gains importance. In essence, network facilities delivered to the end application or the end user should be as robust as possible, within the constraints imposed by the physical network. For example, currently, applications utilizing wireless networks deal with loss of connectivity or even lost data by reinitiating the connection or reissuing the data transfer. While this mode of operation may be acceptable today for certain

H. Schmeck, T. Ungerer, and L. Wolf (Eds.): ARCS 2002, LNCS 2299, pp. 131–145, 2002.
© Springer-Verlag Berlin Heidelberg 2002

applications, degradation in quality will become a serious issue that must be addressed at various levels as the technology matures and other more sophisticated applications evolve.

Like other networks, wireless network quality is subject to network factors such as congestion, traffic spikes, and link failures. However, in addition, wireless networks are also susceptible to environmental factors that affect network quality when a mobile device is within specific regions within a coverage area. Examples include physical obstructions such as walls or other structures, electrical disturbances from other devices, or even factors such as weather. When a mobile device is within such areas in the scope of a wireless network, communication bandwidth, latency, and packet loss are generally affected. In this project we focus on network quality issues that are a direct result of location and environmental factors, and propose methods for detecting and adapting to them.

We postulate that through lightweight monitoring in software, it is possible for mobile devices and their communicating partners to detect when a wireless node is (imminently) entering and departing a "trouble spot", i.e. a region within the coverage area that is characterized by degraded network quality. If devices, protocols or applications are forewarned about imminent quality degradation, they can take preemptive or corrective action, if they so desire. For example, transport protocols may decide to increase acknowledgment timeout durations or the number of retransmissions. Applications may defer critical actions such as database commits until the device is clear of the trouble spot. Low level protocols or the device itself may wish to take power-saving actions or to hibernate. Such measures will lead to increased overall effectiveness in the wireless environment, and are also likely to be crucial to certain classes of applications. In this paper we describe our work in constructing software frameworks that detect trouble spots in IEEE 802.11b networks, comment on the accuracy of these methods, and provide an application level example of using trouble spot information to improve throughput.

2   Related Work

Two major aspects, related to quality variations and trouble spots in wireless networks, are: (1) detecting and predicting areas that can cause degraded network performance; and (2) providing this information to entities that may find it useful. In the past, most efforts have focused on correcting trouble spot related problems, while little has been done to integrate their prediction with taking early corrective measures. Typically, most projects require certain tradeoffs, ranging from modifying existing applications or protocol implementations to adding new hardware. In addition, existing approaches focus only on a specific facet of wireless communications, such as improving the performance of a given protocol over wireless links, e.g. TCP. Balakrishnan et al. [ ] classify different approaches to this problem into three different groups: (1) end-to-end strategies, where the TCP sender is responsible for handling losses through selective acknowledgments or explicit loss notifications; (2) split-connection techniques that hide the wireless link from the sender by terminating the TCP connection at the base station; (3)link-layer modifications that hide link-related losses from the TCP sender by using local retransmissions and forward error correction over the wireless link. One deficiency of most of these projects is that they require low level modifications (e.g. firmware modifications in Snoop [ ]) that detracts from their usability. Furthermore, all are corrective in nature, and do not make provisions for predicting trouble spots and taking preventive measures.

Another research direction that is less closely related, concerns location determination. While such techniques may not be directly related to improving performance, they can be valuable as auxiliary tools. Once a device associates degraded performance with a certain location, it can reasonably expect a similar experience on subsequent revisits, and can take preemptive action. Location determination also frequently involves trade-offs; an example system is Cricket [ ] that necessitates additional hardware in the mobile device and in the infrastructure.

Although approaches such as those mentioned above can be useful in certain cases, we believe that a need exists for a trouble spot detection tool that can be easily integrated into various systems without the use of special hardware. Our project makes no assumptions about location awareness and the data it generates depends only on the accurate measurement of network parameters. Applications or protocols may then decide if, and how, the data provided by our tool will be used. To the best of our knowledge, few other projects have proposed this approach in the context of IEEE 802.11b networks.

3   Monitoring Software

The trouble spot detection framework presented in this paper is based on monitoring network parameters from within the mobile device; our experimental platform is based on the IEEE 802.11b standard. Such local area wireless networks are currently the most popular, and in widespread use. Possible reasons for the popularity of 802.11b networks include their network compatibility, use of unregulated frequencies, and (relatively) high bandwidth. However, as with most devices, there are variations in adherence to the standard as well as in the interpretation of unspecified aspects, both in hardware and device drivers. For our purposes, we wish to measure general network artifacts such as packet loss and round-trip time, and wireless-specific parameters such as signal strength, bitrate, and noise, although the latter measurements are only as reliable as the data provided by wireless NIC device drivers. In this section, we describe our experimental setup and project scenario, and briefly highlight the relevant aspects of wireless networks that affect the above parameters and are subject to variability due to device driver differences.

Our experimental setup consists of portable laptop computers with PCMCIA wireless NICs that are operating in infrastructural mode. One base station is used. It should be noted that the base station does not play a direct role in

our experiments (and our proposed scheme), unlike projects such as Snoop [ ]
that modify base station firmware/software. Our monitoring software executes
as a background process on the laptop computers and injects minimally sized
packets into the network to measure round-trip times and packet loss; sampling
is done at a rate of 10 per second. Signal strength is also monitored at the same
frequency by querying the device driver, which in turn reads the value from the
device hardware. Figure 1 depicts our experimental setup and proposed scheme
for supporting network quality detection and adaptation in a typical wireless
and wired network scenario.

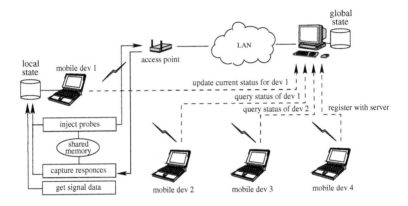

Fig. 1. Project schematic and operational overview

3.1   Hardware

For the purpose of performing our experiments we evaluated the Compaq WL110
(orinoco_cs driver), the SMC 2632 (orinoco_cs driver) and the Aironet 4800b
(airo_cs driver) wireless PCMCIA cards. Despite the relatively small number of
devices used, we came across a number of inconsistencies in the cards' hardware
implementation and in the drivers used. While the field of wireless LANs using Linux is an emerging one and serious attempts for standardization are yet
to be witnessed, these inconsistencies make the creation of a general purpose
tool, independent from the underlying hardware, difficult to achieve. Wireless
802.11b PCMCIA cards are essentially capable of providing information on signal strength, noise, signal quality and bitrate. Bitrate may be automatically
adjusted by the card and can therefore be a good indicator of network quality,
but according to the standard, it may be set, via software, to a fixed value.
Moreover, cards do not reliably supply either bitrate, noise, or signal quality information. For example, in some of the device drivers we analyzed, noise was set
to a hardcoded value and the kernel tables were not updated when appropriate.
Consequently, signal quality becomes irrelevant, since it is normally computed

as a direct function of noise. In other cases, the hardware itself is suspect. For example, using the same device driver, a card from one manufacturer registered significant noise levels when used near a microwave oven, while another did not register any noise. Yet another problem with certain cards is their reported values of signal strength; one card displayed 0% signal strength even when network performance was entirely satisfactory. Based on these experiences, we selected the Compaq WL110 card with the orinoco_cs driver as the one providing the most stable information for our experiments.

3.2 Methodology

To determine the influence of location and environment factors on wireless network performance, we propose a lightweight and realtime monitoring strategy; each mobile device monitors local conditions and takes adaptive action, while simultaneously recording status information in a landline database (see Figure 1). Communicating partner devices (both landline and wireless) consult the database either on demand or via periodic updates and take appropriate actions. To prototype this scenario, we implemented a tool that is designed to be: (1) lightweight – it should impose as little overhead as possible on both the mobile device and the network (both wired and wireless components); (2) transparent to the user – the tool is initiated as a background process during system startup and continues to operate as long the system is up and running; (3) flexible – it should facilitate interfacing with a more comprehensive monitoring system or graphical tool, in addition to working as autonomous monitoring software.

While the manner in which signal and noise related data is retrieved is quite straightforward (the device driver updates kernel tables and standard interfaces are available to access them), measuring round-trip time and packet loss is somewhat more difficult. There are several different techniques that can be employed for this purpose. One obvious strategy is to mimic the way *ping* works, i.e. by using ICMP echo request packets [ ]; another is to use UDP datagrams sent to idle ports, and exploit the default response of conforming UDP implementations. While it is widely known that ICMP echo request packets are often filtered due to security concerns (and this can easily turn into an obstacle to our goals), experiments showed that in practice this approach caused far fewer problems than the UDP one. Thus far, we have not encountered an access point that is set to filter ICMP echo request packets, and since the wireless portion of the network is under analysis, ideally, it is the access point that should serve as the target of the probes. For this reason, we chose to mimic the ping approach.

The prototype implementation of our monitoring tool runs as a *daemon* process that does not require user interaction or intervention. When started, the tool spawns three threads: an *injector*, a *capturer* and a *signal data processor*, each performing a specific task. The injector constructs ICMP echo request packets and sends them to the access point. The capturer thread monitors incoming traffic and processes the returned ICMP echo reply packets. The signal data processor parses the /proc file system and retrieves data for the signal strength. Based on the data collected, a local adaptive action may be taken. In other words, the mobile device possesses all the information needed about local conditions, and can take preemptive or corrective action as appropriate; an example of such an action is described in section 5.

Alternatively or additionally, the monitoring software on a given mobile device can be integrated into a larger system. A number of mobile devices, each working separately, but requiring information about the current state of their peers can register with a central server (or a number of central servers, if distributed control is required) that stores data for each registered device and supplies it to its peers upon request or through periodic updates. The peers can then also take preemptive or corrective actions, thereby improving the overall robustness or performance characteristics of the wireless system. In both scenarios, but especially important for the hybrid (database supported) model, is the ability of each monitor to be able to predict imminent trouble spots, before the device actually enters them, so that the mobile device has a reasonable opportunity to notify the appropriate server. Since the same network that is susceptible is also used to send updates to the database, it may not be possible to guarantee that device status information will always be delivered to the external system and database when a device enters a trouble spot.

4   Experimental Results

The goal of this project is to determine the feasibility of characterizing and predicting network behavior, based on the quality of service provided by the wireless connection at a given location and under the influence of certain environmental factors. We denote coverage according to the severity of the degradation in performance as *good*, *average* and *poor*. Good coverage implies maximal throughput, minimal latency, and only occasional packet loss; "poor" implies little or no connectivity. Areas of "average" coverage are characterized by high packet loss and lowered bandwidth; these areas typically surround poor areas for a distance of a few meters. Our preliminary analysis suggests that it is possible to devise a more fine grained categorization; we are currently investigating the need and usefulness of using a greater number of classifications. The qualitative characterizations of poor, average, and good may be viewed from the network perspective as: *trouble spot* – areas with poor network quality, where the mobile host is practically disassociated with the access point; any network activity is impossible; *preamble/postamble to the trouble spot* – areas with variable network performance where communication is sometimes possible, but the mobile host experiences significant network problems; performance and reliability is severely degraded; *normal* – the least interesting case; there may be transient errors in the network, but these do not influence its performance. The results of the experiments that are discussed below pertain to a number of measurements over a fixed path, while moving the mobile device at a constant speed through the coverage area. The path, shown in Figure 2, contains two trouble spots. Due to the difficulty of recreating linear patterns of trouble spots, the path involves movement of the mobile host into the trouble spot, turning around and retracing

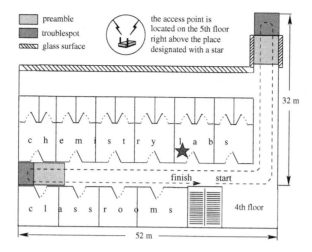

preamble
troublespot
glass surface

the access point is located on the 5th floor right above the place designated with a star

32 m

c h e m i s t r y l a b s

finish   start

c l a s s r o o m s

4th floor

52 m

Fig. 2. Diagram of the test environment

the incoming route. While this is equivalent to a trajectory that passes *through* a trouble spot, it also shows how the network reacts when the direction of movement of the mobile device changes in relation to the access point. Given the range of 802.11b networks and the fact that such networks are usually installed within buildings, mobility rates are typically that of human movement; our experiments were therefore conducted at normal walking pace.

The experimental results that we present, indicate the raw measurements of round-trip time, packet loss, and signal strength (individually), when a mobile device traverses the path shown in Figure 2 at a constant rate; the duration of the traversal is 120 seconds in all cases. For each metric, we then attempt to categorize each instantaneous position along the route as good, average, or poor, based on data trends in the measured values of that parameter. We also perform this characterization by using all three metrics in combination. It should be noted that in each case, the software makes a decision on the status of a point on the path based only on data available up to that point. Finally, we evaluate the accuracy of each of the four methods of classifying network regions by comparing the perceptions of each method to the known characteristics of the region that were determined through careful experimentation and human observation (i.e. as shown in Figure 2).

4.1   RTT-Based Classification

The software framework measures round-trip time (RTT) at the rate of ten times per second by injecting sequenced packets into the network and recording the duration until the corresponding response is received. A frequency distribution of RTT measurements is constructed, using 10 millisecond ranges. Responses that

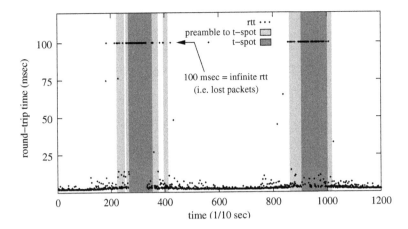

Fig. 3. RTT raw data and the corresponding network performance estimate

do not arrive within a conservative threshold are assumed to signify "infinite" RTT (i.e. lost packets), but to unify the algorithm, are assigned an artificial value of 100 milliseconds[1]. By analyzing the frequency distribution and using experimentally determined ranges, the software identifies the mobile device as being in a normal, preamble/postamble, or trouble spot region.

Figure 3 shows a scatter-plot of the RTT measurements; normal values are in the 2-5 milliseconds range, while values in the 10-20 millisecond range can be seen in a limited portion of the graph. The two trouble spots are clearly seen even from the raw data. In the first conglomeration of samples with high RTT values, it is easy to distinguish even the preamble to the trouble spot. The shaded areas in Figure 3 show the classification by the software system of the different region categories (unfilled areas are judged to be normal, light shaded areas are preambles/postambles, and dark shaded areas are deemed to be trouble spots). Through visual inspection of the figure, it can be seen that the software decisions are reasonably accurate; later in this section we quantify the degree of accuracy.

4.2   Packet Loss

The injector and capturer components of the software measure packet loss by periodically harvesting unacknowledged probes from RTT measurements. Packet loss, by definition, can only be inferred locally by a mobile device long after its actual occurrence. Therefore, this metric is less likely to be of value in early warnings of impending trouble spots, however, it is useful in detecting the emergence of a mobile device from a trouble spot.

Figure 4 shows a plot of the instantaneous (not cumulative) number of packets lost during each second, as the mobile device traverses the standard path.

---

[1] This value was selected as being far above any plausible real RTT, and is valid for 802.11b networks.

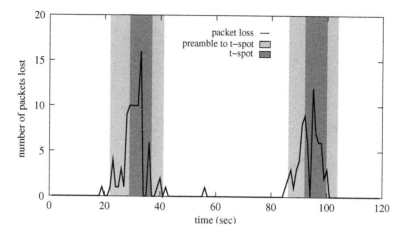

Fig. 4. Packet loss raw data and the corresponding network performance estimate

Again, using a frequency distribution and distinct ranges, software decisions about the status of each point along the path are shown as shaded areas. It can be discerned from a comparison of Figures 3 and 4 that both schemes possess the same view of trouble spots, but their interpretations of preamble/postamble areas are considerably different.

4.3 Signal Strength

Instantaneous measurements of signal strength, sampled at the rate of 10 per second, are shown in the graph in Figure 5. Being an electrical, rather than a network measure, much greater continuity of trend is exhibited by this metric – it gradually decreases as the mobile devices moves away from the base station, and increases as the device moves toward it. By using a threshold corresponding to 15% of the maximum, the software classifies regions as "good" and "poor" for values above and below the threshold, with an "average" performance for values roughly equal to 15%.

As with the previous two metrics, there is a clear indication of the two trouble spots. The shape of the curve facilitates early decision making and allows the communication device to undertake corrective measures, while it still has connectivity with the rest of the network. We expect even better results, once we are able to augment this metric with signal quality, which normally takes noise into account.

4.4 Combinations

In the previous subsections we presented the decisions made by our monitoring software as to the presence of trouble spots and preambles/postambles, based

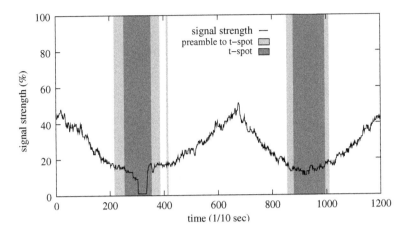

Fig. 5. Signal strength raw data and the corresponding network performance estimate

on three different metrics used in isolation. Since all three metrics are available to the software, it is also possible to combine them and perhaps gain a greater degree of confidence in the identification of trouble spots and preambles. In order to measure this, we employed a "majority" rule using the three metrics in combination; a given point is deemed to be "good", "average" or "poor" based on the largest number of metrics that characterize it as such (and deemed to be "average" when there is no clear majority). Figure 6 shows the superimposed metrics; the shaded regions again depict judgment points of the monitoring in determining the three types of regions. Using the combined metrics, regions quite similar in appearance to the others are visually observed.

4.5   Accuracy

Based on the decision graphs presented, we can safely argue that we have two trouble spots, each surrounded by a preamble and a postamble. However, the true accuracy of these heuristic decisions by the software still remains to be verified. In order to do so, we need a reference map that represents the "actual" network zones that can be used to measure the deviation of the four methods. In this exercise, we constructed this reference map based on multiple manual observations measured along the path: (a) intervals 0-220, 411-860 and 1021-1200[2] correspond to areas with good network performance; (b) intervals 221-265, 356-410, 861-900 and 1006-1020 correspond to preambles/postambles to trouble spots; and (c) intervals 266-355 and 901-1005 correspond to trouble spots. Based on the above reference regions, we compared the decisions made by the software using RTT, packet loss, signal strength, and all three metrics in combination to

---

[2] time intervals are measured in tenths of a second

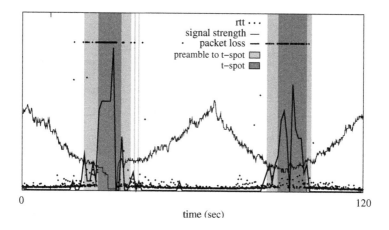

Fig. 6. Combined graph

our known view of the different regions. True-positives and true-negatives, or the percent of time when the software determines correctly that the device is, or is not, in a zone of a certain type, should be as close to 100% as possible. False-positives, when the software believes that it is in a zone of certain type and in fact it is not, should be near 0%. Similarly, false negatives should also be near 0%.

Table 1 shows the accuracy of determining network zones through RTT alone. It can be seen that this method very accurately determines normal regions, and identifies trouble spots quite well, but the accuracy for identifying average areas is not as high.

Tables 2 and 3 show the accuracy measures when using signal strength and packet loss metrics in isolation. With these metrics, "good" areas are identified correctly with a high degree of accuracy, but the identification of "average" and "poor" areas exhibit a very large percentage of erroneous conclusions.

Finally, Table 4 shows the accuracy levels of detecting different zones in an 802.11b network when all three metrics are used in combination, i.e. it quantifies the veracity of Figure 6 when compared against the true locations of different types of zones in the coverage area. It is clear from the table that the combined metrics provide the best results. In particular, using the combined metrics correctly identifies trouble spots almost 95% of the time. False-positive readings in "good" zones, and false-negative readings in both "good" and "poor" zones are at very acceptable levels of just a few percent (or less). Accuracy of detecting "average" zones is also better as compared to any of the metrics used in isolation, although it is still not near the 100% mark. This is intrinsic to "average" areas; the degree of nondeterminism that is present in these zones will necessarily result in a lowered degree of confidence in identifying them.

	Good		Average		Poor	

Table 1. Round-trip Time						
	pos	neg	pos	neg	pos	neg
true	99.65%	90.57%	81.29%	97.99%	88.72%	100.00%
false	2.75%	0.25%	1.75%	2.42%	0.00%	1.83%

Table 2. Signal Strength						
	pos	neg	pos	neg	pos	neg
true	98.82%	89.71%	56.77%	97.89%	93.85%	96.92%
false	3.00%	0.83%	1.83%	5.58%	2.58%	1.00%

Table 3. Packet Loss						
	pos	neg	pos	neg	pos	neg
true	98.82%	94.29%	67.74%	95.52%	84.62%	97.50%
false	1.67%	0.83%	3.75%	4.17%	2.08%	2.50%

Table 4. Combined						
	pos	neg	pos	neg	pos	neg
true	99.76%	93.43%	85.16%	98.85%	94.87%	100.00%
false	1.92%	0.17%	1.00%	1.92%	0.00%	0.83%

5   Application-Level Adaptation

The long-term goal of this project is to devise lightweight and accurate schemes to monitor mobile devices within a wireless network, with a view of detecting their movement into and out of trouble spots. Our approach is to signal any perception of trouble spot or preamble/postamble and leave it up to the programmer to decide how and when this information will be used. In addition, we also intend to investigate techniques that utilize this location information, to adaptively deliver more effective network services to user applications. In order to validate this premise and to demonstrate the viability of our approach, we undertook a simple case study involving file transfers between a mobile device and a landline host. This exercise postulates that when mobile devices move in and out of trouble spots during file transfers, using TCP, the transport layer assumes that there is network congestion or a rate control issue. In other words, the TCP protocol, intended for long-haul wired networks, cannot distinguish between trouble spots and typical Internet congestion that occurs in routers, and therefore invokes standard *slow start* and *congestion avoidance* [ ]algorithms that degrade overall throughput. Our hypothesis is that if monitoring software could detect an imminent trouble spot, the default action of TCP could be overridden, thereby delivering higher performance. To experimentally verify this, we modified the TCP protocol implementation in the Linux kernel to differentiate between trouble spots and other network effects. We changed the default behavior of the TCP stack with particular reference to its slow start and congestion avoidance algorithms.

It is known that slow start and congestion avoidance are two phases in a TCP connection that are invoked when the sender senses that maximum network capacity is reached. In order to describe and justify our modifications when wireless trouble spots are encountered, we provide some details of these two algorithms, including the criteria for their invocation and the consequences of their activation.

5.1   TCP Issues and Algorithms

To achieve high performance, a TCP connection should attempt to utilize the entire network bandwidth available. This means that the sender should inject enough data to keep the "pipe" full, but the rate at which it sends data should not exceed the rate at which the receiver or any intermediate router can handle it. This principle, called "conservation of packets", implies that the network is operating at full capacity (i.e. utilizing the entire sliding window size) and also that a new packet is injected only after an old packet loaves [ ]. Violating this principle leads to underutilization of network resources or alternatively to overutilization, which results in increased number of packet retransmissions. Either situation is undesirable and leads to lowered bandwidth and an increase in the time required to complete a transfer. These problems occur when the connection is unable to reach equilibrium, either because the sender has an unrealistic estimate of the rate at which it should operate, or there are insufficient network resources along the path [ ]. However, when a TCP connection starts for the first time, or when it is restarted after a timeout, the sender has no way of knowing its ideal transmit rate. The "standard" TCP implementations paces packet injection by using acknowledgments to clock the sending of new data, but this can only be done after the connection reaches steady state. Therefore, initially, and every time the clocking mechanism is disrupted due to a timeout, the rate at which data is sent is drastically reduced and the process of establishing the clock is restarted. This process is controlled by the two algorithms mentioned previously, namely slow start and congestion avoidance.

As a result of our experiments, we came to think that the major cause for invoking the two algorithms is (a) packets being dropped and (b) packets arriving out of order. These are usually manifested in the form of selective acknowledgments [ ] received by the sender. In a wired network both events would normally suggest congestion (i.e. packets are being dropped at the routers or the receiver, or alternate routes are being used). This classic characteristic of TCP results in a saw-tooth throughput pattern in the presence of congestion, and leads to reduced overall bandwidth for a given connection.

5.2   Trouble Spot Handling

While selective acknowledgments and time-outs generally indicate congestion in conventional networks, this is not necessarily the case in wireless ones. As discussed in [ ], one characteristic feature of 802.11b is a high bit-error rate in trouble spots, which in turn leads to an increased number of damaged packets and hence, to packets considered lost. In addition, multipath causes packets to arrive out of sequence. As a result, trouble spots cause unmodified TCP implementations to (erroneously) invoke congestion related algorithms (usually slow start followed by congestion avoidance) in an attempt to fix a problem that is actually due to the location of the mobile device. Even worse, as a result of these algorithms, TCP will unnecessarily spend a great portion of its time, operating with a decreased window size, thereby substantially affecting performance for a given connection.

It is exactly this behavior that we try to prevent using our trouble spot detection methodology. We want to be able to provide TCP with "hints" about what it should do when we are reasonably sure that current network problems are due to damaged packets as a result of multipath or signal attenuation [ ]. This decision is taken heuristically; if the device is in, or is entering, a trouble spot, and recent events do not suggest network congestion, then lost packets and/or selective acknowledgments are likely to be due to the trouble spot. In these situations the monitoring software can notify the TCP stack that adaptive actions should be taken. For example if we are entering a trouble spot, the size of the congestion window [ ]³ should be kept down, while when moving out of trouble spot its size should be increased much faster in contrast to conventional TCP practice.

In order to measure the effectiveness of the above approach, we modified the TCP implementation in the Linux kernel to use the adaptive actions above, when a mobile device entered the trouble spots, in our test environment, shown in Figure 2. The mobile device was engaged in a large file transfer, and measurements were made with an unmodified as well as a modified kernel. We observed rates of improvement ranging from 3% up to 14.5%, which indicates that TCP is very sensitive to the way the experiment is performed and that precise coordination of our tool and the kernel is required. Nevertheless, the results are very encouraging and indicate the high degree of effectiveness of this scheme.

6   Discussion and Future Work

The existence of trouble spots within wireless networks leads to disruptions in connectivity and degraded performance of user applications. Although trouble spots cannot be eliminated, their detrimental effects can be considerably diminished by detecting them and preemptively adapting to them. In this paper, we have demonstrated a lightweight and highly effective scheme for monitoring network quality as a mobile device moves through a wireless coverage area; this scheme is able to distinguish between normal, average, and poor network regions

---

³ a variable that directly controls the transmission rate of the sender; the sender's output routine sends the minimum of the congestion window size and the size of the sliding window negotiated by the receiver

with a very high degree of accuracy. By using a combination of network and interface card metrics (i.e. round-trip time, packet loss, and signal strength), the software classifies each point within the coverage area into one of the three categories, with error rates of only a few percent. Furthermore, we have shown that this status information can be used to adapt to current conditions, leading to significant improvements in application effectiveness. We believe that our scheme will be effective even in the presence of multiple access points, but this has to be further investigated and enhancements will be made if necessary. In addition, we intend to continue our research in the following directions: (1) measure and analyze the overheads involved in trouble spot detection; (2) devise schemes to make the process more efficient and accurate; and (3) investigate the use of trouble spot adaptation in group communications protocols [9], where the level of disruption due to intermittent connectivity and network quality is extremely high. We believe that the outcome of these efforts will contribute to enhancing the effectiveness and service levels as wireless networks become increasingly commonplace.

Acknowledgments

This work was supported in part by NSF grant ACI-9872167 and DoE grant DE-FG02-99ER25379.

References

1. Balakrishnan, H., Seshan, S., Amir, E., Katz, R.: "Improving TCP/IP Performance over Wireless Networks", *In Proc. 1st ACM International Conference on Mobile Computing and Networking (MOBICOM)*, November 1995 133, 134
2. Balakrishnan, H., Padmanabhan, V., Seshan, S., Katz, R.: "A Comparison of Mechanisms for Improving TCP Performance over Wireless Links", *IEEE/ACM Transactions on Networking, December 1997* 132
3. Priyantha, N., Chakraborty, A., Balakrishnan, H.: "The Cricket Location-Support System", *In Proc. of the 6th Annual ACM International Conference on Mobile Computing and Networking (MOBICOM)*, August 2000 133
4. Jacobson, V.: "Congestion Avoidance and Control", *In Proc. ACM SIGCOMM 88*, August 1988 143, 144
5. Stevens. W.: "TCP Slow Start, Congestion Avoidance, Fast Retransmit, and Fast Recovery Algorithms", *RFC-2001*, January 1997 142
6. Mathis, M., Mahdavi, J., Floyd, S., Romanow, A.: "TCP Selective Acknowledgment Options", *RFC-2018*, October 1996 143
7. Postel, J.: "Internet Control Message Protocol", *RFC-792*, September 1981 135
8. Eckhardt, D., Steenkiste P.: "Measurement and Analysis of the Error Characteristics of an In-Building Wireless Network", *In Proc. of the SIGCOMM '96 Symposium on Communications Architectures and Protocols*, pp. 243-254, Stanford, August 1996, ACM 144
9. Pascoe, J., Sibley, G., Sunderam, V., Loader, R.: "Mobile Wide Area Wireless Fault Tolerance", *Computational Science - ICCS 2001*, Eds. V. Alexandrov, J, Dongarra, B. Juliano, R. Renner, K. Tan, *Springer-Verlag Lecture Notes in Computer Science LNCS 2073*, pp. 385-394, May 2001 145

Session IV

Processor Architecture

Design Tradeoffs
for Embedded Network Processors

Tilman Wolf[1] and Mark A. Franklin[2]

[1] Department of Computer Science, Washington University,
St. Louis, MO, USA
wolf@ccrc.wustl.edu
[2] Departments of Computer Science and Electrical Engineering,
Washington University, St. Louis, MO, USA
jbf@ccrc.wustl.edu

Abstract. Demands for flexible processing have moved general-purpose processing into the data path of networks. With the development of System-On-a-Chip technology, it is possible to put a number of processors with memory and I/O components on a single ASIC. We present a performance model of such a system and show how the number of processors, cache sizes, and the tradeoffs between the use of on-chip SRAM and DRAM can be optimized in terms of computation per unit chip area for a given workload. Based on a telecommunications benchmark the results of such an optimization are presented and design tradeoffs for Systems-on-a-Chip are identified and discussed.

1 Introduction

Over the past decade there has been rapid growth in the need for reliable, robust, and high performance communications networks. This has been driven in large part by the demands of the Internet and general data communications. To adapt to new protocols, services, standards, and network applications, many modern routers are equipped with general purpose processing capabilities to handle (e.g., route and process) data traffic in software rather than dedicated hardware. Design of the network processors associated with such routers is a current and competitive area of computer architecture. This paper is aimed at examining certain tradeoffs associated with the design of these embedded network processors.

In the current router environment, single processor systems generally cannot meet network processing demands. This is due to the growing gap between link bandwidth and processor speed. Broadly speaking, with the advent of optical WDM links, packets are arriving faster than single processors can deal with them. However, since packet streams only have dependencies among packets of the same flow but none across different flows, processing can be distributed over several processors. That is, there is an inherent parallelism associated with the processing of independent packet flows. Thus, the problems of complex synchronization and inter-processor communications, typically encountered with parallelization arising from scientific applications, are not present. From a functional

H. Schmeck, T. Ungerer, and L. Wolf (Eds.): ARCS 2002, LNCS 2299, pp. 149–164, 2002.
© Springer-Verlag Berlin Heidelberg 2002

and performance standpoint it is therefore reasonable to consider developing network processors as parallel machines.

There are a host of advantages associated with integrating multiple processing units, memory, and I/O components on a single chip and developing what is referred to as a SOC (System-On-a-Chip) network processor. Chief among them are the ability to achieve higher performance and, by using fewer chips, lower cost. Such implementations are however limited by the size of the chip that is feasible (for cost and technology reasons), the packaging technology that can be utilized (to achieve given pin requirements), and the power which can be dissipated (at a given frequency).Therefore, one important design decision for such multiprocessor chips is how many processors and how much associated cache should be placed on a single chip. This is important since, for a given chip size, more processors imply smaller caches and smaller caches lead to higher fault rates. High fault rates, in turn, impact performance and also the required off-chip memory bandwidth. Bandwidth requirements for off-chip memory access and network traffic I/O are yet another important design constraint. In this paper, we address these optimization issues. In particular, our contributions are:

- Development of a performance model for a general single chip multiprocessor oriented towards network processing, but applicable across a range of application domains. Such a model easily accommodates future technology changes that drive the design space.
- Exploration of the design tradeoffs available and development of optimal architecture configurations. In particular the model permits examination of the interactions between number of processors, size of on-chip caches, type of on-chip cache (SRAM, DRAM), number of off-chip memory channels, and characteristics of the application workload.
- Development of selected network processor design guidelines.

Two metrics are associated with the performance model presented. The first is processing power per unit chip area, and the second is the total processing power for a fixed size chip. Model evaluation is performed for a realistic network processor workload over a range of design parameters. The derived set of design curves can be used as guidelines for future network processor designs.

Section 2 that follows characterizes the overall system design in more detail. Section 3 covers the analysis of the optimization problem. Section 4 introduces the application workload that was used for the optimization results that are shown in Section 5. Section 6 summarizes the work and presents conclusions.

2   Multiple Processor Systems-On-a-Chip

For the remainder of the paper we focus on a single SOC architecture consisting of multiple independent processing engines (Figure 1). The memory hierarchy consists of on-chip, per-processor instruction and data cache, and shared off-chip memory. A cluster of processors shares a common memory channel for off-chip

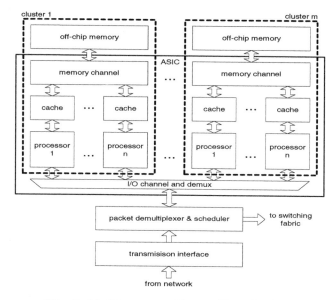

Fig. 1. Multiprocessor Router Port Outline

memory accesses. The I/O channel is used by the system controller/scheduler to send packets requiring processing to the individual processors.

Typically, a packet is first received and reassembled by the *Transmission Interface* on the input port of the router. The packet then enters a *Packet Demultiplexer* which uses packet header information to determine the flow to which the packet belongs. Based on this flow information the *Packet Demultiplexer* now decides what processing is required for the packet. The packet is then enqueued until a processor becomes available. When a processor becomes available, the packet and the flow information is sent over the I/O channel to one of the processors on the network processor chip. After processing has completed, the packet is returned to the *Packet Demultiplexer* and enqueued before being sent through the router switching fabric to its designated output port. A more detailed functional description of the above design can be found in [ ]. Here, we consider the single chip design optimization problem associated with selection of the:

– Number of processors per cluster.
– Instruction and data cache size per processor.
– Cache memory technology (SRAM vs. DRAM).
– Bandwidth and load of the memory channels.
– ASIC size.
– Application workload.

Table 1 lists the parameters that are considered. The processors are assumed to be simple pipelined, general purpose RISC cores (e.g., MIPS [ ], ARM [ ],

or PowerPC [ ]). VLIW or superscalar processors are not considered since they
require significantly more silicon real-estate than simple RISC cores. A study of
different multi-processor architectures [ ] has shown that single chip multipro-
cessors are highly competitive with super-scalar and multithreaded processors.
Also, super-scalar processors are optimized for workloads with few complex tasks
rather than many simple and highly parallelized tasks that are found in the network processor environment.

Table 1. System Parameters

Component	Symbol	Description
processor	clk_p	processor clock frequency
program	f_{load}	frequency of load instructions
	f_{store}	frequency of store instructions
	mi_c	i-cache miss probability for cache size c_i
	md_c	d-cache miss probability for cache size c_d
	$dirty_c$	prob. of dirty bit set in d-cache of size c_d
	$compl$	complexity (instr. per byte of packet)
caches	c_i	instruction cache size
	c_d	data cache size
	$linesize$	cache line size of i- and d-cache
	$t_{cache.dram}$	time for cache access (only DRAM)
off-chip memory	t_{mem}	time to access off-chip memory
memory channel	$width_{mchl}$	width of memory channel
	clk_{mchl}	memory channel clock frequency
	ρ	load on memory channel
I/O channel	$width_{io}$	width of I/O channel
	clk_{io}	clock rate of I/O channel
cluster	n	number of processors per cluster
ASIC	m	number of clusters and memory channels
	$s(x)$	actual size of component x, with $x \in \{ASIC, p, c_i, c_d, io, mchl\}$

3   Analysis

Given that we are interested in the amount of traffic the system can handle, we
view the design problem as one of selecting the parameter values which maximize
the throughput assuming chip area constraints, reasonable technology parameters, and the operational characteristics of a benchmark of network processing
programs.[1]

---

[1] In this treatment we do not consider latency issues and assume that these requirements are met if the design can keep up with the incoming packet rate.

Throughput in this environment corresponds to the number of packets that can be processed in a given time. This is determined by a combination of the instruction processing requirements of a given application (e.g., number of instructions necessary for routing table lookup, packet encoding, etc.), and the number of instructions that can be executed per second on the network processor. We assume that all packet processing tasks are performed in software on the RISC microprocessors. Thus, the throughput is proportional to the number of Instructions Per Second (IPS) that can be executed on the system. Given a typical RISC instruction set, network application benchmark characteristics, and various other parameters (e.g., CPU clock rate, cache miss times, etc.), an optimal system configuration, that maximizes IPS, can be determined.

3.1   Configurations

We begin by defining the fundamental chip area limitations for this system. The network processor chip size limits the number of processors, the amount of instruction and data cache per processor, and the number of memory channels that may be present. Let $s(ASIC)$ be the size of the network processor chip, $s(p_k)$, $s(c_{i_k})$, and $s(c_{d_k})$ respectively the sizes of a processor k, instruction cache c_{i_k}, and data cache c_{d_k}, and $s(mchl)$ and $s(io)$ the sizes of a memory channel and an I/O channel. With n processors per cluster and m clusters, all valid solutions must satisfy the following inequality:

$$s(io) + \sum_{k=1}^{n \cdot m} \left(s(p_k) + s(c_{i_k}) + s(c_{d_k}) \right) + \sum_{k=1}^{m} s(mchl) \leq s(ASIC). \qquad (1)$$

With identical processors, cache configurations, and I/O channels this becomes:

$$s(io) + m \cdot [s(mchl) + n \cdot (s(p) + s(c_i) + s(c_d))] \leq s(ASIC). \qquad (2)$$

Further, we can assume that the best performance is achieved with a set of design parameters which result in an area as close to $s(ASIC)$ as possible. That is, we need to investigate only configurations that try to "fill" the available chip area. Another potential constraint concerns chip I/O pin limitations with a given packaging technology. We show later that this is not a significant constraint for the optimized systems considered.

3.2   Single Processor

Consider first the performance model for a single processor in terms of the number of instructions per second (IPS) that can executed by the processor. This metric is highly dependent on the processor architecture, however it does capture the effect of application instruction mix and memory hierarchy performance.

The number of executed instructions per second for a single processor, IPS_1, depends on the processor clock speed and the CPI:

$$IPS_1 = \frac{clk_p}{CPI} \tag{3}$$

In an ideal RISC processor, where there are no cache misses, branch mispredictions, or other hazards, all instructions can be pipelined without stalls and the CPI is 1. While in a realistic system the CPI increases with the occurrence of hazards, for this analysis, we only consider memory hazards since other hazards, like branch mispredictions, are relatively rare and cause only brief stalls (1-2 cycles) in the short pipeline RISC processors considered here. This model constraint can be easily removed if greater accuracy is required. If SRAM is used as cache memory, a cache access can be done in one processor clock cycle and no stall cycles are introduced by cache hits. If DRAM is used for the instruction and data caches, then the basic pipeline clock cycle increases from 1 to $t_{cache.dram} \cdot clk_p$. Thus:

$$CPI = \begin{cases} 1 + p_{miss} \cdot penalty, & for\ SRAM \\ t_{cache.dram} \cdot clk_p + p_{miss} \cdot penalty, & for\ DRAM \end{cases} \tag{4}$$

where p_{miss} is the probability for an instruction cache miss or a data cache miss. The probability that a cache miss occurs, depends on the application being executed and the parameters associated with the caches. Using load and store frequencies and cache miss probabilities results in:

$$p_{miss} = mi_c + (f_{load} + f_{store}) \cdot md_c. \tag{5}$$

Note that Equation 5 considers only cache misses resulting from memory reads. Writes to memory, which are caused by replacing dirty cache lines, do not cause processor stalls. Assuming no contention for the memory channel, the miss penalty of a cache miss in turn depends on the memory access time and the time it takes to transfer a cache line over the memory bus (in processor clock cycles):

$$penalty = clk_p \cdot \left(t_{mem} + \frac{linesize}{width_{mchl} \cdot clk_{mchl}} \right). \tag{6}$$

With a cache miss, one cache line of size $linesize$ is transferred over the memory channel. Additionally, if the replaced cache line was dirty, one cache line is written back to memory. The off-chip memory bandwidth generated by a single processor, $BW_{mchl,1}$, therefore depends on the number of instructions executed and how many off-chip accesses are generated. Thus:

$$BW_{mchl,1} = IPS_1 \cdot linesize \cdot (mi_c + (f_{load} + f_{store}) \cdot md_c \cdot (1 + dirty_c)). \tag{7}$$

The I/O bandwidth for a processor depends on the *complexity* of the application that is running. *Complexity* in the context of network processors is defined as the number of instructions that are executed per byte of packet data (header and payload). Applications with a high complexity require little I/O bandwidth, since more time is spent processing. Thus, the I/O bandwidth of a single processor, $BW_{io,1}$, is

$$BW_{io,1} = 2 \cdot \frac{IPS_1}{compl}. \tag{8}$$

The factor of 2 is present since every packet has to be sent first from the scheduler to the processor chip, and then later back out to the network. In the next section, this basic model is extended to the multiple processor situation.

3.3   Multiple Processors

Consider the case where multiple processors in a cluster share a common memory channel. Since the processors contend for the memory channel, it is necessary to account for the delay t_Q that is introduced by queuing memory requests. Equation 6 becomes:

$$penalty = clk_p \cdot \left(t_{mem} + t_Q + \frac{linesize}{width_{mchl} \cdot clk_{mchl}} \right). \tag{9}$$

To model the queuing delay, we approximate the distribution of memory requests due to cache misses by a exponential distribution. This reflects the bursty nature associated with memory locality processes.[2] Thus, the queuing system can be approximated by a M/D/1 queuing model. The deterministic service time corresponds to the duration of a cache line transfer over the memory channel. Given the load, ρ, on the memory channel, the average queue length for an M/D/1 queue can be expressed as:

$$N_Q = \frac{\rho^2}{2(1 - \rho)}. \tag{10}$$

Multiplying by the time associated with a single non-blocked request, we obtain the average time for a request entering the system as:

$$t_Q = \frac{\rho^2}{2(1 - \rho)} \cdot \frac{linesize}{width_{mchl} \cdot clk_{mchl}}. \tag{11}$$

The obtained cache miss penalty for the multiprocessor case (Equation 9) can now be used with Equation 4 to determine the CPI of a processor and Equation 3 then provides the number of instructions executed. If we know the number of processors, n, then multiplying by IPS_1 by n will result in the overall

---

[2] Using a cache simulator, we measured the distribution of memory request interarrival times for the benchmark applications (Section 4). This was compared to an exponential distribution with the same mean. For $2kB$ instruction and data cache, the standard deviation of the measured interarrival times, on average, comes within a factor of 0.70 of the standard deviation of the exponential distribution.

$IPS_{cluster}$. Using Equation 7 for the memory bandwidth generated by a single processor, n is the maximum number of processors that can be accommodated in a cluster without exceeding a selected load ρ:

$$n = \left\lfloor \frac{width_{mchl} \cdot clk_{mchl} \cdot \rho}{BW_{mchl,1}} \right\rfloor, \tag{12}$$

$$IPS_{cluster} = n \cdot IPS_1. \tag{13}$$

Knowing n, the size of such a cluster, $s(cluster)$, can be determined as the sum of all of its components (the I/O channel is not considered here, since it is shared over several clusters). Since n processors in a cluster share a single memory channel:

$$s(cluster) = s(mchl) + n \cdot (s(p) + s(c_i) + s(c_d)). \tag{14}$$

Before turning to the optimization problem, we briefly discuss workloads that consist of multiple applications.

3.4 Multiple Applications

So far we have considered only a single program to be executed on the processors. A more realistic assumption is that there is a set of programs that make up the processor workload. The above analysis can easily be extended to accommodate such a workload notion.

Let the network processing workload W consist of l applications $a_1, a_2, ..., a_l$. Each application i is executed on a fraction q_i of the total data stream ($\sum q_i = 1$). The actual number of instructions that are executed by an application a_i depends on q_i and on its complexity, $compl_i$. Let r_i be the fraction of instructions executed that belong to application a_i.

$$r_i = \frac{q_i \cdot compl_i}{\sum_{k=1}^{l} q_k \cdot compl_k}, \quad i = 1, ..., l \tag{15}$$

The fraction r_i determines the contribution of each application to memory accesses and associated pipeline stalls. The load and store frequencies $f_{load,i}$ and $f_{store,i}$ of each application a_i, the cache miss rates $m_{ic,i}$, $m_{dc,i}$, and the dirty bit probability $dirty_{c,i}$ are determined experimentally. The resulting average cache miss probability $p_{miss,W}$ for workload W is

$$p_{miss,W} = \sum_{i=1}^{l} r_i \cdot (mi_{c,i} + (f_{load,i} + f_{store,i}) \cdot md_{c,i}). \tag{16}$$

Similarly, the memory bandwidth $BW_{mchl,1,W}$ of a processor for workload W becomes:

$$BW_{mchl,1,W} = IPS_1 \cdot linesize \cdot \sum_{i=1}^{l} r_i \cdot (mi_{c,i} + (f_{load,i} + f_{store,i}) \cdot md_{c,i} \cdot (1 + dirty_{c,i})). \tag{17}$$

The new definitions of $p_{miss,W}$ and $BW_{mchl,1,W}$ can be replaced in the above formulas to obtain n and IPS.

3.5   Optimization

The optimization process can be targeted either to a single cluster or to an entire chip containing multiple clusters:

- Processor cluster: The optimization of a processor cluster for different configurations helps to identify and understand basic design tradeoffs. It does not take into account global system components, like the I/O channel, and ASIC size constraints.
- Complete ASIC: The optimization of the complete system accounts for ASIC size and includes the I/O channel.

Based on the optimization goal, different optimization functions can be chosen. For the processor cluster, we define the number of instructions per second per area ($IPSA_{cluster}$) as:

$$IPSA_{cluster} = \frac{IPS}{size(cluster)}. \tag{18}$$

To find the maximum $IPSA_{cluster}$, theoretically any parameter shown in Table 1 can be varied. Practically, though, certain parameters, like $s(x)$ or $linesize$, are fixed and the optimization space can be limited to a smaller set of variables, such as clk_p, c_i, c_d, ρ, and whether the cache is implemented with on-chip SRAM or DRAM.

The complete ASIC optimization considers an integrated system consisting of several processor clusters on one chip. The number of clusters, m, is limited by the area constraint (Equation 2). The goal is to maximize the total number of instructions per second, IPS_{ASIC}, that can be executed on the ASIC.

$$IPS_{ASIC} = m \cdot IPS_{cluster}. \tag{19}$$

Due to the limited number of possible configurations, either optimization problem can be solved by exhaustive search over the configuration space.

4   Workload Definition

To properly evaluate and design network processors it is necessary to specify a workload that is typical of that environment. This has been done in the development of the benchmark CommBench [7]. Applications for CommBench were selected to include a balance between header-processing applications (HPA) and payload-processing applications (PPA). HPA processes only packet headers which generally makes them computationally less demanding than PPA that process all of the data in a packet.

For each application, the following properties have been measured experimentally: computational complexity, load and store instruction frequencies, instruction cache and data cache miss rate, and dirty bit probability. The complexity of an application can be obtained by measuring the number of instructions that are required to process a packet of a certain length (for header-processing applications, we assumed 64 byte packets):

$$compl = \frac{instructions\ executed}{packet\ size} \tag{20}$$

The cache properties of the benchmark applications were also measured to obtain $mi_{c,i}$, $md_{c,i}$, and $dirty_{c,i}$. This was done with the cache size ranging from $1kB$ to $1024kB$. For this purpose, a processor and cache simulator (Shade [ ] and Dinero [ ]) where used. A 2-way associative write-back cache with a linesize of 32 bytes was simulated. The cache miss rates were obtained such that cold cache misses were amortized over a long program run. Thus, they can be assumed to represent the steady-state miss rates of these applications.

We consider two workloads for the evaluation of our analysis: considered:

- Workload A - HPA: Header-processing applications.
- Workload B - PPA: Payload-processing applications.

These workloads are such that there is an equal distribution of processing requirements over all applications within each workload. Table 2 shows the aggregate complexity and *load* and *store* frequencies of the workloads. Note that the complexity of payload processing is significantly higher than for header processing. This is due to the fact that payload processing actually touches every byte of the packet payload and typically executes complex transcoding algorithms. Header processing on the other hand, typically only reads few header fields and does simple lookup and comparison operations. The aggregate cache miss rates for instruction and data cache are shown in Figure 2. Both workloads achieve instruction miss rates below 0.5% for cache sizes of $8kB$ or more. The data cache miss rate for workload A also drops below 0.5% for $8kB$. For workload B, though, the data cache miss rate only drops below 1% for $32kB$ or larger caches.

Table 2. Computational Complexity and Load and Store Frequencies of Workloads

Workload	$compl_W$	$f_{load,W}$	$f_{store,W}$
A - HPA	9.1	0.2319	0.0650
B - PPA	249	0.1691	0.0595

5   Evaluation

For the optimization of the network processor we have to define a design space that reflects current ASIC technology. Table 3 shows the values, or ranges of values, of each system parameter considered. For the feature size of components, we assume $.25\mu$m technology.

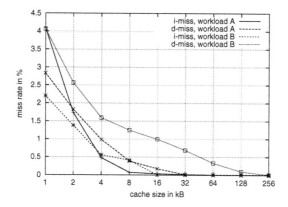

Fig. 2. Aggregate Cache Performance of Workloads

Table 3. System Parameters for Optimization

Parameter	Value(s)	Parameter	Value(s)
clk_p	$50MHz\ldots400MHz$	ρ	$0\ldots1$
c_i	$1kB\ldots1024kB$	$width_{io}$	up to $64bit$
c_d	$1kB\ldots1024kB$	clk_{io}	$200MHz$
$linesize$	$32byte$	$s(ASIC)$	$100mm^2\ldots400mm^2$
t_{mem}	$40ns\ldots80ns$	$s(proc)$	$2mm^2$
$t_{cache.dram}$	$15ns$	$s(c_i),\ s(c_d)$	SRAM: $0.15mm^2$ per kB
$width_{mchl}$	$4bit\ldots64bit$		DRAM: $0.015mm^2$ per kB
clk_{mchl}	$200MHz$	$s(mchl),\ s(io)$	$10mm^2 + width \cdot 0.25mm^2$

Given the analysis of Section 3 and the workload and system properties of Section 4, the optimal configuration of a network processor can now be determined.

5.1   Cluster Optimization

This optimization looks only at the configuration of a cluster without considering ASIC chip size constraints or the I/O channel. Under these conditions, no area fragmentation occurs and design tradeoffs can be easily observed. For the two workloads, and the SRAM and DRAM configurations, we evaluate the effect of memory channel bandwidth and load, processor speed, and off-chip memory access time.

As base parameters, we use a memory channel bandwidth of $BW_{mchl} = 800MB/s$, a off-chip memory access time of $t_{mem} = 60ns$, and a processor clock speed of $clk_p = 400MHz$. Starting out with this configuration, we vary different parameters to see their effects on the overall system performance. Table 4 shows the optimal configuration for the base parameters.

For workload A, an $8kB$ instruction cache is sufficient to achieve very low instruction cache misses (see Figure 2). Workload B, requires a $16kB$ instruction cache. Since there is no "knee" in the data cache miss curve, the optimization results are $16kB$ and $32kB$ for data caches, which achieve less than 0.3% miss rate for workload A and less than 1% for workload B. Larger caches do not improve the miss rates significantly, but require much more chip area. The memory channel load for these configurations ranges from 69% to 79%. The number of processors per clusters is 6 and 16 when SRAM is present, and about 6 time larger, 40 and 91, when DRAM is present. The DRAM results stem from a combination of several effects: a) the processor speed is limited by the on-chip DRAM access time, b) the limited processor speed permits more processors to share a single memory channel, and c) DRAM takes about one tenth the area of SRAM. Despite the slower processing speed of DRAM configurations, they still achieve $50\% - 75\%$ of the $ISPA$ rating of the SRAM configurations.

Table 4. Optimal configuration of cluster with base parameters of $BW_{mchl} = 800MB/s$, $t_{mem} = 60ns$, and $clk_p = 400MHz$

Workload	On-chip Memory	n	c_i (kB)	c_d (kB)	ρ	$IPSA$ $(MIPS/mm^2)$
A - HPA	SRAM	16	8	16	0.72	50.31
B - PPA	SRAM	6	16	16	0.69	25.55
A - HPA	DRAM	91	8	16	0.78	25.20
B - PPA	DRAM	40	16	32	0.79	19.38

One important observation is that increasing processor speed only affects SRAM cache configurations. This can be seen in Figure 3, where the $IPSA_{cluster}$ for different workloads and on-chip memory configurations is plotted over a set processor clock speeds. In the SRAM case, the total processing per area increases with faster processor clocks, since IPS_1 from Equation 3 increases. For DRAM cache, though, the effective processor speed is bound by the time it takes to access on-chip DRAM.

The effect of the memory channel load, ρ, on the $IPSA_{cluster}$ is shown in Figure 4. Also shown on this figure is N_Q, the queue length associated with the M/D/1 model of the memory channel. The largest number of instructions executed can be achieved for memory channel loads of $\rho = 0.6 \ldots 0.85$, which corresponds to the region where the queue length is small (< 3). While smaller loads cause lower queuing delays, they also require more chip area per processor since fewer processors share the fixed size channel. Higher loads increase the queuing delay significantly, which in turn causes processors to stall very long on cache misses.

Figure 5 shows the $IPSA_{cluster}$ for different memory channel bandwidths. For SRAM configurations, a faster memory channel improves the $IPSA_{cluster}$

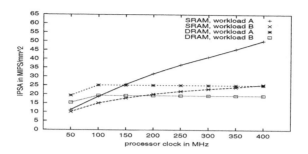

Fig. 3. Optimal $IPSA_{cluster}$ for different processor speeds ($BW_{mchl} = 800MB/s$ and $t_{mem} = 60ns$)

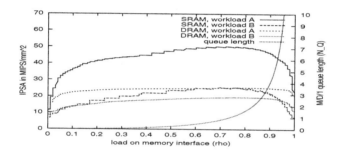

Fig. 4. Optimal $IPSA_{cluster}$ for different memory channel loads ρ ($BW_{mchl} = 800MB/s$, $t_{mem} = 60ns$, and $clk_p = 400MHz$)

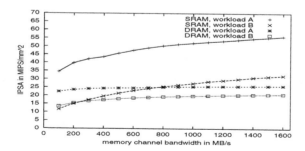

Fig. 5. Optimal $IPSA_{cluster}$ for different memory channel bandwidths ($t_{mem} = 60ns$ and $clk_p = 400MHz$)

by about $20MIPS/mm^2$, from $100MB/s$ to $1600MB/s$. This is due to the reduced transfer time for a cache line. These improvements are less significant for the DRAM configuration, since the processors operate at a much slower rate (bound by the on-chip DRAM access time) and the reduction in memory transfer time has less of an impact on the total CPI_{DRAM} (see Equation 4).

Different types of off-chip memories with different access times can also be used. The effect of the memory access time t_{mem} on the processing power per area is very limited. The total $IPSA_{cluster}$ decreases slightly for slower memories (2-5% for $t_{mem} = 80ns$ over $t_{mem} = 40ns$), but the memory access time is only a small component in the cache miss penalty (Equation 6). More important is the actual memory bandwidth and the load on the memory channel as shown in Figures 4 and 5.

5.2   ASIC Optimization

For the ASIC optimization, ASIC size constraints have to be considered as well as the I/O channel. To illustrate the optimization space, Figure 6 shows the optimal IPS_{ASIC} of a $400mm^2$ ASIC with workload A and SRAM caches. The memory channel bandwidth is $800MB/s$, the processor clock speed is $400MHz$, and the off-chip memory access time is $60ns$. One can see that there is a distinct optimum for $8kB$ instruction and $16kB$ data cache. Cache configurations that vary significantly from this optimum show a steep decline in overall performance. This emphasizes the importance of an optimally configured system.

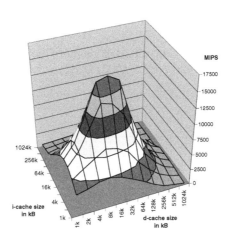

Fig. 6. Total processing capacity, IPS_{ASIC}, for different instruction and data cache sizes (BW_{mchl} = $800MB/s$, t_{mem} = $60ns$, clk_p = $400MHz$ and $s(ASIC) = 400mm^2$)

Table 5. ASIC configurations with maximum processing power ($s(ASIC) = 400mm^2$)

Workload	Cache Type	m	n	c_i (kB)	c_d (kB)	ρ	t_{mem} (ns)	BW_{mchl} (GB/s)	clk_p (MHz)	I/O pins	IPS (MIPS)
A - HPA	SRAM	3	20	8	8	0.8	40	1.6	400	365	19700
B - PPA	SRAM	6	10	4	8	0.86	40	1.6	400	389	12600
A - HPA	DRAM	1	145	8	16	0.63	40	1.6	$\geq 67^3$	148	9450
B - PPA	DRAM	1	64	16	16	0.92	40	1.6	$\geq 67^3$	131	8050

The maximum IPS_{ASIC} found in any system configuration is shown in Table 5 for both workloads and cache technologies. It is not surprising that the optimum is achieved for the fastest technology parameters in all categories ($BW_{mchl} = 1.6GB/s$, $t_{mem} = 40ns$, and $clk_p = 400MHz$ for SRAM caches). The maximum processing capacity is almost $20000MIPS$ for an SRAM cache configuration with $8kB$ for data and $8kB$ for instructions. The DRAM cache configurations, again, achieve about half the performance of the SRAM caches. Note however, that the optimal DRAM configurations obtained do not take into account other factors which would likely make this design infeasible. For example, electrical bus loading would preclude having 145 processors associated with a single memory bus. Nevertheless, with improved DRAM implementations, the model will permit analysis of alternative configurations.

One important thing to note in Table 5 is that the maximum number of I/O pins (that is the number of data pins for the memory channels and the I/O channel) does not exceed 400. Even when adding pins that are necessary for signaling, control, and power, the total pin count does not go beyond current packaging technologies.

6   Summary and Conclusions

In this paper, we consider a multiprocessor System-on-a-Chip that is specialized for the telecommunications environment. Network traffic can be processed by special application software that executes on a set of processors contained on a single chip. The problem analyzed is that of determining the optimal number of processors, associated cache sizes, and memory channels that should be present in such a design given a set of defining parameters and constraints with the principal constraint being the total chip area available.

An analytical model of the system has been presented that reflects the computational power per area of a cluster and the total processing power of an ASIC. Using application statistics from a telecommunications benchmark, a workload was defined and used in the optimization process. Results for various cluster and

---

[3]   As explained in Section 5.1, the processor clock speed has no impact on the performance, as long as it is faster than the on-chip DRAM access time. Thus, any frequency above $67MHz$ will achieve the same performance in this configuration.

ASIC configurations were presented and analyzed. The following key technology tradeoffs for System-on-a-Chip designs can be derived:

- The processor clock frequency has significant impact on configurations with on-chip SRAM caches. For on-chip DRAM caches, it does not improve the performance for clock rates higher that the memory access speed.
- Higher memory channel bandwidth improves both SRAM and DRAM configurations. The impact is larger for SRAM configurations. The optimal memory channel load for SRAM caches is in the range of 65% to 85% and for DRAM caches in the range of 70% to 92%.
- For the workload considered, the access delay of off-chip memory has little impact on the system performance.
- Optimal DRAM cache configurations achieve on average only half of the processing power of SRAM cache configurations, however, with current technologies, other implementation constraints likely make them a less desirable alternative than SRAM.
- Tradeoff trends are the same for both of the workloads considered. This indicates that they are independent of the particular workload for which the system is optimized.

These general observations along with the use of the model can be utilized to guide the design of network processors.

References

1. ARM Ltd. *ARM9E-S - Technical Reference Manual*, Dec. 1999. http://www.arm.com. 151
2. R. F. Cmelik and D. Keppel. Shade: A fast instruction-set simulator for execution profiling. In *Proc. of ACM SIGMETRICS*, Nashville, TN, May 1994. 158
3. P. Crowley, M. E. Fiuczynski, J.-L. Baer, and B. N. Bershad. Characterizing processor architectures for programmable network interfaces. In *Proc. of 2000 International Conference on Supercomputing*, Santa Fe, NM, May 2000. 152
4. J. Edler and M. D. Hill. *Dinero IV Trace-Driven Uniprocessor Cache Simulator*, 1998. http://www.neci.nj.nec.com/homepages/edler/d4/. 158
5. IBM Microelectronics Division. *The PowerPC 405^{TM} Core*, 1998. http://www.chips.ibm.com/products/powerpc/cores/405cr_wp.pdf. 152
6. MIPS Technologies, Inc. *JADE - Embedded MIPS Processor Core*, 1998. http://www.mips.com/products/Jade1030.pdf. 151
7. T. Wolf and M. A. Franklin. CommBench - a telecommunications benchmark for network processors. In *Proc. of IEEE International Symposium on Performance Analysis of Systems and Software (ISPASS)*, pages 154–162, Austin, TX, Apr. 2000. 157
8. T. Wolf and J. S. Turner. Design issues for high performance active routers. *IEEE Journal on Selected Areas of Communication*, 19(3):404–409, Mar. 2001. 151

Reconfigurable RISC – A New Approach for Space-Efficient Superscalar Microprocessor Architecture

Sascha Wennekers[1] and Christian Siemers[2]

[1] Technical University Clausthal
Julius-Albert-Str. 4, 38678 Clausthal-Zellerfeld, Germany
`sascha.wennekers@tu-clausthal.de`
[2] University of Applied Sciences Heide
Fritz-Thiedemann-Ring 20, 25746 Heide, Germany
`christian.siemers@computer.org`

Abstract. This approach modifies a RISC processor by integrating an additional Fetch Look-Aside Buffer (FLAB) for instructions. While the first fetch of any instruction results in normal execution, this instruction is combined in parallel with former instructions for later execution and saved inside the FLAB. The architecture works like a dynamic Very-Long-Instruction-Word architecture using code morphing. Extensive simulations indicate that this approach results in average instructions per cycle rate up to 1.4. The more important fact is that these values are obtained at moderate hardware extensions. The Space-Time-Efficiency E is defined and shows values from 0.5 to 1 for all modified architectures, relative to the RISC processor.

1 Introduction

The development of microprocessors in the last three decades seems to be mostly dominated by ever increasing clocking rates. This results in high power dissipation as well as increasing power densities on the surface of the devices: The values have passed the power density of a hot plate and are expected soon to reach nuclear reactor power densities.

New architectural concepts were taken into consideration as the second best choice for improvements. While there were some exceptions to this rule like the introduction of RISC and superscalar processors as well as other concepts, the focus on the development of faster clocking rates has returned soon afterwards.

But since the last two years the upcoming ubiquitous computing has changed the point of interest from performance to performance per power or even power dissipation itself. The focus on electrical power necessary for specific computations has been changed so that power is considered to be a 'First-Class Architectural Design Constraint' [Mudge_2001].

The first in [Wennekers_2001] introduced and now extended approach for a modified processor architecture meets this new architecture paradigm. Based on a well-

H. Schmeck, T. Ungerer, and L. Wolf (Eds.): ARCS 2002, LNCS 2299, pp. 165–178, 2002.

known RISC architecture two major modifications are added to obtain superscalarity without the necessity for expensive hardware extensions: A Fetch Look-Aside Buffer (FLAB) is integrated to store modified instructions for later fetches at the same address, and some executing parts inside the processor are identified for 'natural' partitioning for parallel execution.

The later means that those parts inside the real processor were identified that could be used for execution in parallel without any or with only negligible additional effort. This includes that no part of the CPU is doubled like inside superscalar architectures – with one inexpensive exception as described later.

The question arises how to compare this architecture with well-known architectures in research and practice. The basic roots are located inside the >S<puter concept first published in [Siemers_1997]. This approach introduced a new scheduling algorithm for superscalar processor architectures and replaced the execution pipelines by one or more configurable data path systems. Once configured the system called s-unit could work as long as no new reconfiguration occurred.

The Universal Configurable Block/Machine-concept UCB/UCM [Siemers_2000a] introduced real reconfigurability [Siemers_2000b] enabling the *application* to decide to reconfigure (while inside sequential system the *machine* decides to fetch and execute the next instruction). It considered the blocks to work independent from but with communication to each other and gave the UCM the ability to schedule frequently used program parts into exclusive UCBs.

Inside the actual architecture the already mentioned modified instructions are stored inside a configuration containing more than one instruction as well as additional information. This is equivalent to the >S<puter model and the UCBs, but the comparison of the execution model with the definition in [Siemers_2000b] shows the reconfiguration is not completely met.

The paper will show that the global execution principle consists of the composition of long instructions during execution. The way this architecture acts can be described as dynamic Very-Long-Instruction-Word (dVLIW) using code morphing. The algorithm located inside the FLAB morphs incoming code during runtime to composed (very long) instructions. The execution itself uses either the original instruction (if no composed instruction is available) or the morphed instruction. Nevertheless we call our architecture 'reconfigurable RISC' or 'rRISC' due to the roots it was derived from.

The remainder of this paper introduces the micro-architecture for reconfigurable RISC and describes the modified architecture and the impacts on the pipelining in chapter 2. The corresponding instructions for parallel execution are identified and classified in chapter 3. Chapter 4 discusses the way the translation of instructions into the configuration works and how the information is stored within the FLAB. The performance side of this microprocessor is concluded with simulation results in chapter 5. These values were obtained introducing a model called Small RISC Machine (SRM), which was completely described in VHDL to be cycle-accurate during simulation.

Chapter 6 discusses the efficiency of the architectural approach. For this purpose the Space-Time-Efficiency $E_{S/T}$ is defined with respect to [Flynn_1999]. This attempt presents a metric for comparing all obtained values of this project but shows a lack when comparing with other architectures.

Finally the advantages of our approach but also open questions are discussed in the summary and outlook (chapter 7). It is important to note that the defined efficiency shows the relationship between (silicon) space and (execution) time but obviously not power consumption.

2 Micro-Architecture for Reconfigurable RISC

The micro-architecture of the rRISC-machine may be described as an extension of a standard RISC-like processor. Fig. 1 shows the typical structure of a 4-stage RISC processor using fetch, decode/load, execute and write-back stage. The new Fetch Look-Ahead Buffer (FLAB) is added to the classical structure and holds the capability of translating and storing code for future execution. This model shows the micro-architecture of the concrete model SRM too.

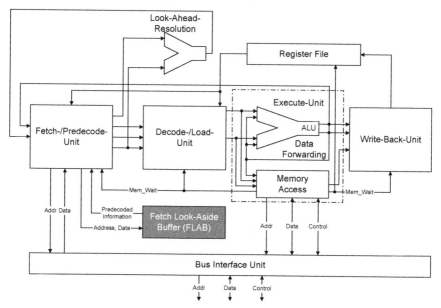

Fig. 1. rRISC Block Structure

Every cycle the processor fetches the next instruction from code memory, this fetch is additionally performed in the FLAB. From this point of view the FLAB acts like a fully-associative cache memory. If the FLAB access does not hit, the fetch from memory is used and the rRISC architecture works as a RISC-like processor.

In this case the fetched instruction is not only decoded for further execution but also analyzed for integration inside the FLAB. The FLAB integration phase works completely parallel to (and independent of) the decode/load phase. The instruction is not stored directly but computed to a configuration in combination with previous instruction. The FLAB acts like a trace cache but does not store the original infor-mation, and the algorithm is described in chapter 4.

The pipelining system is changed in three major parts: The fetch stage works not only via the bus interface but in parallel using the FLAB, the FLAB itself is considered to morph the actual instruction within one cycle into a new or existing FLAB line, and the complete execution through decode/load, execution, write back and interfacing to the register file must work for parallel operations.

2.1   Fetch Operation

The fetch operation starts with parallel accesses to main (or cache) memory and to the FLAB. As soon as the FLAB working like a fully-associative cache responds with a FLAB hit the memory access is aborted. If on the other side the fetch access to main memory is blocked by data access through memory access unit, the FLAB access still works, if a FLAB hit occurs, and avoids pipeline stalls resulting from concurrent memory accesses in this case.

This principle avoids any performance degradation inside the fetch unit because all operations are performed in parallel. The only additional path is a condition whether the FLAB hits or not (similar to cache hits), but this effect is neglected.

2.2   FLAB Operation

As discussed later in this paper the FLAB performs several operations beside serving fetch requests. These operations result in the composition of the FLAB lines from the incoming and previous instructions.

In most cases the algorithm consists of three operations: test of the suitable instruction class, test for integration capabilities and test for data hazards. With carefully designed instruction coding the first test is rather simple and similar to a corresponding part inside the decode sub-unit. The second test, which might even include the first, tests the corresponding space inside a FLAB line and is again very simple.

The third part must use parallel checks for any data dependency. The parts inside a FLAB line, where information about previous generated data are located, are well-defined and consist of all destination registers. Therefor any test for dependency must compare source registers with previous destination registers, and if such dependency occurs, the FLAB line is closed without integrating the actual instruction.

The FLAB operations were carefully analyzed for their runtime, and the result is that the complete FLAB operation will not use more time than the decode phase. This encourages to assume that the FLAB operation completes within 1 cycle and runs fully parallel to decode/load phase.

2.3   Parallel Execution

The first effect of parallel execution inside the rRISC architecture is that the pipeline structure from fetch to write back is spread. Fig. 2 shows the resulting fine structure.

The execution unit is carefully partitioned into parts with independent execution. The independence is based on the operations and shown in the next chapter: While addition and subtraction will use the same silicon part, addition and load or move will not. This results in parallel execution using only independent parts with no impact on execution speed.

The pipeline is of course spread (additional signals are shown with broader lines) but the influence on the overall speed and clock frequency is neglected. Especially the configuration time for the execution unit is the same compared to the known RISC architecture, because the information for execution is simply stored in the pipeline stage registers between decode/load and execution unit.

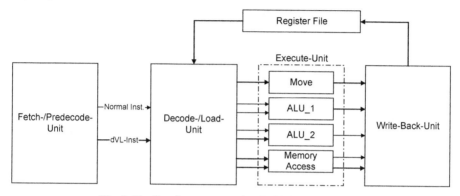

Fig. 2. Pipeline fine-structure for rRISC implementation

The analysis of all delays inside the modified pipeline results in no clock speed degradation. Therefor all modification is considered to be delay-time neutral.

3   Instruction Classes for Parallel Execution

As introduced in previous work [Wennekers_2001] the instruction are classified for the determination of usable instructions for integration. The following classes are received:

- *M-class* (Memory): All memory access operations like load, store, push and pop (as stack operations) are classified in this class.
- *C-class* (Control Flow): This class includes conditional and unconditional branches and jumps as typical control flow operations, independent of the addressing format.
- *NOP-class* (No Operation): As described in the previous work it makes sense to classify this operation on its own for compressing this fill operation inside the code.
- *I-class* (Internal operations): All integer operations, arithmetical and logical, as well as move, copy and exchange operations are included inside. This class is further divided into several subclasses:
- *MC-subclass* (Move and Copy): All copy and exchange instructions using internal registers as source and destination.
- *A-subclass* (Arithmetical): This subclass contains all arithmetical operations on integer with the exception of decrement and increment.

- *DI-subclass* (Decrement/Increment): The decrement and increment operations, often used for loops with predetermined length, build their own subclass as explained below.
- *L-subclass* (Logical): Logical as well as shift and rotate operations are classified for themselves.
- *FP-class* (Floating-Point): Executing internally too, all floating-point operations are included within their own class.
- *OT-class* (Other operations): Further instructions which influence the control flow may be wait, stop and others. These instructions may influence the operational mode of the processor and have substantial differences to the branches and jumps. Other instructions in this class are call to and return from subroutine and flag modification instructions like Set Carry which also influence the control flow but in a more indirect way.

These 6 classes and 4 subclasses are discussed for parallel execution using exclusive parts of the processor. The main goal of this work was to identify natural parallel resources inside a typical processor architecture. For all simulation purposes, a simple microprocessor model called Small RISC Machine (SRM) was used containing all further described resources.

As discussed in our previous work, it is assumed that a memory sub-unit is always existing for exclusively executing the M-class members (refer to fig. 1). The first approach called rRISC level 1 connected one M-class member with one C-class instruction, which will typically execute inside the fetch unit with support by e.g. the look-ahead unit, and one I-class instruction for parallel execution.

The subclasses MC, A, DI and L were carefully chosen for independent hardware regions inside the execution unit. Even the decrement/increment operation, which could be executed using the adder block with one constant operand, may receive exclusive hardware with little effort. The simulated model did not support floating-point operations, but these operations would be good candidates for parallel execution too.

Table 1 defines the level 2 and 3 for the rRISC-model using the SRM machine. The inexpensive execution for move-instructions – this is a simple data transfer – helped to decide to use up to 4 moves within one configuration and execute them in parallel. This is the only exception from the rule of using only single instances of any operation. Level 2 already uses these moves and one other internal instruction from A-, L- and DI-subclass.

Level 3 finally supplies the full parallelism even for internal operations at the above defined classification. Of course this classification could be refined but it was decided to stop, because any refinement would also result in more efforts for storing and transporting the configuration.

The NOP instruction as a special case was also defined to be integratable. This eliminates all effects from NOP, but if there are wanted (like lengthening a waiting loop), integration must be avoided. In any way, the NOP instruction was not used during simulation.

The overview of the rRISC classes contains 2 values for each degree of parallelization. The first number counts the maximum number of instructions (except NOP instructions), the second takes into account that all moves may consist of two partial moves. A combination like move/move high word with the same destination register, which loads a complete word of immediate data into the register but uses 2 instructions, will be compressed into one instruction inside the FLAB. This results in $p_{max} = 13$ for this approach.

Table 1. Summary of rRISC levels for the SRM

	Instructions	Parallelization degree
Level 1	1 M-class 1 C-class 1 I-class	3 (4)
Level 2	1 M-class 1 C-class 1 AL-subclass (A, DI, L) 4 MC-subclass	7 (11)
Level 3	1 M-class 1 C-class 1 A-subclass 1 L-subclass 1 DI-subclass 4 MC-subclass	9 (13)

4   Fetch Look-Aside Buffer

Fig. 3 shows the way the Fetch Look-Aside Buffer (FLAB) is coupled with the fetch unit. During fetch phase the FLAB looks like a fully associative cache memory to the processor. A cache hit cancels the normal fetch, and the FLAB line is going into execution. If a FLAB miss occurs, the normal fetch is finished. During the next phase the fetched instruction is available for being translated for a new FLAB line. The data from fetch unit include all necessary address informations.

Inside the Fetch Look-Aside Buffer all translated information is stored. Fig. 4 depicts the format for level 3. The information include start address, number of instructions and/or end address and the instructions themselves. For easy execution these instructions are stored in pre-decoded format.

4.1   PDSP – Procedural-Driven Structural Programming

The algorithm performs some binary translation and is called PSDP (Procedural-Driven Structural Programming) [Siemers_2000b]. Summarized three major stages are performed, which include checking for integration capability, data dependencies and availability. In particular the following steps are taken:

1. The actual instruction is tested whether it belongs to a class with integration capabilities. If this is not true, any FLAB line under construction will be closed and eventually stored. The classes for integration in the simple RISC machine in

fig. 1 are defined in table 1. In addition to this list, the NOP instruction is also integratable.

2. If the integration test is true, the corresponding line part is tested for availability. Any occupation results in closing the FLAB line. For all but MC-class and NOP only one resource is available in the SRM. For the move and copy instructions all parts are tested, and for the NOP instruction the number of instructions is just incremented.

3. In parallel to the resource checking part data dependencies are tested. This compares all registers for read-after-write-hazards, and for this example it is defined that the algorithm finishes for the actual line if this occurs. In general, even RAW dependencies may be integrated in the structure [Siemers_2000a].

4. As special case the mov/movh instruction pairing is checked in the SRM. This pairing is defined by a mov-instruction with immediate addressing followed by a movh with the same destination register. The necessity for these pairs arises from data constants in the source code, which uses the full data width but are stored only with fractional portions inside the code. This pair is stored as one move-instruction with a full-width data constant as operand.

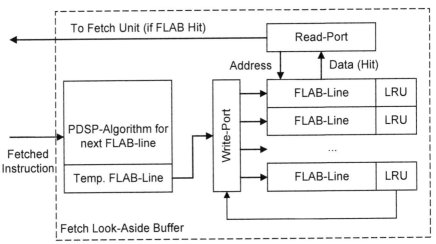

Fig. 3. FLAB Fine Structure

Start Address	No. of Inst.	Class-M code (memory access)	Class-C code (control flow)
		4 * Class-MC code (move and copy)	
Class-L code (logical)		Class-A code (arithmetical)	Class-DI code (decrement/increment)

Fig. 4. Structure of FLAB Line

As described earlier in this paper the algorithm was implemented and carefully tested for execution speed. All steps may execute in parallel to each other, and at the end of the cycle the result is stored. This enables the algorithm to execute within one clock cycle, and a critical path analysis shows that no clock speed reduction will occur.

The translation into one FLAB line will finish under some circumstances. First, a non-integratable instruction may occur. In this case, the actual FLAB line is closed and no new will be opened. Second, the actual instruction is of C-class type. In most cases, this will be a conditional branch instruction, and the actual way is unknown. Therefor, the FLAB line is closed, the C-class instruction is integrated, and no new line is opened (in both cases, this is done with the next integratable instruction).

Third, data dependencies will be recognized and fourth, the resource for the specific instruction is already occupied. In these case, the actual line is closed and a new is opened storing the actual instruction. In all cases, when a FLAB line is closed it is only stored when more then 1 instructions are configured within the line. As replacement strategy, least-recently-used was chosen.

The following example shows the effect for level 1 and 3. This example is part of the array initialization algorithm published in [Kelly_1998]:

The translation for level 1 results in 2 FLAB lines because the resource for the decrement instruction (DEC) is occupied by the SUB-instruction. However, level 3 contains enough resources to store the complete loop body inside 1 FLAB line. This results in 4 instructions per cycle during execution after correct branch prediction.

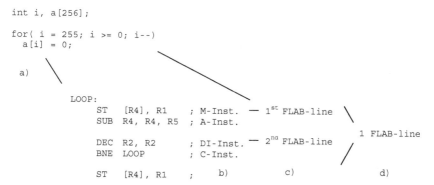

Fig. 5. Example for PDSP algorithm: a) C-sourcecode b) assembler code c) Level 1 translation d) Level 3 translation

4.2   Branch Prediction

The branch prediction is a problem that must be solved within the rRISC architecture. The actual model uses a dynamic 1-bit branch prediction. The branch target address is stored inside the FLAB line, and the last direction (taken/not taken) is always stored after execution. Other prediction strategies may be used instead.

The behavior for misprediction is a critical point for the rRISC architecture, because this could lead to performance reduction. If a branch inside the FLAB line is executed, the net effect for the execution time is 0 (zero branch time), but what happened when the branch direction is mispredicted?

For the estimation of this effect, a rRISC-architecture with k pipeline stages is assumed. Furthermore, at the end of stage kf the fetch has finished, and at the end of stage kst the status flags or conditions for the branch are available using data forwarding. If $kexe$ defines the stage where operations would be irreversible, then

$$kexe \geq kst - kf \qquad (1)$$

must be valid, if execution shall not lead to clock cycle losses, compared with the corresponding RISC-model. Inside the simulated SRM model, any misprediction leads to 2 cycles waiting time which is exactly the value without using the FLAB.

5   Performance Simulations for rRISC

For quantitative results, the rRISC model was simulated in all levels including level 0 for a RISC processor with 1-bit branch prediction. The following programs were used for this purpose:

- INIT_ARR: Initialization of a 1-dimensional integer array (see fig. 5 for inner loop).
- MOV_AVRG: Computing the moving average of 4 elements within an integer array of 64 elements.
- PARITY: Computing the even parity bit for all possible 8-bit values.
- WORDCOUN: The well-known UNIX-tool for a book text.
- CRC-8: Computing the cyclic redundancy check sum as used for ATM headers. The first part computes the syndrome-table, the second one the error table, the third part tests the tables with correct headers, headers with 1-bit error and with 2-bit errors.
- SEL_SORT: The selectionsort algorithm is used for 2 arrays containing 100 members each.
- QUICKSRT: The quicksort algorithm sorts the same 2 arrays containing 100 elements each.

The rRISC architecture SRM (Small RISC Machine) was described as VHDL-model on RT-level. This resulted in cycle-accurate instruction counts. Fig. 6 presents the results for the basic RISC-model as well as for models with 12 FLAB-lines inside the levels 1–3 of the rRISC architecture. With the exception of the INIT_ARR program, which is optimal for execution, all programs show positive effects for higher levels but are limited to IPC-values less than 2. Level 3 was additional simulated for 64 FLAB-lines to explore saturation effects.

All tested programs show a saturation using 64 FLAB lines, most of them at values much lesser. This encourages to use only small numbers of buffer lines for this architecture. On the other side, higher levels (2 and 3) show performance reduction when the number of lines is very small. Fig. 7 presents the effect for the CRC-8 program, 3rd part, but some other show the same effect.

The effect is based on the small number of lines. For level 2 and 3, more possibilities exist inside a program to obtain a FLAB line with 2 or more instructions, and therefor lines are earlier replaced. As result the extensive use of FLAB lines is self-blocked.

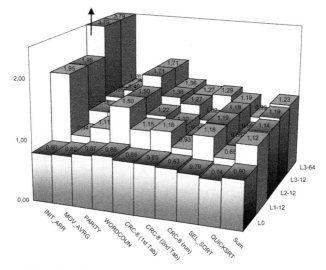

Fig. 6. IPC values for test programs and rRISC levels 0 .. 3 (single port)

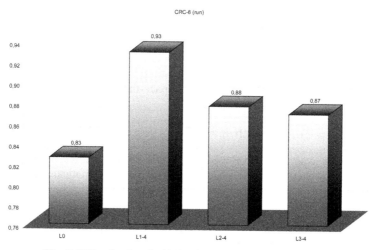

Fig. 7. IPC reduction for higher levels with small buffer sizes

Last-not-least the impact of single-ported and dual-ported memory architecture, referred as von-Neuman and Harvard-model, is shown in fig. 8. The difference between both memory port architectures is nearly constant 0.12 IPC. This was surprising, because some positive effect for the single port system could be expected. It was implemented inside the simulation model that a fetch is blocked for the external bus system when a data memory access occurs, but not for the FLAB. This should decrease the difference between both memory systems.

The reason for this behavior was identified in the fact that in most cases the M-class instructions could not be integrated into a FLAB line due to data dependencies. A change of the PDSP-algorithm and storage of a FLAB line containing a M-class instruction even if only 1 instruction is inside will positively impact the single-ported values.

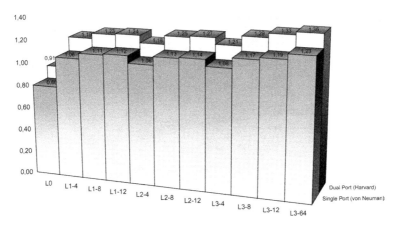

Fig. 8. IPC-values for single- and dual-ported memory architecture

6   Space-Time-Efficiency

One important question already mentioned in the introduction is the efficiency of the architecture. For this purpose the space-time relationship as discussed in [Flynn_1999] is taken for a definition of the space-time-efficiency. This relationship results in Eq. 2:

$$A \cdot T^n = Const. \quad \text{with } n = 1 \ .. \ 2 \tag{2}$$

This equation was first developed for single operations but is now used for complete microprocessors and related designs. For arithmetical operations, the constant n is near to 2. This is used to define the space-time-efficiency $E_{S/T}$ as

$$E_{S/T} = \frac{1}{T \cdot \sqrt{A}} \tag{3}$$

With definition (3), values relative to the rRISC-L0 architecture can be estimated. For this purpose, the inverted IPC-values were used for the execution time T, and the (weighted) number of generated signals inside the design can be taken for the space A. As a Register-Transfer-Level VHDL-model was used for cycle-accurate simulation, the number of signals could be determined rather precise.

Fig. 9 presents the values derived from eq. (3) using measured values for the performance and estimated for the space. Two different models were estimated. The original 16-bit processor model shows a relative great efficiency reduction, because the basic model is quite small. The 32-bit values were estimated from scaling up the 16-bit design. In this case the space used for the FLAB buffer and the translation algorithm was reduced, relative to the basic model.

We found the 32-bit-values to be more realistic, as microcontroller in this area have always 32 bit intrinsic data width. The efficiency shows with 40% reduction for the L3-12 model a rather smooth efficiency reduction and with values near 1 for the L1-4 model nearly the same value as in the basic model.

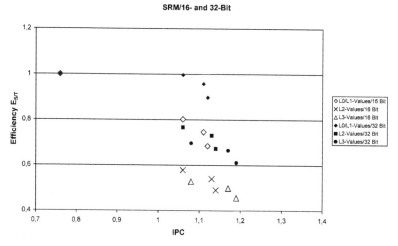

Fig. 9. Relative Space-Time-Efficiency for various rRISC-Level

7   Summary and Outlook

This work introduces an alternative way for superscalarity inside microprocessors, probably well-suited for microcontroller in the embedded world. The integrated Fetch Look-Aside Buffer, which acts like a trace-cache but stores more than 1 instruction for further execution, enhances the performance in connection with the configurable way the processor executes more than 1 instruction. IPC-values up to 1.4 are reported. The size of 8–12 FLAB lines seems to be the best trade-off between performance enhancement and efficiency reduction.

The way this model executes instructions has its roots in the area of reconfigurable computing but shows now much similarity to Very-Long-Instruction-Word architectures. While well-known members of this architecture class, e.g. the EPIC architecture from Intel, receive compile-time composed instructions during fetch, the rRISC architecture composes them during runtime. This dramatically downsizes the memory interface and might be well-suited for embedded systems reducing system costs. This could be named dynamical VLIW-architecture.

The way the instructions are composed shows similarities to code morphing [Kelly_1998]. Instructions are composed as long as no dependency or resource problem occurs avoiding any control function or any performance degradation during runtime.

Some questions are still open. The first is that the algorithm for translation and storing the configuration was not changed but has some impact on the results. This is obviously for M-class operations, where the expected value improvement for single port architecture failed to come.

The second question is, whether the space-time-efficiency, which reduces rather moderate compared to other superscalar architectures, also indicates a good power-performance-ratio, which would be of much more interest. Future work will address this question, but until now quantitative values are missing.

The third question concerns the optimal structure inside. There is a great degree of freedom for choosing combinations of operations, even multiple units might be useful. Algorithms from digital signal processing e.g. would tend to have more than one port to data memory, others could prefer more arithmetical capacities. This question will be addressed by intensive simulations of realistic benchmarks and by exploring the design space.

References

[Flynn_1999]   Flynn, M. J., Hung, P., Rudd, K.W.: Deep-Submicron Micro-processor Design Issues. - IEEE Micro 19(4), pp. 11 .. 22, 1999.

[Kelly_1998]   Edmund J. Kelly et.al., "Memory Controller for a Microprocessor for Detecting a Failure of Speculation on the Physical Nature of a Component Being Addressed". United States Patent No. 5,832,205, published Nov. 3rd, 1998.

[Mudge_2001]   Mudge, Trevor: "Power: A First-Class Architectural Design Constraint". IEEE Computer 34(4), pp. 52 .. 58 (2001).

[Siemers_1997]   Christian Siemers, Dietmar P.F. Möller, "Der >S<puter: Ein dynamisch rekonfigurierbares Mikroarchitekturmodell zur Erreichung des maximalen Instruktionsparallelitätsgrades". Vortragsband der 14. ITG/GI-Fachtagung Architektur von Rechensystemen ARCS '97, Rostock, September 1997, S. 133 .. 142. VDE Verlag, Berlin und Offenbach, 1997 (in German language).

[Siemers_2000a]   Christian Siemers, Sybille Siemers, "Reconfigurable Computing based on Universal Configurable Blocks – A New Approach for Supporting Performance- and Realtime-dominated Applications". In: Proceedings of the 5th Australasian Computer Architecture Conference ACAC-2000, Canberra, ACT, January 31 – February 3, 2000. Australian Computer Science Communications, Vol. 22, Number 4, pp. 82 .. 89.

[Siemers_2000b]   Christian Siemers, "Reconfigurable Computing between Classifications and Metrics – The Approach of Space/Time Scheduling" in: Proceedings of Tenth International Conference on Field Programmable Logic and Applications, FPL'2000 Villach, Austria, August 2000. Springer Lecture Notes in Computer Science 1896, pp. 769 .. 772.

[Wennekers_2001] Sascha Wennekers, Christian Siemers, "Reconfigurable RISC – ein neuer Mikroarchitektur-Ansatz zur flächen- und energie-effizienten Erhöhung der Instruktionsrate". Mitteilungen – Gesellschaft für Informatik e.V., Parallel-Algorithmen und Rechnerstrukturen, ISSN 0177-0454 Nr. 18, S. 11 .. 20 (2001). (in German language).

Cached Two-Level Adaptive Branch Predictors with Multiple Stages

Colin Egan[1], Gordon Steven[1], and Lucian Vintan[2]

[1] University of Hertfordshire,
Hatfield, Hertfordshire, U.K. AL10 9AB
{c.egan,g.b.steven}@herts.ac.uk
[2] University "Lucian Braga" of Sibiu, 2400, Romania
vintan@cs.sibiu.ro

Abstract. In this paper, we quantify the performance of a novel family of multi-stage Two-Level Adaptive Branch Predictors. In each two-level predictor, the PHT of a conventional Two-level Adaptive Branch Predictor is replaced by a Prediction Cache. Unlike a PHT, a Prediction Cache saves only relevant branch prediction information. Furthermore, predictions are never based on uninitialised entries and interference between branches is eliminated. In the case of a Prediction Cache miss in the first stage, our two-stage predictors use a default two-bit prediction counter stored in a second stage. We demonstrate that a two-stage Cached Predictor is more accurate than a conventional two-level predictor and quantify the crucial contribution made by the second prediction stage in achieving this high accuracy. We then extend our Cached Predictor by adding a third stage and demonstrate that a Three-Stage Cached Predictor further improves the accuracy of cached predictors.

1   Introduction

The advent of superscalar processors has given renewed impetus to branch prediction research. On a scalar processor, an incorrect branch prediction costs only a small number of processor cycles and only one or two instructions are lost. In contrast, in a superscalar processor many cycles may elapse before a mispredicted branch instruction is finally resolved. Furthermore, each cycle lost now represents multiple lost instructions. As a result branch mispredictions are far more costly on a superscalar processor.

This renewed interest in branch prediction led to a dramatic breakthrough in the 1990s with the development of Two-Level Adaptive Branch Predictors by Yale Patt's group [1] and by Pan, So and Rahmeh [2]. More recently two-level branch predictors have been implemented in several commercial microprocessors [3], [4]. However, although high prediction rates are achieved with Two-Level Adaptive Branch Predictors, this success is obtained by providing very large arrays of prediction

H. Schmeck, T. Ungerer, and L. Wolf (Eds.): ARCS 2002, LNCS 2299, pp. 179–191, 2002.
© Springer-Verlag Berlin Heidelberg 2002

counters or PHTs (Pattern History Tables). Since the size of the PHT increases exponentially as a function of history register length, the cost of the PHT can become excessive, and it is difficult to exploit a large amount of branch history effectively. Two-level Adaptive Branch Predictors have two other disadvantages. Firstly, in most practical implementations each prediction counter is shared between several branches. There is therefore interference or aliasing between branch predictions. Secondly, large arrays of prediction counters require extensive initial training. Furthermore, the amount of training required increases as additional branch history is exploited, further limiting the amount of branch history that can be exploited.

We have developed [5] a family of Two-Level Branch Predictors that addresses the three problems of conventional two-level predictors: cost, interference and initial training. We have called these novel predictors Cached Correlated Branch Predictors. By replacing the second level PHT with a cache, we significantly reduce the cost. At the same time, our predictors outperform traditional implementations. For equal cost models, this performance advantage is particularly significant. These advantages are achieved for three reasons. Firstly, our cached predictor only holds those prediction counters that are actually used. Secondly, interference between branches is eliminated; each branch prediction is determined solely by historical information related to the branch being predicted. Thirdly, a simple default prediction mechanism is included that is initialised after a single occurrence of each branch. This avoids the high number of initial mispredictions sustained during the warm-up phase of conventional two-level predictors and minimises the impact of misses in the Prediction Cache.

In an earlier feasibility study [6] we presented a Cached Correlated Branch Predictor that used a fully associative Prediction Cache. Although the concept of a cached PHT was successfully demonstrated, a fully associative cache would be too costly in practice. In contrast, all the Cached Correlated Branch Predictors presented in this paper, use a set-associative Prediction Cache that is indexed by hashing the PC with the history register. We also quantify the crucial role played by a second prediction stage in our cached predictor and we then extend cached prediction techniques to three-stages for the first time.

2   Two-Level Branch Prediction

Recent research on branch prediction has focused almost exclusively on Two-Level Adaptive Branch Predictors, which are usually classified using a system proposed by Yeh and Patt [7], [8]. The six most common configurations are GAg, GAp, GAs, PAg, PAp and PAs. The first letter specifies the first-level mechanism and the last letter the second level, while the "A" emphasises the adaptive or dynamic nature of the predictor. GAg, GAp and GAs rely on global branch history while PAg, PAp and PAs rely on local branch history.

GAg uses a single global history register, that records the outcome of the last k branches encountered, and a single global PHT containing an array of two-bit prediction counters. To generate a prediction, the k bit pattern in the first-level global history register is used to index the array of prediction counters in the second level PHT. Each branch prediction therefore seeks to exploit correlation between the next branch outcome and the outcome of the k most recently executed branches. The prediction counter in the PHT and the global history register are updated as soon as the branch is resolved. Finally, a separate BTC is still required to provide branch target addresses.

Unfortunately, since all the branches in a GAg predictor share a common set of prediction counters, the outcome of one branch can affect the prediction of all other branches. Although this branch interference limits the performance, the prediction accuracy improves as the history register length is increased. At the same time, the number of counters in the PHT also increases, which in turn increases both the number of initial mispredictions and the cost of the PHT. Eventually, the increased number of initial mispredictions negates the benefit of additional branch history and the prediction accuracy stops improving.

Several researchers have attempted to reduce interference in the PHT. The Gshare Predictor [9], [10], for example, hashes the PC and history register bits before accessing the PHT, in an attempt to spread accesses more evenly throughout the PHT. Alternatively, the Bimodal Predictor [11] uses twin PHT arrays to decrease destructive interference between branch predictions and to maximise positive interference. Finally, the Agree Predictor [12] also attempts to maximise positive interference.

GAp was first proposed by Pan et al [2] and called Correlated Branch Prediction. Like GAg, GAp uses a single history register to record the outcome of the last k branches executed. However, to reduce the interference between different branches, a separate per-address PHT is provided for each branch. Conceptually in GAp, the PC and the history register are used to index into an array of PHTs. Although this ideal model eliminates interference between branches, it leads to an exceptionally large PHT array. For example, with a 30-bit PC and 12-bit history register, 2^{42} counters would be required. In practice, to limit the size of the predictor, only a limited number of PHT arrays is provided; each PHT is therefore shared by a group of PCs with the same least significant address bits. Since a separate set of PHT counters is provided for each set of branch addresses, this configuration is classified as GAs. However, while the size of the PHT array is significantly reduced, branch interference is now reintroduced. As in the case of GAg, a separate BTC is provided to furnish branch target addresses in both the GAp and GAs configurations.

The Two-Level Adaptive Branch Prediction mechanism originally proposed by Yeh and Patt in 1991 [1] was later classified as PAg. PAg uses a separate local history register for each branch, or a Per-address history register, and a single shared global PHT. Each branch prediction is therefore based entirely on the history of the branch being predicted. The local history registers can be integrated into the BTC by adding a history register field to each entry. Since all branches share a single PHT, PAg is also characterised by interference between different branches. Interference can be reduced by providing multiple PHTs. If we retain the Per-Address Branch History Table and provide a separate PHT for each address or a Per-Address PHT, we have the PAp configuration. As in the case of GAp, the size of the PHT array is excessive, and the initial training problem is exacerbated. A separate PHT is therefore usually provided for sets of branches, giving rise to the PAs configuration.

We have emphasised that most branch prediction research is based on Two-Level Adaptive Branch Predictors. Yet, branch prediction is a specific example of a general

Time Series Prediction problem that occurs in many diverse fields of science. It is therefore surprising that there has not been more cross-fertilisation of ideas between different application areas. A notable exception is a paper by Mudge's group [13] that demonstrates that all Two-Level Adaptive Predictors implement special cases of the Prediction by Partial Matching [PPM] algorithm that is widely used in data compression. Mudge uses the PPM algorithm to compute a theoretical upper bound on the accuracy of branch prediction. Another exception is a recent attempt to use Neural Networks for dynamic branch prediction [14].

3   Two Stage Cached Correlated Prediction

The high cost of Two-level Adaptive Branch Predictors is a direct result of the size of the second level PHTs which increase exponentially in size as a function of History Register length. In a Cached Correlated Predictor [5], [6], the second-level table is therefore replaced with a Prediction Cache, while the first level is unchanged. Unlike PHTs in conventional two-level predictors, the number of entries in a Prediction Cache is not a direct function of the History Register length. Instead, the size of the cache is determined by the number of prediction counters that are actually used. This number increases only slowly as a function of History Register length. Since the Prediction Cache only needs to store active prediction counters, most of the entries in a traditional PHT can be discarded. However, to implement caching, a tag field must be added to each entry and the size of the tag field increases linearly as a function of History Register length. A Cached Correlated Branch Predictor will therefore only be cost effective as long as the cost of the redundant counters removed from the PHT exceeds the cost of the added tags. Two Cached Correlated Branch Predictors are presented in this section. The first predictor employs a global history register, while the second employs multiple local or per-address history registers.

3.1   Global Cached Correlated Predictor

Figure 1 shows a four-way set-associative Global Cached Correlated Branch Predictor. Each entry in the Prediction Cache consists of a PC tag, a history register tag, a two-bit prediction counter, a valid bit and a LRU (Least Recently Used) field. A four-way set-associative BTC is also provided to furnish the branch target address. Each BTC entry is augmented with a two-bit default prediction counter and consists of a branch target address, a branch address tag, the two-bit prediction counter, a valid bit and a LRU field.

Both the global Prediction Cache and the BTC are accessed simultaneously to provide two predictions. The length of the pipelength need not therefore be increased, and there is no significant increase in the clock cycle time. The BTC is accessed using the least significant bits of the PC, while the Prediction Cache index is obtained by hashing the PC with the global history register bits. As long as there is a miss in the BTC, the predictor has no previous record of the branch and defaults to predict not taken. Whenever there is a BTC hit a prediction is attempted. If there is also a hit in the Prediction Cache, the corresponding two-bit counter from the Prediction Cache entry is used to generate the prediction. In this case the prediction is based on the past behaviour of the branch with the current history register pattern. If, however, there is a miss in the Prediction Cache, the prediction is based on the default prediction counter held in the BTC and is therefore based on the overall past behaviour of the branch. Once the branch outcome is known, the relevant saturating counters are updated in both the Prediction Cache and the BTC. In the case of misses in either cache, new entries are added using an LRU replacement algorithm. Finally, the global history register is updated.

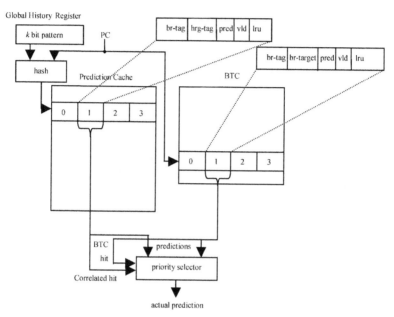

Fig. 1. A Global Cached Correlated Branch Predictor

Adding a default prediction counter to each BTC entry has several advantages. Firstly, the default predictor is initialised after only one execution of the branch. In contrast, with a k bit history register, up to 2^k Prediction Cache entries must be initialised for each branch before the two-level predictor is fully trained. Adding a default predictor should therefore significantly reduce the number of initial mispredictions. Secondly, the default predictor minimises the impact of misses in the Prediction Cache.

The hashing function to access the Prediction Cache requires careful consideration. Both a BTC and an instruction cache are usually indexed by the least significant bits of the PC. However, this solution is completely unsatisfactory for a Prediction Cache. Consider, for example, a four-way set-associative cache. In the absence of collisions with other branches, each branch is restricted to only four entries. However, if k history register bits are used by the predictor, as many as 2^k cache entries may theoretically be required for each branch. Although most history register patterns will never occur, a PC indexed cache will clearly suffer from excessive collisions, even with modest history register lengths.

A second alternative is to use the history register to index the Prediction Cache. This solution also has disadvantages. Firstly, if only a small number of history register bits is used, only part of the Prediction Cache will be used. Secondly, when the number of history register bits exceeds the number of bits in the cache index, sufficient collisions occur to prevent the predictor from reaching its full potential.

We found that the most accurate predictions were obtained when the history register bits were XORed with the PC bits to form the Prediction Cache index. A single XOR followed by truncation was found to be non-optimum. Instead, the following hashing algorithm was adopted. First, the PC was concatenated with the history register. Second, the resulting bit pattern was divided into groups that contained the same number of bits as the required index. Finally, all the groups were XORed to generate the Prediction Cache index.

3.2   Local Cached Correlated Predictor

The Local Cached Correlated Predictor (Figure 2) also replaces the PHT with a Prediction Cache. A local Cached Correlated predictor is more complex than a global Cached Correlated predictor. Since a history register is now required for every branch, a local history register field is added to each BTC entry. As with the Global Cached Correlated Predictor, a prediction counter is ncluded in each BTC entry.

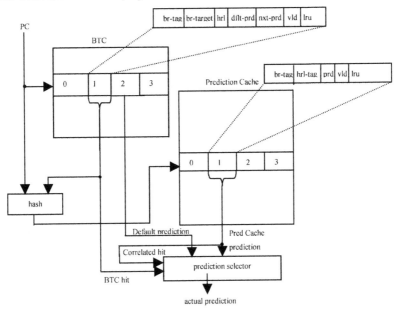

Fig. 2. A Local Cached Correlated Branch Predictor

To avoid two sequential table accesses, the first to access the BTC to furnish the local history register and a second to access the Prediction Cache, the access time can be reduced to one clock cycle by caching the next prediction for each branch in the BTC. As a result, the next time there is a hit in the BTC, the prediction will be available after only one table access. Once the counters have been updated the revised prediction from the Prediction Cache must now be cached in the BTC. There is, however, a possibility that the attempt to obtain the next prediction for a branch may result in a Prediction Cache miss. Therefore a valid bit must also be associated with the cached prediction bit in each entry.

The BTC is accessed using the least significant bits of the PC. On a BTC hit, the history register associated with the PC is obtained along with a default prediction. The history register is then hashed with the PC and the resulting bit pattern is used to access the Prediction Cache. Whenever possible a prediction counter stored in the Prediction Cache is used to make a prediction. However, in the case of a Prediction Cache miss and a hit in the BTC, the prediction from the BTC is used.

Hybrid predictors [9], [15] also use two or more predictors to generate each prediction. A hybrid predictor chooses dynamically between two or more distinct predictors on the basis of each predictor's past success. In contrast, our priority prediction mechanism uses the Prediction Cache whenever possible, and only uses the prediction counter in the BTC when no other prediction is available.

4   Two Stage Predictor Performance

In this section, we quantify the performance of two-stage Cached Correlated Predictors. First we compare their performance with conventional two-level predictors. We then quantify the crucial contribution of the second stage. Our simulations used a set of eight integer programs known collectively as the Stanford benchmarks. Since the programs are shorter than the SPEC benchmarks, each branch is executed fewer times. The branches are therefore more difficult to predict and the initial training problems are more acute. As a result, a classic BTC only achieves an average misprediction rate of 11.86% with the Stanford benchmarks. The benchmarks were compiled for the Hatfield Superscalar Architecture [16], a high-performance multiple-instruction-issue architecture developed to exploit instruction-level parallelism through static instruction scheduling. The HSA instruction-level simulator was then used to generate instruction traces for the branch prediction simulations. All the predictors simulated use a four-way set-associative BTC with 1K entries; sufficient entries are always available to minimise BTC misses. A four-way set-associative organisation is also always used for the Prediction Cache.

4.1   Global Cached Predictors

For comparative purposes, we first simulated a GAg predictor, a GAs predictor with 16 sets and a GAp predictor. The best misprediction rates were achieved by the GAp predictor (Figure 3). The average misprediction rate initially falls steadily as a function of the history register length before flattening out at a misprediction rate of around 9.5%. The best misprediction rate of 9.23% is achieved with the 26 history register bits. In general, however, there is little benefit from increasing the history register length beyond 16 bits.

The average misprediction rates achieved with a Global Cached Correlated Predictor are also shown in Figure 3. The number of entries in the Prediction Cache is varied from 1K to 64K. Initially, the misprediction rate steadily improves as a function of history register length for all cache sizes. However, after history register lengths of 12 bits, the limited capacity of the 1K Prediction Cache prevents further improvement. In contrast, with larger Prediction Cache sizes, the prediction rate continues to improve until a history register length of 26 bits is reached. Not surprisingly, the larger the Prediction Cache the better the misprediction rates. The lowest misprediction rate of 5.99% is achieved with a 32K entry Prediction Cache and a 30-bit history register. This represents a 54% reduction over the best misprediction rate achieved by a conventional Global Two-Level Adaptive Predictor.

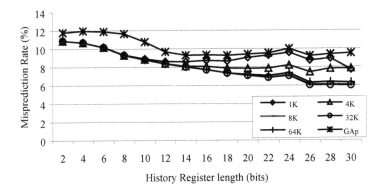

Fig. 3. Global Cached Correlated misprediction rates

The high performance of the Cached Predictor depends crucially on the provision of the two-stage mechanism. Without the default prediction counters in the BTC, Prediction Cache misses result in an excessive number of mispredictions. To quantify the contributions of the default prediction counters, we repeated our simulations with the BTC counters removed (Figure 4). The best misprediction rate achieved rose to 9.12%. Removing the second stage therefore degrades the prediction accuracy by 52%. As a result, the Prediction Cache performance is now only marginally better than a conventional Two-Level Adaptive Predictor and only 12 bits of history register information can be exploited. Even worse, as the history register length is increased beyond twelve bits, the prediction accuracy is degraded catastrophically.

4.2   Local Cached Predictors

Again for comparative purposes, we first simulated conventional PAg, PAs and PAp predictors. Conventional local predictors achieve average misprediction rates of around 7.5%, significantly better than GAg/GAs predictors. The best conventional local performance of 7.35% is achieved with a PAp predictor and a 30-bit history register length (Figure 5). Local predictors are therefore able to benefit from longer history registers than their global counterparts.

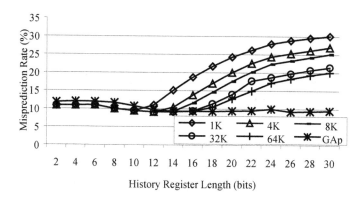

Fig. 4. Global Cached Correlated misprediction rates (no default predictor)

The misprediction rates achieved by a Local Cached Correlated Predictor are also recorded in Figure 5. The number of entries in the Prediction Cache is varied between 1K and 64K. Initially the misprediction rate falls steadily as a function of history register length for all cache sizes. Then as more and more predictions need to be cached, the larger caches deliver superior prediction rates. However, no significant benefit is derived from increasing the cache size beyond 8K. The best misprediction rate of 6.19% is achieved with a 64K cache and a 28-bit history register. This figure is slightly worse than the best global predictor, but represents a 19% improvement over the best PAg/PAp configuration.

In Figure 6, we record the impact of removing the default prediction stage from our Global Cached Correlated Predictors. Again, the impact is severe. The best misprediction rate rises to 8.21%, an increase of 33%. This figure is achieved with 12 history register bits and a 32K Prediction Cache. Overall, the performance is now worse than a conventional Two-Level Adaptive Predictor. We conclude that Local Cached Predictors are ineffective without a default prediction mechanism and are unable to exploit more than around 12 bits of branch history information.

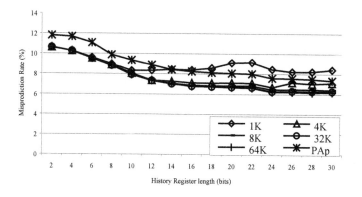

Fig. 5. Local Cached Correlated misprediction rates

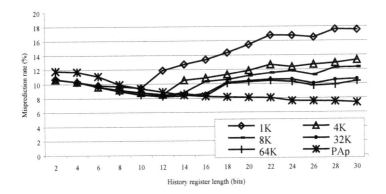

Fig. 6. Local Cached Correlated misprediction rates (no default predictor)

5   Three Stage Predictor

The simulation results in the previous section suggest that a Cached Predictor can deliver a higher prediction accuracy than a conventional Two-Level Adaptive Predictor. However, this superiority is crucially dependent on the provision of default prediction counters in the BTC. Default prediction counters improve performance for two reasons. Firstly, each counter is initialised after only a single execution of a branch. In contrast, a branch may have to be executed many times before a useful entry is made in the Prediction Cache. Furthermore, several entries must be initialised for each branch. Secondly, the Prediction Cache is of finite size and is therefore unable to retain all the relevant branch prediction information. In the absence of a default predictor, a high proportion of Prediction Cache misses will generate mispredictions.

Furthermore, the best misprediction rates were achieved with long history registers. For example, the best Global Cached Predictor achieved a misprediction rate of 5.99% with a 30-bit History Register, while the best Local Cached Predictor achieved 6.19% with 28 bits. This is remarkable, since Prediction Caches using 30-bit history registers require considerable initiation. We therefore believed that there was scope for introducing a third prediction level of intermediate complexity. This third prediction stage would use fewer history register bits than the main Prediction Cache, but, unlike the BTC, would not throw away all the history register information.

These considerations led to the development of a Three-Stage Cached Predictor with the following stages: a Primary Prediction Cache with k history register bits, a Secondary Prediction Cache with $^k/_2$ history register bits and a default BTC predictor. Two clock cycles are therefore required to generate a prediction. However, as described earlier, the prediction in the two Prediction Caches can be cached in the BTC to reduce the access time to one clock cycle. Our expectation was that the new Secondary Prediction Cache, with only half the number of history register bits, would be initialised more rapidly than the Primary Prediction Cache. It would therefore be able to generate more accurate predictions than the BTC when there were misses in the Primary Prediction Cache.

A Three-Stage Predictor can be viewed as a practical implementation of Prediction by Partial Matching [13]. Predictions are generated as follows. If there is a miss in the BTC, the predictor has no knowledge of the branch and defaults to predict-not-taken. However, whenever there is a BTC hit, a prediction is attempted on a strict priority basis. Whenever possible, the Primary Prediction Cache is used, then the Secondary Prediction Cache, and finally the BTC.

5.1   Three Stage Predictor Performance

We repeated our simulations using both Global and Local versions of our Three-Stage Cached Predictors. As before, the size of the Primary Prediction Cache was varied between 1K and 64K. The Secondary Prediction Cache was always half the size of the Primary Cache and used exactly half the number of history register bits. The results for the Global Three-Stage Predictors are summarised in Figure 7. As expected, the three-stage predictor consistently outperforms the simpler global two-stage predictor, particularly when a large number of history register bits is involved. The best misprediction rate of 5.57% is achieved with a 32K Primary Prediction Cache and a 30-bit history register. This represents a 7.5% improvement over the best Two-Stage Global Predictor.

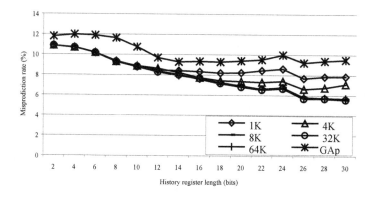

Fig. 7. Global Three Stage misprediction rates

The results for the Local Three-Stage Cached Predictor are summarised in Figure 8. Again, the three-stage predictor consistently outperforms its two-stage counterparts. The best misprediction rate of 6.00% is achieved with a 64K Primary Prediction Cache and a 28-bit history register, an improvement over the best Local Two-Level Predictor of 3.2%.

Three-Stage Predictors therefore consistently recorded a small but significant improvement over their two-stage counterparts. Furthermore, this improvement was not necessarily achieved by increasing cost. For example, a Global Three-Stage Predictor with an 8K primary cache and a 4K secondary cache outperforms a Global Two-Stage Predictor with a 32K Prediction Cache.

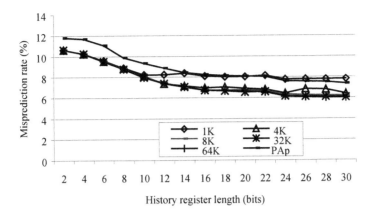

Fig. 8. Local Three Stage misprediction rates

6   Conclusions

Our simulations show that a Cached Correlated Branch Predictor is significantly more accurate than a conventional Two-level Adaptive Predictor. In earlier work, we also demonstrated that cached predictors are more cost-effective than conventional predictors [5], [6]. Our best global predictor is 54% better than the best GAs predictor and our best local predictor is 19% better than the best PAg/PAp predictor. We ascribe this higher accuracy to our more disciplined approach. Our predictions are always based on counters that have been trained using at least one previous encounter with the branch being predicted. Furthermore, there is never any interference between branch predictions.

The higher accuracy depends crucially on the addition of default predictors in the BTC. Removing the default prediction counters degrades the performance of the best global predictors by 52% and the best local predictor by 33%. As history register lengths increase, two-level predictors require an increasing number of counter initialisations and therefore suffer an increasing numbers of initial mispredictions. In contrast, the default counter is initialised after only one execution of a branch, significantly reducing the number of initial mispredictions.

Even higher prediction accuracy was achieved with our Three-Stage Cached Predictors, which can be viewed as a practical implementation of Prediction by Partial Matching. The best three-stage predictor delivered a misprediction rate of 5.43%, a 35% improvement over the best conventional Two-Level Adaptive Predictor, and a 4.6% improvement over the best two-stage cached predictor.

A major advantage of Cached Correlated Branch Predictors is their ability to exploit correlations from a large number of history bits. In our two-stage Combined Cached Predictor, this advantage is exploited to combine local and global history information in a single predictor. This combined predictor delivered a misprediction rate of 5.68%, 29.4% better than the best conventional two-level predictor. Finally, a three-stage combined predictor delivered a misprediction rate of 5.42%, the lowest misprediction rate reported in this paper.

References

1. Yeh, T. and Patt, Y. N.: Two-Level Adaptive Training Branch Prediction, Micro-24, Albuquerque, New Mexico, (1991), 51-61.
2. Pan, S.; So, K. and Rahmeh, J. T.: Improving the Accuracy of Dynamic Branch Prediction Using Branch Correlation, ASPLOS-V, Boston, (1992), 76-84.
3. IA-64 Application Developer's Guide, Intel, (2000).
4. Kessler, R. E.: The Alpha 21264 Microprocessor, IEEE Micro, (1999), 24-36.
5. Egan, C.: Dynamic Branch Prediction in High Performance Superscalar Processors, PhD thesis, University of Hertfordshire, (2000).
6. Steven, G. B.; Egan, C.; Quick, P. and Vintan, L.: A Cost Effective Cached Correlated Two-level Adaptive Branch Predictor, 18th IASTED International Conference on Applied Informatics (AI 2000), Innsbruck, (2000).
7. Yeh, T. and Patt, P.: Alternative Implementations of Two-Level Adaptive Branch Prediction, ISCA-19, Gold Coast, Australia, (1992), 124–134.
8. Yeh, T. and Patt, Y. N.: A Comparison of Dynamic Branch Predictors that use Two Levels of Branch History, ISCA - 20, (1993), 257-266.
9. McFarling, S.: Combining Branch Predictors, Western Research Laboratories Technical Report TN-36, (1993).
10. Chang, P., Hao, E., Yeh. T. and Patt, Y. N.: Branch Classification: A New Mechanism for Improving Branch Predictor Performance, Micro-27, San Jose, California, (1994), 22-31.
11. Lee, C. C., Chen, I. K. and Mudge, T. N.: The Bi-Mode Branch Predictor, Micro-30, Research Triangle Park, North Carolina, (1997), 4-13.
12. Sprangle, E., Chappell, R. S., Alsup, M. and Patt, Y. N.: The Agree Predictor: A Mechanism for Reducing Negative Branch History Interference, ISCA '24, Denver, Colorado, (1997), 284-291.
13. Chen, I. K., Coffey, J. T. and Mudge, T. N.: Analysis of Branch Prediction via Data Compression, ASPLOS VII, (1996), 128-137.
14. Steven, G., Anguera, R., Egan, C., Steven, F. and Vintan, L.: Dynamic Branch Prediction Using Neural Networks, DSD 2001, Poland, (2001), 178-185.
15. Chang, L, Hao E. and Patt, Y. N.: Alternative Implementations of Hybrid Branch Predictors, Micro-29, Ann Arbor, Michigan, (1995), 252-257.
16. Steven, G. B., Christianson, D. B., Collins, R., Potter, R. D. and Steven, F. L.: A Superscalar Architecture to Exploit Instruction Level Parallelism, Microprocessors and Microsystems, 20 (7), (1997), 391– 400.

Session V

Middleware and Verification

On the Combination of Assertions and Virtual Prototyping for the Design of Safety-Critical Systems

Tim Oodes, Holger Krisp, and Christian Müller-Schloer

Institute of Computer Engineering, Architecture and Operating Systems
University of Hannover, Appelstraße 4, D-30167 Hannover
`{oodes;krisp;cms}@irb.uni-hannover.de`

Abstract. Embedded systems for safety-critical applications need design methods, which comply with the requirements of such sensitive systems. This paper proposes a new approach to the design of such systems and presents first results. We introduce the method of Virtual Prototyping in combination with assertions for an UML-based system design. This means that we build an abstract model of a heterogeneous embedded system including functional and especially timing constraints from the very beginning. The Unified Modeling Language (UML) has been extended to model complex heterogeneous systems rather than just software. The Virtual Prototype is made executable on an open simulator platform. From the simulation we derive information about the system's functional and timing behavior, which is fed back to the UML system level. This paper discusses the assertion-based design process and its implementation by corresponding design tools, and it shows how assertions can vastly improve the quality of embedded system design.

1 Introduction

This paper proposes a new approach to the design of systems and presents first results. It concentrates on formal methods and tools to make safety-critical systems more reliable. By "systems" we mean mainly but not exclusively "embedded systems" used for the control of complex technical devices like cars, production lines or telecommunication systems. They are characterized by

- the heavy usage of invisible computing power; this means that a large part of the design effort is spent on software design;
- distribution of computing resources over typically tens of processors;
- communication via local or remote connections like e.g. the CANbus;
- real time requirements;
- complex I/O consisting of peripherals, sensors and actuators;
- a closed control loop via the system-under-control.

This notion of a system largely extends the system view taken by the integrated circuit community (system on a chip). A system in our sense is truly heterogeneous

H. Schmeck, T. Ungerer, and L. Wolf (Eds.): ARCS 2002, LNCS 2299, pp. 195-208, 2002.

spanning a variety of different design domains like software, hardware (ASICs), communication and mechanical subsystems. Moreover, the system designer is confronted with a large variety of modeling methods and languages for each of these domains.

The development of system design methods and tools is directed by three major trends:

- Design space extension,
- Need for efficiency improvement and
- Functionality increase.

Design space extension: The design of heterogeneous systems demands the mastering and integration of many methods and tools already in use for the single domains. Since a single formal system description language has proven unrealistic, we must provide design methods, which allow for multi-language approaches. This means e.g. the combination of a software simulator, a hardware emulator and a differential equation solver. In addition to this *horizontal* extension of the design space we witness also a *vertical* extension towards the higher system levels. Here high-level formal system descriptions are necessary.

Efficiency: Generative approaches are commonplace on the lower design levels (e.g. the translation from high level language to machine code). If we want to extend automatic synthesis to the system level we need formal system level models, which can be subjected to rigorous examination by validation and verification tools. A concise and validated (if not verified) system model is also a guarantee for the success of the subsystem integration further down in the design process. High time pressure usually demands the parallel development of subsystems with the result that overall system test during large parts of the design process must be based on a fully virtual or mixed real/virtual prototype.

Functionality: More powerful microprocessors attract more complex applications. This in turn requires RTOS support which then complicates the test phase, especially if hard real time constraints are to be fulfilled. This is even more serious due to the increased usage of embedded control systems in safety-critical applications (like the upcoming X-by-wire technology for cars).

The current situation in the area of systems design is rather fragmented and lacks integration. There are, however, promising starting points and building blocks available:

Simulation tools have developed from single domains (like MATLAB/Simulink for control system design or MODELICA/DYMOLA for continuous time systems) partially to tools covering a wider range. The open system simulator ClearSim-MultiDomain [Sch01], developed at IRB/University of Hannover, combines a very efficient software simulation (almost real time) with a variety of other executable modeling languages like EFSM (extended finite state machines), MODELICA, VHDL, SDL and MATLAB/Simulink.

For *system level modeling*, the telecom-oriented protocol description language SDL has become popular and tool-supported in recent years. Its main disadvantage, lacking real-time support, is overcome by a variant, SDL.Realtime [Wel01]. Despite its generic name suggesting a wider applicability, UML (Unified Modeling Language) is in use exclusively for the domain of software design. Moreover, its real-time support is not adequate for the design of heterogeneous embedded hardware/software systems. Nevertheless, we think that UML is a very good candidate for a general system description language.

Safety-critical systems such as an ABS for airplanes are usually verified by exhaustive test. This is clearly not possible for more complex or consumer-oriented lower-cost systems. Formal verification is promising but difficult to handle by the average design engineer. A more pragmatic solution is the design-by-contract method proposed by B. Meyer [Mey01]. It provides a syntax for the insertion of so-called assertions into the code. Assertions check the validity of logical conditions and fire exception handling procedures in case of violation. It seems obvious to extend this idea to timing assertions to support the design of safety-critical real-time systems

The design method described in this article builds on a system design and validation process (fig. 1), which generates an executable system model (a virtual prototype) from UML models. Simulation is carried out by ClearSim-MultiDomain, which predicts function as well as timing. Safety-critical requirements are introduced in terms of assertions into the system-level UML diagrams. Logical values as well as timing assertions are possible. From the graphical input, the assertions are captured in form of a well-defined language, ADL (Assertion Definition Language [ADL01]). ADL can be translated back into natural language to support communication with the possibly non-technical customer. ADL is also the basis for an automatic insertion of assertions into the C code and the virtual prototype. During the following simulation, assertions act like "intelligent printf's" allowing for a systematic debug process. For real-time systems, the combination of timing assertions and the timing predictions of the system simulator is crucial. Assertions can be debug-time-only (non-resident) or left in the final product (code resident) forming the basis for an on-board diagnosis system.

The proposed combination of (1) our UML-based high-level system design, (2) the virtual prototype simulation and (3) the instrumentation with assertions has the following advantages:

- Safety requirements like parameter ranges or time constraints can be enforced through formal constructs inserted into the graphical system design.
- Assertions formally reflect the requirements from the usually non-formal specification.
- Assertions are inserted into the code without manual interaction.
- A back-annotation into natural language supports contract transparency.
- Assertions if properly allocated allow to catch a large number of design errors already during virtual prototype simulation, i.e. in the early design phases.
- Code-resident assertions serve as hooks for on-board diagnosis.
- Non-resident (i.e. debug-time-only) assertions can be made time-invisible by the simulator. Hence they don't influence the timing predictions.

The remaining part of the paper will first briefly review our UML- and simulation-based system design method thereby largely referring to previous publications. Then it introduces the usage of assertions for timing and variable value supervision, their classification and the code-resident vs. non-resident variants. The following chapter covers the possibilities of assertion instrumentation into the virtual prototype with the help of the assertion definition language ADL. Finally we will discuss the multiple ways of using assertions in the overall design process of safety-critical systems.

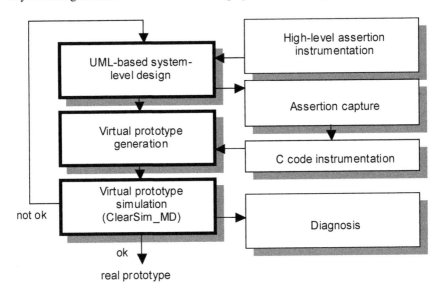

Fig. 1: The basic design process (left) based on the simulation of virtual prototypes with Clear-Sim-MD. The picture omits for reasons of simplification the refinement steps which follow after the system level design. The right side shows the safety-critical extensions

2   UML-Based System Design for Embedded Systems

The most important and far-reaching decisions in system design are made in the early design phase when the designer defines the overall system structure that is able to fulfill the given requirements (in terms of function and timing).

We use the Unified Modeling Language (UML) for high-level system design. UML is normally used for the structured development of (large) software systems. In this context, UML classes represent portions of software. However, we can "misuse" UML to describe systems in a far more general way if we attach additional properties like timing or a binding to a specific processor type to the objects where necessary. It is important to construct already this high level view of the embedded system in such a way that it can be validated by simulation. This means that we need a structural as well as a functional and executable description.

It should be emphasized that we do not try to find a general system description language for all the different domains involved. Rather, we use UML to define the top-level system structure (also called communication skeleton) in terms of a modi-fied class diagram. The single classes corresponding to the submodules of our embed-ded system will later have to be modeled with conventional domain-specific methods and tools. In addition we exploit three more UML diagrams to present different useful views on the system to the designer: the Use Case Diagram, the Statecharts and the Sequence Diagram.

Use Case Diagrams are the external user's view of a system and its environment. They describe primary and secondary functions (requirements) and show the main services the system offers to human users and external systems. Use cases are easy to grasp also by non-technical persons and should be the basic platform for customers and system designers to jointly discuss and develop the system's requirements (Fig. 2).

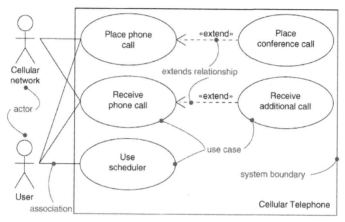

Fig. 2: A Use Case Diagram of a cellular telephone

The use cases are also the starting point for the designer to partition an embedded system into different classes. These classes realize the use cases. The result is a Class Diagram, which describes the modules of the total system and their relations to each other.

The following example clarifies how we use an UML *Class Diagram* to model the structure of embedded systems. An embedded system may be composed of modules as shown in the example in fig. 3. A fan, controlled by a microcontroller C167, generates an airflow whose speed is measured at the end of a wind tunnel. All data are transferred via a CANbus with 2 microcontrollers C505 driving the CANbus. This embedded system leads to the Class Diagram also shown in fig. 3.

The Class Diagram is the base for the automatic Virtual Prototype (VP) generation (more details about the VP simulation in chapter 3). From it we extract the top-level communication structure of our embedded system. Modules are extracted to a module list, relations between modules like communication links result in a net list, which is used in the subsequent steps of building the VP.

In order to make the class diagram executable, the classes' behavior has to be defined. This can be done using domain-specific design tools. During system design, however, this step has to be deferred. For the time being we are content with a gross behavioral description of function and timing of the submodules. We use UML *Statecharts* to define the behavior of the classes (subsystems). These classes are described in terms of states and event driven transitions forcing the subsystem from one state to another (see fig. 4 and fig. 5).

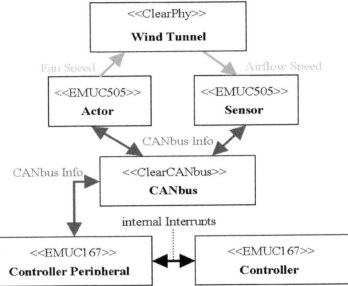

Fig. 3: Example embedded system consisting of 3 microcontrollers and a wind tunnel as system-under-control and the corresponding Class Diagram

The description of class behavior by Statecharts may be implemented in two refinement steps. One rudimentary description sketches the gross behavior (see fig. 4). A fine description, which is also made with the help of Statecharts, can be transformed into a finite state machine (EFSM) model (see fig. 5) and also used to generate C code.

In any case, the state model is the input for the automatic generation of a Virtual Prototype. In case a state description is not adequate for specific domains, other models (Modelica, MatLab/Simulink, C) can be used for refinement.

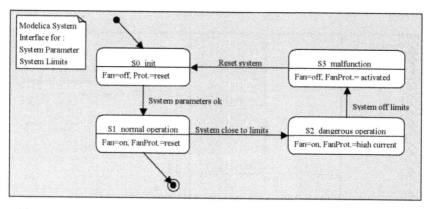

Fig. 4: A Statechart as a rudimentary description destined to be refined by Modelica

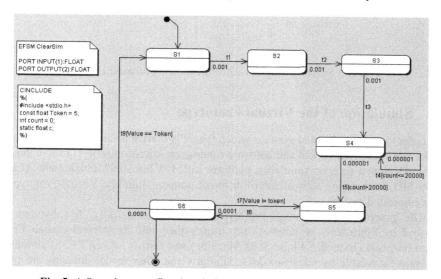

Fig. 5: A Statechart as a fine description suitable to be transformed to EFSM

At this point in the design process the timing behavior of the modules is not known yet. Instead we assign timing assumptions to the transitions, which have to be corrected further down in the design process. There is a close relationship between these high level assumptions and the timing assertions to be introduced later in this article.

The forth type of UML diagrams we use are the *Sequence Diagrams*. They visualize the communication between the components of the system for the execution of a scenario. They are useful for the specification of the flow of events and the time relationships (Fig. 6). Hence Sequence Diagrams capture the (time-oriented) dynamic behavior between several objects. We use sequence diagrams for the specification of timing constraints and the back-annotation of the simulation results onto the system level as will be explained below.

A more complete description of the UML-based heterogeneous system design methodology is given in [KRI01].

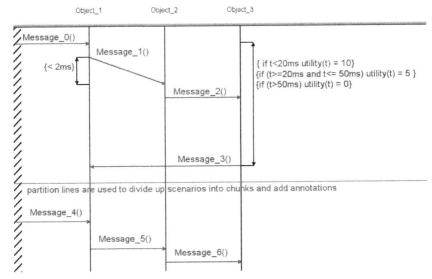

Fig. 6: A Sequence Diagram showing the timing behavior of a system

3   Simulation of the Virtual Prototype

In order to make embedded systems which typically consist of quite different domains (like electrical, mechanical and software running on microcontrollers) executable, we have developed an open simulation platform called "ClearSim-MultiDomain" (Clear-Sim-MD) to integrate subsystems of different domains into one Virtual Prototype of the embedded system.

The generation of a Virtual Prototype is done automatically. A subsystem described by Statecharts is automatically transformed into an internal textual EFSM representation (Extended Finite State Machine) and further into an EFSM simulation module executable by ClearSim-MD. Similarly the other model domains are translated into executable simulation modules. So far ClearSim-MD supports widely used languages like Modelica, MatLab/Simulink, EFSM, SDL and a software-emulation for Infineon C167 and C505 microcontrollers.

ClearSim-MD predicts the function as well as the exact timing of the VP. This is important for the evaluation of the assertions to be discussed in the next chapter.

So far we have shown how to use UML for the specification and description of embedded systems, introducing the Use Case Diagram, Class Diagram, Statechart and Sequence Diagram, and how to translate these models into an executable Virtual Prototype. Next we will introduce assertions and their role in safety-critical system design.

4   Assertions in UML-Based System Design

Assertions are a construct to specify constraints in a software system. We use the term *assertion* in the way Bertrand Meyer [Mey02] defined it: "An assertion is an expression of the element's purpose". Like Meyer we also distinguish between pre-, post-

and process conditions. According to Warmer and Kleppe [War01] constraints are "Restrictions on one or more values of an object-oriented module or system". Assertions in the context of embedded systems design serve two purposes. (1) They monitor the values of specified variables or of expressions built from variables. This way, a variable can be restricted in a limited range. This is the usage of assertions as proposed by Meyer. (2) Moreover, assertions are also ideal for monitoring the timing behavior of an embedded system. So, we can check e.g. if a certain critical section of a program is carried out within a given time limit. So far, we have not seen an implementation of timing assertions mentioned in the literature. - In both cases an assertion, which is, violated leads to a reaction by some kind of monitoring system.

Depending on the location of an assertion at the beginning or the end of a function, we talk about pre- or postconditions. A process condition makes sure that the assertion is monitored during the whole run time of the program.

The introduction of the concept of assertions into (embedded) systems design poses two problems: (1) How and where are assertions inserted into the model? (2) How can we organize the proper reaction of internal or external monitors to the possible violation of assertions?

4.1   Internal vs. External Monitoring

Assertions may be used for debugging purposes only. In this case they are called "non-resident" since they are removed from the code after the test phase. Accordingly the monitors reacting to violations are external, i.e. not part of the target system. They rather belong to the simulation system (in case of a virtual prototype) or to the test and measurement system in case of a real prototype. Code-resident assertions remain in the final target system to observe, log and possibly correct critical parameters. The monitor in this case has to be part of the target system, i.e. it is internal. Internal monitors can also be viewed as on-board diagnosis systems.

In case of a diagnosis system there exist several possibilities how to react upon assertion violations: Values slightly out of range can be pushed back into the specified range (Meyer's "correct values and continue"). More serious violations might require a system reset or lead to "organized panic" (Meyer in [Mey01]).

The combination of assertions with a full functional and timing simulator allows to enforce constraints already during the early design phases. Its advantage in comparison to a test of the real prototype is that non-resident assertions can be skipped in terms of virtual time calculation. Hence they will not distort the exact timing predictions of the test run, as is always the case with the real test instrumentation.

4.2   Assertion Instrumentation

It is the final goal of a system design methodology to let the designer interact with only high level system representations as introduced in chapter 2 above. This is of course also valid for the insertion of assertions. E.g. general physical constraints (or other obvious constraints taken from the system's specification) will be inserted as assertions into the Class Diagram as they are relevant for a whole subsystem (a class of the Class Diagram).

For the insertion of assertions at a finer granularity we see two possibilities: Assertions can be graphically inserted into the Statecharts (see fig. 7).

This method is advantageous for value range assertions as well as for timing-constraints. Alternatively, timing assertions e.g. of the type min/max time or time-out can be inserted into a Sequence Diagram.

This usage of assertions on the high system level means that not only software systems can be monitored but also – on a rather abstract level – the behavior of subsystems from other domains like electro-mechanical subsystems or sensors. Of course in this case the assertions are restricted to the Virtual Prototype.

So we can summarize the design flow with assertions as follows: First, the designer models the Virtual Prototype with UML diagrams. Starting point for the designer is a requirement analysis with use cases that helps him to divide his system into classes (subsystems). After he has defined the system's structure by a class diagram, he will insert some already known safety-critical constraints (e.g. based on physical limits or other obvious constraints). Then the projected behavior of the different classes will be specified by rudimentary Statecharts. These diagrams import assertions from the Class Diagram level and will be augmented by additional "local assertions", relevant only inside the subsystem itself. So we distinguish between "global assertions" relevant on the upper level of the embedded system (Class Diagrams and rudimentary Statecharts) and "local assertions" relevant on the subsystem level (e.g. fine Statecharts or Modelica, MatLab/Simulink etc.). The system model described so far is then transformed automatically from the instrumented UML diagrams into an executable Virtual Prototype.

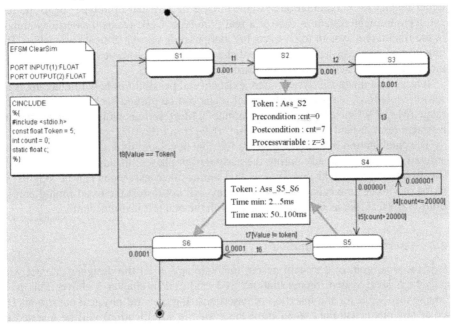

Fig. 7: A Statechart with functional and timing constraints (assertions)

So far, we have implemented an assertion instrumentation method into an SDL model for software subsystems only. A more general assertion instrumentation as described above will be based on graphical primitives inserted into the UML diagrams. Presently we are assessing the possibility to use OCL [War01] (possibly in a slightly modified version) to introduce constraints into the system level UML diagrams.

Having explained the concept of assertions according to B. Meyer and their usage on the embedded system level we will discuss their transformation into target code with the help of the Assertion Definition Language (ADL) and give a short glance to the Object Constraint Language (OCL) which is in its current version 1.4 (UML1.4/OCL1.4) an interesting candidate for high level input of assertions.

5   ADL Supports UML-Based System Design

The objective of the Assertion Definition Language (ADL) is to instrument C-Code, C++-Code and also Java-Code with assertions and to support test scenarios for software (TDD Test Data Description). The latter aspect is not our focus. ADL is also able to use a Natural Language Definition to present its assertions in natural language, which could be used for a non-technical client to crosscheck the final assertions of the embedded system with his expectations and requirements.

Assertions are written in ADL as a description of how the functional behavior is affected by the input state, and the resulting changes on the output state. This is referred to as the pre/post conditions [Oba01]. Figure 8 shows an example of an ADL definition of a function "integer square root" and illustrates the generation of program code by an ADL-Translator (ADLT). The outputs of ADLT are Assertion Checking Objects (ACO) and Assertion Checking Functions (ACF), which we use to instrument C-Code. Additionally we use the Documentation output for a description of assertions in natural language.

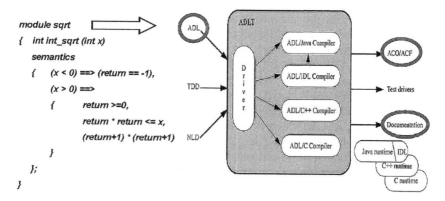

Fig. 8: An example of a function "integer square-root" defined in ADL and translated to Assertion Checking Objects/Functions to instrument C Code

We have examined the suitability of ADL to insert the assertions from high-level UML diagrams into the low level C Code generation. First results show that ADL serves this purpose quite adequately. A (so-far manually written) ADL assertion specification is automatically translated into instrumented C code. As ADL is an open and well documented software it seems obvious that by translating OCL to ADL we will be able to close the remaining gap between system level assertion specification and implementation level assertion instrumentation into C code.

So far we have shown what a closed design process - from system level to the real prototype via a simulated virtual prototype - under inclusion of assertions could look like. In the final chapter of this paper we want to show how this basic mechanism can be used for the design of safety-critical systems.

6   Assertion-Based Design of Safety-Critical Systems

In previous chapters we have discussed the UML Diagrams, Virtual Prototyping in combination with assertions and the usage of ADL (and OCL). So we are now able to extend the design flow of figure 1 to give a more general description of our approach. Figure 9 illustrates the UML-based system design process and especially the flow of assertions in more detail.

Based on the Use Cases and the Class Diagram the embedded system is partitioned into subsystems. Already on the level of Class Diagrams some obvious constraints are attached to the classes. More detailed assertions can be introduced at the levels of the rudimentary and refined Statecharts in the form of graphical add-ons. It is important for our approach that on this abstraction level only assertion tokens are defined as placeholders, which so far carry no values. - With the focus on assertions, now we will explain some details of their further processing.

The module "Assertion Capture" extracts the assertion tokens from a Statechart and builds an assertion table. The values of the assertions are entered into the table by the system designer. They will be possibly changed after a later simulation run of the Virtual Prototype. Where necessary the designer now selects the desired reactions on assertion violations by assigning the assertion tokens to certain reaction classes. In case of using OCL for the instrumentation of assertions into UML diagrams the Assertion Capture module will additionally translate OCL to ADL.

The output of Assertion Capture in combination with the assertion table values is transferred to the ADL translator (ADLT) which generates C code in form of Assertion Checking Objects and Assertion Checking Functions to instrument the C code generated by our Virtual Prototype Builder. Additionally the ADL translator outputs the assertions in natural language for a crosscheck by the client. Therefore ADLT uses a natural language definition file (NLD).

The process of building the VP is synchronized with the ADLT to generate simulation modules including the assertions of the UML level.

The systematic insertion and corresponding check of assertions opens a number of possibilities for their further usage:

(1) Back-Annotation: We have already stated that the ultimate goal of a system design process is to allow the system designer to interact with the design process exclusively from the high-level system point of view. This means that eventual assertion violations must be reported back to the levels of Class Diagrams, Statecharts and Sequence Diagrams. We use graphical representations of assertion violations to achieve this goal.

(2) Assertion correction: The values, which are assigned to the assertion tokens, usually are not final but best guesses. It might turn out during the analysis of the VP that some of them are too narrow, some are too loose. Therefore during a step that we call "assertion sharpening/loosing" the designer goes back to the assertion table to make the necessary corrections. This step can even be partially automated if we assign range parameters (like a relative sharpness) to the assertions.

(3) Automated diagnosis generation: Code resident assertions require defined reactions. Based on the assertion structure it is possible to generate the skeleton of a diagnosis system, which has to be filled in later by the software implementing the desired, the reactions.

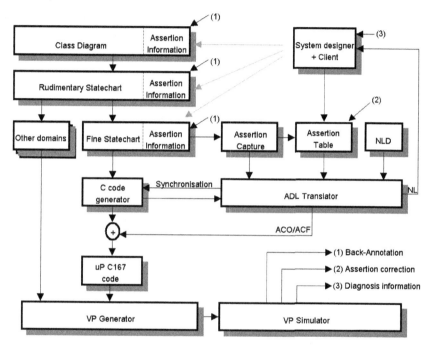

Fig. 9: The UML-based system design using Virtual Prototyping in combination with assertions

7 Summary and Status of Work

We have introduced the concept of an assertion-based design method and associated tools for safety-critical systems. The standard design process for heterogeneous systems based on the simulator ClearSim-MD has been implemented and tested for several applications. In the present version, we support several popular modeling methods for non-software domains like EFSM, Modelica and MatLab/Simulink. Target software is written in C or graphically in SDL.RT. For SDL.RT we have implemented the graphical input of assertions and their processing down to the code level as well as a means for back-annotation to the SDL.RT source level. However, for the future we favor an UML-based approach since UML is widely supported and offers a rich variety of diagrams. We have adapted UML for the use as a general system design language. The automatic translation from Class Diagrams and Statecharts into an executable Virtual Prototype works already in a prototype version. Presently we are developing the Assertion Capture module. First results with (so far manually written) ADL specifications are encouraging. The shift from assertion definition by ADL to a high-level constraint definition by OCL is in its conceptual phase.

References

[ADL01] The Open Group, http://adl.opengroup.org, 1999
[KRI01]   Krisp, H., Müller-Schloer, C.: "Objektorientierte Modellierung und Simulation eingebetteter Systeme mit ClearSim-MultiDomain und UML", ASIM 2001, (15. Symposium Simulationstechnik), Paderborn, September 2001, S. 79-84
[Mey01] Meyer, B.: "Building bug-free O-O software: An Introduction of Design by ContractTM", http://www.eiffel.com/doc/manuals/technology/contract/page.html
[Mey02] Meyer, B.: "Object-Oriented Software Construction", 2nd Edition, Prentice Hall 2000
[Oba01] Obayashi, M., Kubota, H., McCarron, S.P., Mallet, L.: "The Assertion Based Testing Tool for OOP: ADL2", ICSE 1998
[Sch01]   Scherber, S.: "Modellierung und Simulation software-intensiver eingebetteter Systeme", Shaker Verlag 2001
[War01] Warmer, J., Kleppe, A.: "The Object Constraint Language", Addison-Wesley 1999
[Wel01] Welge, R.: "SDL.RT basierter Entwurf und Implementierung zeit- und sicherheitskritischer Systeme", PhD Thesis (University of Hannover) 2001

Ubiquitous Access to
Wide-Area High-Performance Computing

Frank Burchert, Stephan Gatzka, Christian Hochberger,
Chang-Kun Lee, Ulrike Lucke, Djamshid Tavangarian

University of Rostock, Department of Computer Science,
Chair of Computer Architecture
Albert-Einstein-Str. 21, D - 18059 Rostock, Germany
Tel. +49 (0)381 / 498 - 3386 Fax: - 3440
burchert | gatzka | hochberg | lckun | ulrike.lucke | tav @informatik.uni-rostock.de

Abstract. Existing architectures for wide-area high-performance computing often suffer from their inefficient access mechanisms. Especially due to the challenge of ubiquitous computing, flexible access to those infrastructures is needed. Different possibilities to fulfil these requirements are discussed in this paper. Starting with the Hypercomputer as a Java-based architecture for wide-area high-performance computing, access mechanisms for web computing as well as mobile computing are presented. With the Home@Globe system, interactive applications on distributed servers can be run using a web browser. Also, using the Kertasarie VM, resource constrained client devices can be integrated into the system. The successful integration of these four mechanisms is explained by means of an application scenario from the field of agricultural science.

1 Introduction

1.1 Motivation

The capabilities, computational performance and data throughput of desktop computers are continuously growing, but usually they are available only for single users. Furthermore, dedicated high-performance machines need to be integrated into standard computing processes. Different services like the access to applications, information, storage or specific hardware can be offered world-wide by connecting these resources via internet. Since the early '90s, several architectures have been developed to implement this idea. The basic requirements for those systems are:

- The system is widely distributed, and its components and configuration can be changed dynamically.
- The developed or used software must be platform independent and interoperable with other technologies.
- The system shall provide a high degree of performance.
- Because of the use of the internet for communication, security aspects need to be considered.
- The use of the system shall be flexible and easy.

In order to allow or assure a widespread use of existing, powerful infrastructures for high-performance computing, especially their access mechanisms have to be improved. A command line or application program interface is not acceptable for most types of users. Also, there is a continuous trend towards the integration of applications into the

H. Schmeck, T. Ungerer, and L. Wolf (Eds.): ARCS 2002, LNCS 2299, pp. 209–223, 2002.
© Springer-Verlag Berlin Heidelberg 2002

world wide web, and to offer them as services via web browser interfaces. This functionality is implemented in portals, e.g. for application service providing (ASP).

Furthermore, the challenge of ubiquitous systems asks for mechanisms to integrate computers into every-day life [1]. This especially requires a large number of various client devices, like smart labels, information appliances or Personal Digital Assistants (PDAs). These devices are constrained in resources and power consumption, and for this reason special considerations must be given to these aspects.

This paper gives an overview on the successful integration of mobile components into distributed high-performance architectures.

1.2 Scenario of Use

An example for the resulting hardware infrastructure is depicted in Figure 1. There are high-performance server farms, which are interconnected by communication networks like the internet. Additionally, wireless networks can be integrated. Different client devices are completing the scenario, for instance desktop systems with enhanced multimedia capabilities, or portable computers like a PDA.

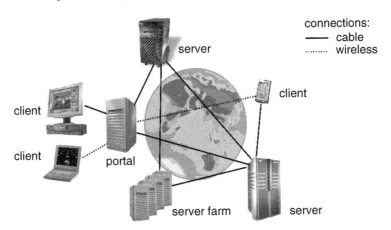

Fig. 1.   Ubiquitous Access to Wide-Area Resources

A system of flexible and powerful software is needed for the management and access of the hardware components, as well as to provide services to the users. A server can act as a portal, e.g. for the combination or web integration of services, which requires further tools.

The main software components as the pivotal points of such an architecture are subject of this paper. In chapter 2, the Hypercomputer as the infrastructure for wide-area high-performance computing for this work is described. The web portal Home@Globe offers access to high-performance and interactive applications through standard web browsers. It is presented in chapter 3. Finally, chapter 4 presents the Kertasarie VM and Tiny RMI implementation for resource-constrained devices. References of these components are given in the corresponding chapters. In order to intensify the motivation of this work, some example applications are given in the following section.

1.3 Example Applications

There are a lot of application scenarios, where on one hand powerful computational resources are needed, yet on the other hand the user needs to be extremely mobile. For instance, in agricultural sciences input data is often gathered outdoors. Since their calculation is resource-intensive and Therefore must take place on a central server, a connection between the mobile measurement device and the server is needed. The client is thus only responsible for the submission of data and the user interface.

A distributed high-performance application that has been implemented is the analysis of water tickling in soils, respectively the simulation of this process. Figure 2 depicts this scenario schematically, together with a sample simulation output.

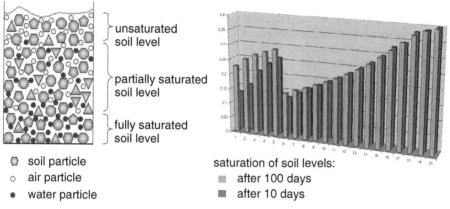

Fig. 2.   Principles and Output Visualization of Soil Simulation

The soil section to be analyzed consists of different soil particles and numerous spaces between them. These can be filled with water or air particles. The deeper a level is, the more water it contains. The movement of water is caused by gravity (downwards) and capillary effects (isotrop), and it depends on the soil type, vegetation, evaporation and so on. The simulation figures out the degree of saturation in the soil levels, following a model based on the hydraulic conductivity of different soil types and rainfall tables troughout several days. The water movement and thus the new water volume of each soil level are calculated. The diagram shows the results for 20 soil levels, where the upper 5 levels consist of a more pervious material than the lower 15 ones. Basically, during a period with continuous rainfall, the water is tickling down, until each soil level is fully saturated. This equals 40 % of the soil volume, which is reached only by level 20 in the diagram.

The combination of mobile devices and distributed high-performance applications could also be used for the cultivation of forests. Foresters often need to decide which trees must be cut down in order to leave enough space for the healthy trees. The main problem is to optimize the amount of valuable wood in a forest. A forester can record various attributes of trees, submit this data, and as a result he gets the trees to cut down. Another application can be found within sports. The analysis of motion sequences of sportsmen requires much computational power. Coaches can input different parameters via mobile devices, submit them for analysis and receive the results within a short period of time.

Moreover, the system can be used without the high-performance facility for conventional interactive and client-server applications on mobile devices, like distributed information systems, e.g. for medical diagnosis.

2 Distributed High-Performance Computing: Hypercomputing

Starting in 1996, the project *Hypercomputing* was one of the first distributed computing initiatives in Germany [2], and was supported by partners from university as well as from industry. The following sections give an overview of the system. Detailed information can be found in the final project report [3].

2.1 Project Principles

The Hypercomputer offers an infrastructure for the concurrent job execution in a wide-area network of workstation clusters. A cluster can be configured to use conventional batch queueing systems. Interfaces to LSF, DQS, NQS and Codine [4] have been implemented. Several types of resources are combined: from the local environment (local-area or cluster computing) as well as remote resources (wide-area, Meta-, Hyper- or Grid computing). The clusters are arranged in a network of neighbourhood relationships.

The system is scalable due to its dynamic resource management, which is transparent to the user. Due to load balancing mechanisms, all available resources and services are used effectively. Furthermore, the architecture is based on a security concept, consisting of authentication, encryption, logging and accounting. A user interface is offered locally on shell level as well as remotely via WWW. All components are implemented in Java and thus executable on VMs on different platforms.

These are significant advantages compared to other projects, which are developed using platform dependent mechanisms or do not offer the full bandwidth of functionality of the Hypercomputer. For instance, the project Metacomputing is focused on dedicated parallel machines [5]. The meanwhile widespread GRID technology formerly suffered from security aspects or data management [6]. Finally, existing tools (e.g. PVM, MPI, or batch queueing systems) are not that comfortable and portable [7].

The following subsection gives an overview on the software architecture of the Hypercomputing system.

2.2 System Architecture

The components of the Hypercomputer are designed as independent modules and thus easy to extend, to replace or to reuse [8]. All software has been written in Java. Each Hypercomputing cluster has a master host, on which the following servers are providing the core functionality of the system (see Figure 3):

- resource management
- job management
- performance management
- security management

The management of resources includes their detection and periodical measurement as well as the information exchange with neighbour clusters. For measurement tasks, the functions of the Hypercomputer or a batch queueing system can be used.

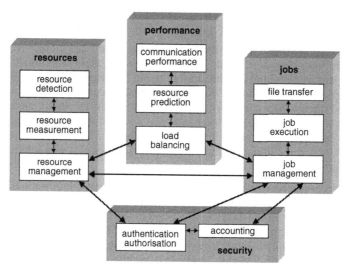

Fig. 3.   Components of the Hypercomputing Architecture

The job server is responsible for all tasks related to the execution of jobs, i.e. their reception from the user, the determination of suitable execution resources, the transport of the job and its data through the Hypercomputer, the observation of job execution, and the notification of the user. In local environments, batch queueing systems can be used for these tasks. The Hypercomputer extends their mechanisms for heterogeneous wide-area networks by defining an overall, flexible and platform independent infrastructure, which is locally adopted to existing systems.

For best use of the Hypercomputing resources, performance management has been integrated. It consists of a flexible load balancing module, a component for resource prediction in order to consider future conditions, and especially an evaluation of communication performance, which has a strong influence in wide-area networks. The load balancer is able to manage various algorithms, which are sorted in a decision tree. Thus, for different types of jobs, users, external constraints and so on, different load balancing strategies can be applied.

All components are accessing security mechanisms in order to mutually authenticate users as well as system modules. The authentication is based on a distributed, Kerberos-like ticketing system. Furthermore, all resources used by jobs are logged and signed by the job server, and are later analyzed and converted into costs per job and per user by an accounting component.

The Hypercomputer software components are communicating with each other using Java Remote Method Invocation (RMI). This requires no special infrastructure on the servers or clients except for the Java Virtual Machine (JVM). Besides, network connections or lower protocols are fully transparent to the system.

2.3 Applications

The Hypercomputing infrastructure can be used for simultaneous execution of parallel or sequential applications on distributed resources in wide-area networks. Because of the often limited network performance, applications with only minimal communication between their program parts should be preferred. Following Flynn´s classification, these are mainly single program multiple data (SPMD) applications.

In order to evaluate and demonstrate the Hypercomputing infrastructure, several example applications have been developed: programs for the parallel rendering of images or animations, a distributed number crunching program for cracking RSA cryptographic keys, and a parallel simulator for soil analysis (see section 1.3). Compared to a sequential algorithm, a huge speed-up can be gained using the Hypercomputer. Following Amdahl´s law, it is limited by the number of parallel processes respectively the number of hosts used for computation. Because of the overhead for administration of the infrastructure and the limited communication performance of wide-area networks, further latencies arise.

The basic Hypercomputer suffers from two restrictions: Firstly, it doesn't allow interactive applications, since the execution host is generally not known to the user. This restriction is addressed by Home@Globe, presented in the next chapter. Secondly, client software of the hypercomputer relies on Java and Java-RMI. Thus, it can not be used on systems that do not provide this infrastructure (like mobile systems). This restriction is addressed by the Kertasarie VM and TinyRMI as middleware, presented in chapter 4.

3 Web Access to Interactive Applications

Home@Globe is a WWW computing portal, which provides a uniform framework for application service providing (ASP) and distributed high-performance computing. Users can access and run applications through a standard web browser. Machines, data, applications, and other computing services at different places can be managed. Home@Globe provides a suitable remote access to normal desktop applications as well as to distributed parallel applications. The following sections give an overview of the system. Detailed information can be found in [9][10].

3.1 Related Work

There are several projects addressing the problem of remote access. As an example, VNC and WinFrame are closely related to this project. They provide flexible mechanisms to export graphical displays to remote clients in a platform independent manner, but they do not address further issues that arise in a wide-area distributed computing environment.

Other work is done to support the development of computational grids. For instance, WebOS [11] provides operating system services to wide area applications, e.g. resource discovery, remote process execution, and security. The Purdue University Network Computing Hubs (PUNCH) [12] consists of a two-level infrastructure. It supports a network-based desktop environment, and the SCION (Scalable Infrastructure for On-demand Network computing) middleware manages distributed resource back end. PUNCH submits jobs to SCION, which determines the most cost-effective system to run the job. SCION supports physically distributed compute engines and tools, and handles the resource and priority assignment as well as failure recovery.

3.2 System Architecture

The software components of the Home@Globe system provide a suitable remote access to common desktop applications as well as to distributed parallel applications. A user interacts with the system in two ways: by invoking single or parallel server applications. The main components of the Home@Globe architecture are (see Figure 4):

- a central server, which provides applications and data
- a HTTP server for the communication with the user
- a Hypercomputing system for distributed applications
- the client

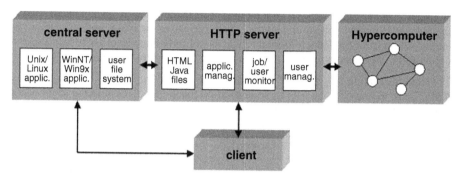

Fig. 4.   System Architecture of Home@Globe

The central server is managing several types of applications, that can be run by the user. These are applications for Unix or Linux as well as Windows variants. Furthermore, the personal data of each user is handled in a local file system. The central server can be distributed on different hosts in a local- or wide-area environment.

The HTTP server is the main communication element of a Home@Globe architecture. It provides HTML and Java classes to establish the connection between the user's browser and the application, for the input of high performance parallel applications, and for remote displaying of applications. Therefore, management information on applications as well as users is stored here. Furthermore, monitoring of users and their jobs is done on this server. The HTTP server can be implemented hierarchically.

In order to avoid making the application server an I/O bottleneck, the application management is responsible for keeping track of the capabilities of each application server. The HTTP server's configuration database contains information about all applications, e.g. user licenses, user priorities, locations of installed software etc. If the number of users or licences on an application server is exhausted, another server which provides the same application can be used.

Besides the central server, a Hypercomputing system can be bound to Home@Globe for the integration of other applications (especially, from the distributed computing area). This is explained in more detail in the following subsection.

The fourth component is the client, which is just a Java-enabled web browser on a workstation, a desktop PC, a network computer (NC), or a notebook. It can be located on any type of platform; Unix, Linux, NT or Windows. Thus, Home@Globe is totally platform independent.

After a user has opened the Java-based Home@Globe web interface and provided that he has authenticated correctly, he can request an application desktop from the central server or the Hypercomputer remotely.

3.3 Integration of the Hypercomputer

The Hypercomputer and Home@Globe mutually extend each others functionality. The original Hypercomputing architecture is not able to deal with interactive applications with graphical user interfaces, but Home@Globe handles a display redirection. On the other hand, the Hypercomputer offers a huge amount of distributed applications to the Home@Globe web computing interface.

Both systems can share some components, for instance the user management. Indeed, the current Home@Globe architecture is using the user database, authentication, and authorisation from the Hypercomputer. This is not only done in order to minimize the expense for implementation, but also to simplify the security mechanisms.

The communication between the components of both systems takes place using Java RMI. Thus, Home@Globe acts as another node for the Hypercomputing architecture, which is able to configure the system and to submit jobs, but is unable to execute any. No modifications of the existing Hypercomputing software have been necessary for its integration into Home@Globe.

4 Access by Mobile Devices

4.1 Java in Embedded Systems

Throughout this chapter, we will focus on PDAs as an example for mobile devices. In the last two years a fusion of PDAs and cellular phones can be seen. This adds substantial capabilities to such devices. This kind of equipment allows network access virtually anywhere. Persistent network connections are conceivable using GPRS technology. Thus, PDAs seem to be an ideal portal to access the Hypercomputer from every place. There are some severe restrictions on these devices, however. Typical PDAs like the 3Com Palm series offer only very limited resources. The constraints by name are computing power, memory (up to 8MBytes), a limited display (160x160 pixel) and bounded network capabilities (with respect to bandwidth and latency).

Accessing the Hypercomputer mandatorily requires Java RMI as a middleware infrastructure. RMI is so tightly integrated into the language concepts of Java that it is not possible to use RMI without Java. The use of RMI yields to the deployment of a Java infrastructure. Unfortunately, common Java implementations require considerably too many resources in terms of computing power and memory in order to use them on a PDA. There are three major components that are not suited to run on a PDA: the virtual machine itself, Sun's implementation of RMI and the available Java GUI systems.

Over the last two years, several Java virtual machines, that are especially designed for embedded systems and particularly PDAs were introduced. Examples are the KVM by Sun [13], IBM's J9 [14], Esmertec's JBed [15] and a VM by Kada Systems [16]. All these developments have one thing in common: they do not support reflection. Reflection is a concept to gain information about classes, fields and methods. It is a mandatory component of the Java API to allow object serialization and remote method invocation. Another VM implementation of Sun which supports reflection, the CVM, is much to large (about 2 MBytes of code) to be run on a restricted device like a PDA. To sum up, there is no virtual machine implementation available that is designed for PDAs and supports Java RMI. This led us to the development of our own VM implementation, called

Kertasarie, which fully supports reflection. This VM, as well as a windowing toolkit suited for limited displays, are described in more detail in the next subsection.

Another drawback is the current RMI implementation of Sun. It was designed for use in well-equipped desktop and server systems and not with limited resources in mind. Therefore, a compatible RMI implementation suited for embedded devices and PDAs was developed. It is described in section 4.3. Finally, the connection of PDAs to the Hypercomputer is described in section 4.4.

4.2 The Kertasarie VM Implementation

The Kertasarie VM was designed with restricted resources in mind [17]. Not only computing power, but also memory is very limited compared to desktop systems. Hence, the major objective was to focus on low memory consumption. Other design goals were:

- full support of the Java 1.2 standard including reflection,
- shifting as many data structures as possible into ROM to gain more object store,
- ease of portability,
- real-time capabilities,
- scalability of VM functionality as well as of the Java API, and
- an integrated Java debugger for remote access to the internal VM structures via a socket connection.

Table 1 shows the code size of the Kertasarie VM compared to the market leaders KVM from Sun and the J9 VM from IBM.

JVM	Binary Code (kB)	API (kB)		Application (kB)	Overall (kB)
		Standard	Specialized		
KVM	581 [1]	-	-	19	600
J9	85	211	98	15	198
Kertasarie	105	440	53	13	171

Tab. 1. Size of different VM implementations

All VMs are running on a PalmOS PDA, which is a typical example of a mobile device. The Kertasarie VM was compiled with full reflection and RMI support. The column „overall" represents the sum of binary code, specialized API and the application. The results show, that the Kertasarie VM is smaller than the other implementations, even though it offers a more extensive functionality. Table 2 shows the results of a simple benchmark [18].

This benchmark consists of 9 tests:

- empty loop iteration (1 000 000 times),
- addition of 1 000 000 values,
- multiplication of 1 000 000 values,

---

[1] The standard API of the KVM can't be tailored to a specific application. Thus, the KVM itself contains the full API.

JVM	Execution Time (s)
KVM	1 142
J9	1 147
Kertasarie	963

Tab. 2. Performance of different VM implementations

- 1 000 000 array assignments,
- 1 000 000 object field accesses,
- 1 000 000 method calls in the same object,
- 1 000 000 method calls in another object,
- throwing and catching of 1 000 000 exceptions, and
- thread switchings between two threads with the same priority, 10 000 times for each thread.

Table 2 shows, that the Kertasarie VM is the fastest among the three tested VMs. It should be noted, that the Kertasarie VM implements a strict „highest priority first" algorithm, including „priority inheritance" to prevent high priority threads from being starved by a low priority thread holding a needed resource. This implementation was chosen with real-time scenarios in mind.

Major attention was put on the ease of portability. The Kertasarie VM is strictly ANSI-C compliant, and all platform dependent code is strongly encapsulated. Until now, the VM has been ported to the following operating systems: Linux, Solaris, LynxOS, PalmOS, and a special operating system inside a PBX (private branch exchange).

The scalability of the VM and the appendant API is addressed in several ways. Firstly, it is possible to exclude at compile time those functions from the VM, that are not needed for a particular application. This can considerably decrease the size of the virtual machine. Another way to reduce the amount of necessary memory is to tailor the API according to a particular application. A tool suite developed for the Kertasarie VM, called Embedded Java Tools (EJT), takes an application as a starting point and builds a new API adapted to this application. Only those classes and methods that are needed to execute the application are adopted into the specially created API. For a typical application, approximately 50 percent of the methods are swept. This VM-independent part of the EJT is the input to another process that takes this API and transforms it into the internal Kertasarie VM structures. One benefit is the reduced size of the classes, because all symbolic references are substituted with pointers to the appropriate VM structures. The table containing the symbolic references in the class-files is now obsolete. Further important advantages are the possibility to shift these generated VM structures into the ROM to save much valuable RAM and to reduce the start-up time.

Existing GUI systems for Java also do not address the restricted resources in terms of display sizes and memory constraints. The standard windowing toolkits like AWT (Abstract Windowing Toolkit) and Java Swing are much too large to deploy them into a PDA. Moreover, the GUI components like buttons, menus, sliders etc. are not designed for small displays. There are notably two existing GUI toolkits designed for use on PDAs: kJava and kAWT.

The kJava [19] native components are tightly integrated into Suns KVM, so an easy integration into the Kertasarie VM is out of question. Besides these drawbacks, kJava only supports the dynamically representable elements, and therefore suffers from displaying menus on PalmOS devices. Recently, the kJava package was migrated into the MIDP (Mobile Information Device Profile) LCD-user interface package, which is even more restricted and heavily tied to the capabilities of cellular phones.

The kAWT [20] was developed to be functionally compatible to the standard AWT package. A major drawback is that kAWT rebuilds its own GUI components and does not use the native operating system components, which decreases the performance.

For the Kertasarie VM, an own GUI system has been developed. A major goal was the usability on PalmOS devices and Linux/Unix desktop systems. The PalmOS implementation supports all native GUI components of the operating system including menus. Figure 5 shows a screenshot of an example application, which is the submission of a batch job to the Hypercomputer.

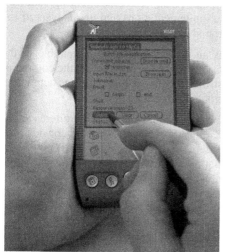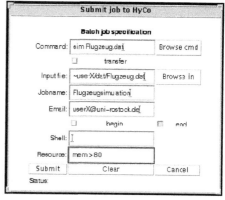

Fig. 5.   PDA with the developed GUI for PalmOS, and the original Hypercomputer GUI with the Java AWT

The Linux/Unix implementation relies on the Gimp toolkit (GTK). It was chosen because it offers a C interface and particularly because it is available in a framebuffer version. This framebuffer version allows an easy integration into various embedded systems.

Using the Kertasarie GUI toolkit, it is now possible to write applications for various embedded devices including PDAs and desktop systems. Especially, rapid prototyping becomes now feasible.

4.3 A minimized RMI variant: TinyRMI

The usage of a middleware like RMI on a mobile device is not only limited by the required virtual machine, but also by the middleware layer itself. The original implementation of RMI by Sun amounts to more than 400 KB of class files. This includes components for distributed garbage collection and activation. Even if those components are not considered, still 200 KB of class files remain.

Thus, it is not only necessary to minimize the resources required by the virtual machine, but also to minimize the size of the implementation of the middleware layer. TinyRMI was designed and implemented with this goal in mind. Primary focus was the minimization of the number and size of the classes. Yet, space should not simply be traded for time and thus the resulting implementation should not be considerably slower than the original implementation.

Other researchers have already implemented special versions of RMI. NexusRMI [21] was intended to provide a uniform interface to remote objects, that can be used with Java as well as with C++. Its main target is high performance computing. JavaParty [22] is targeted for the same area and offers direct usage of various transport layers. Another interesting RMI variant is NinjaRMI [23], which implements other transport protocols besides TCP like UDP, multicast and broadcast. All of these variants were not designed with a minimization of the memory usage in mind. Thus, we decided to design our own variant. A more detailed discussion of these implementations and an analysis of the structure of the Sun implementation can be found in [24].

The resulting TinyRMI implementation has an API that is fully compatible to the reference implementation, while not using exactly the same protocol on the communication channel. TinyRMI doesn't provide distributed garbage collection and activation, but in our opinion these are not required in embedded systems.

Table 3 shows the number of classes and the corresponding sizes of the reference implementation, NinjaRMI and TinyRMI. The other implementations are considerably larger and thus not suitable for embedded systems. The results show that TinyRMI is by far smaller than the reference implementation and noticeably smaller than NinjaRMI. Yet, the full quality of the implementation can only be seen, if not only the classes itself, but also the required Java API classes are counted. Table 4 shows these figures for all three variants. Now the difference between NinjaRMI and TinyRMI becomes substantially larger (almost 70KB). The given figures are based on the standard API by Sun. If we use the specialized API of the Kertasarie VM the required memory space shrinks dramatically, as the last line of Table 4 shows. Compared with the original version of Sun this variant only consumes one fifth of the memory space.

Variant	# of Classes	Size (Byte)
Sun RMI	121	209 573
NinjaRMI	42	68 343
TinyRMI	26	51 060

Tab. 3. Size of the three RMI implementations

Such a clear reduction of the space is often traded for the speed of the corresponding implementation. Table 5 shows communication times for all three variants for two different test cases. The first case is a method call with no parameters and no return value (thus the most simple case that can be thought of). The second case is a method call with an array `long[1024]` as parameter and result value. The table does not only show the

Variant	# of Classes	Size (Byte)
Sun RMI	254	703 836
NinjaRMI	202	458 400
TinyRMI	194	391 122
TinyRMI + KertasarieVM	97	140637

Tab. 4. Overall Size (including API) of the three RMI implementations

average time for the method call, but also the standard deviation of the sample. It turns out, that NinjaRMI is the fastest variant for the simple case, and TinyRMI is the fastest for the complex case, and is considerably faster than the Sun implementation for the simple case. Even more interesting is the fact, that the standard deviation of the TinyRMI results are considerably lower than for both other variants. We currently can't give an explanation of this behaviour, although it is absolutely in the favour of TinyRMI. Several additional test cases and a more thorough analysis of the results can also be found in [24].

Test Case	Variant	Average (ms)	Deviation (ms)
1	SunRMI	3.868	6.785
	NinjaRMI	2.799	4.531
	TinyRMI	3.048	2.903
2	SunRMI	22.104	10.962
	NinjaRMI	52.289	9.698
	TinyRMI	20.693	4.890

Tab. 5. Performance of the three RMI implementations

4.4 Integration of the PDA into the Hypercomputer

In order to use TinyRMI as middleware between the Hypercomputer and the mobile device, the Hypercomputer had to use TinyRMI as middleware layer for its internal communication. This required only the change of an import clause in the sources. No additional changes were required, since the API of TinyRMI is fully compatible to the reference implementation.

On the PDA's side, the implementation of the Hypercomputer client was required. Unfortunately, this implied many more changes, since the GUI differs significantly from the standard AWT used in the Hypercomputer. Thus, the screen layout had to be adapted to the limited display size of the PDA, and the dialogues had to be restructured slightly in order to fit all essential elements on the screen. With these changes, the user was able to submit jobs to the Hypercomputer from his PDA. Network access of the PDA can be established by several alternative layers. Sometimes infrared communication might be sufficient, while at other times a GSM mobile phone connected to the PDA will provide the network access.

5 Conclusion and Further Work

This paper has introduced topical developments offering an ubiquitous access to wide-area high-performance computing systems not only for common desktop computers or web-based systems, but also for small mobile computer systems like PDAs. Based on a concrete application scenario in agricultural science, we have shown the necessity for new access possibilities to (distributed) compute servers that allow mobile systems with strongly restricted resources to act as an access terminal to services of powerful servers via wireless network connections.

The Hypercomputer is the distributed wide-area computing infrastructure to build such a scenario. It has been developed in a recent research project at the University of Rostock. Its architecture is implemented using Java and Java RMI, which allows to combine the distributed wide-area high-performance computing services of the Hypercomputer with any other system that is able to communicate via Java RMI.

A current development is the Home@Globe system, which has been designed to enable web-based remote access to distributed applications via a graphical user interface. It is also mainly realized using the Java technology, and may therefore be easily tied to the Hypercomputer. This leads to a web-based, graphical interface to run interactive jobs in a distributed wide-area environment.

Finally, a highly portable, extra small Java infrastructure called Kertasarie VM has been developed. It is a complete Java 1.2 implementation for resource-constrained devices, offers full RMI support as well as a special GUI system for PDAs, and has proven to be the key technology in this respect. The use of the Kertasarie VM for the mobile access to a Hypercomputing infrastructure by PDA has been demonstrated.

Future work will concentrate on different security aspects, like the security of RMI connections and the encryption of transmitted data. Due to the limitations concerning computing power, only simple encryption policies and algorithms may be engaged, either proprietary or well known like RC4. The exploitation of socket factories within the Java API may be an effective way to secure data transmissions even over wireless media. This reflects the high importance of security aspects especially with respect to ubiquitous environments, since mobile communication is by nature open to several types of attacks - and the vision of ubiquitous computing will surely stay just a vision, if this problem is not fixed.

6 References

1. Weiser, M. The Computer for the Twenty-First Century. Scientific American, September 1991.
2. Tavangarian, D.; Eschholz, P.; Koch, M.; Pitz, C.; Preuß, St. Hypercomputing: A Concept for a Network-based Computer Architecture. In: Proceedings of the International Conference on Parallel and Distributed Processing Techniques and Applications (PDPTA), CSREA Press, Las Vegas (USA), July 1998.
3. Tavangarian, D.; Lucke, U.; Lucke, Th.: "Hypercomputing: Ein verteiltes System zur Bearbeitung von DV-Problemen in Weitverkehrsnetzen", final project report, University of Rostock, 2001.
4. Kaplan, J.A. et.al. A Comparison of Queueing, Cluster and Distributed Computing Systems. NASA Langley Research Center, June 1994.

5. Monien, B. Jahresbericht des Forschungsverbundes NRW-Metacomputing ,Verteiltes Höchstleistungsrechnen' für das Jahr 1997. University of Paderborn (Germany), March 1998.

6. Foster, I.; Kesselman, C. The Grid - Blueprint for a New Computing Infrastructure. Morgan Kaufmann Publishers, Inc., San Francisco 1999.

7. Ungerer, Th. Parallelrechner und parallele Programmierung. Spektrum Verlag, Berlin (Germany), 1997.

8. Tavangarian, D.; Kleinau, U.; Schulz, J. Eine Architektur für Hochleistungs-Datenverarbeitung in Weitverkehrs Workstation Netzwerken. In: Proceedings of the German Conference on Architecture of Computing Systems (ARCS'99), VDE Verlag, Berlin (Germany), October 1999.

9. Lee, Ch.-K.; Hochberger, Chr.; Tavangarian, D. Application Service Providing for Distributed High-Performance Computing. In: Proceedings of the International Conference on High Performance Computing Systems and Applications (HPCS 2001), Kluwer Academic Press, Dordrecht (Netherlands), June 2001.

10. Lee, Ch.-K.; Hochberger, Chr.; Tavangarian, D. Home@Globe: Integration of Distributed High- Performance Computing into Application Service Providing. In: Proceedings of the International Conference on Parallel and Distributed Processing Techniques and Applications (PDPTA 2001), CSREA Press, Las Vegas (USA), June 2001.

11. WebOS, http://www.cs.duke.edu/ari/issg/webos

12. Purdue University Network Computing Hubs, http://punch.ecn.purdue.edu/

13. Sun KVM, http://java.sun.com/products/cldc

14. IBM J9 VM, http://www.embedded.oti.com

15. Esmertec JBed, http://www.jbed.com

16. Kada Systems VM, http://www.kadasystems.com/kada_vm.html

17. Burchert, Fr.; Gatzka, St.; Geithner, Th.; Hochberger, Chr.; Kopp, H.; Tavangarian, D. Providing Java Based Middleware for PalmOS Devices. To appear in: Proceedings of the International ITEA Workshop on Virtual Home Environments, 2002.

18. UCSD Benchmarks for Java, http://www-cse.ucsd.edu/users/wgg/JavaProf/javaprof.html

19. kJava, http://www.microjava.com/technologies/kJava

20. kAWT, http://ww.kawt.de

21. Breg, F.; Diwan, Shr.; Villacis, J.; Balasubramanian, J.; Akman, E.; Gannon, D. Java RMI Performance and Object Model Interoperability: Experiments with Java/HPC++. In: Proceedings of the Workshop on Java for High Performance Network Computing, Palo Alto (California), 1998.

22. Nester, Chr.; Philippsen, M.; Haumacher, B. Effizientes RMI für Java. In: Proceedings of the conference JIT 99, Springer, Berlin (Germany), 1999.

23. Ninja RMI, http://www.cs.berkeley.edu/~mdw/proj/ninja/ninjarmi.html

24. Gatzka, St.; Hochberger, Chr.; Kopp, H. Deployment of Middleware in Resource Constrained Embedded Systems. In: Proceedings of the Workshop on Pervasive computing and information logistics, GI/OCG conference, Vienna (Austria), September 2001.

Filter Similarities in Content-Based Publish/Subscribe Systems

Gero Mühl*, Ludger Fiege*, and Alejandro Buchmann

Department of Computer Science
Darmstadt University of Technology, D-64283 Darmstadt
{fiege,gmuehl}@gkec.tu-darmstadt.de
buchmann@informatik.tu-darmstadt.de

Abstract. Matching notifications to subscriptions and routing notifications from producers to interested consumers are the main problems in large-scale publish/subscribe systems.
Most previously proposed distributed notification services either use flooding or, if filtering is performed, they assume that each event broker has global knowledge about all active subscriptions. Both approaches degrade the scalability of notification services as the former wastes network resources and the latter generates overly large routing tables.
In this paper we describe content-based routing algorithms that exploit filter similarities in order to reduce the size of routing tables and the number of control messages that are exchanged among the brokers in order to keep the routing tables up-to-date. In particular, the proposed algorithms do not assume global knowledge about all active subscriptions. Furthermore, we describe how these optimizations can be supported if the underlying data and filter model is based on structured records.

1 Introduction

Publish/subscribe provides means for the loosely coupled exchange of asynchronous messages. A *publish/subscribe system* consists of a set of nodes that communicate by exchanging notifications with the help of a notification service that is interposed between the producers and consumers. A broad range of applications can benefit from a solution that is based on publish/subscribe. For example, electronic trading platforms including stock exchanges, auction sites, and reverse auction platforms are inherently event-based [3, 19]. Also applications from the area of ubiquitous computing where clients are interested in up-to-date data and bandwidth is scarce or expensive are good candidates.

A *notification* is simply a message that contains some information called its *content*. *Clients* are producers, consumers, or both. *Producers* publish notifications and *consumers* subscribe to notifications by issuing *subscriptions* that are

---

* Supported by the German National Science Foundation (DFG) as part of the PhD program "Enabling Technologies for Electronic Commerce" at Darmstadt University of Technology.

H. Schmeck, T. Ungerer, and L. Wolf (Eds.): ARCS 2002, LNCS 2299, pp. 224–238, 2002.

essentially stateless message filters. Consumers can have multiple active subscriptions and after a client has issued a subscription the notification service is responsible for delivering all future matching notifications that are published until the client cancels the respective subscription.

The expressiveness of the subscription model is crucial for both the flexibility and the scalability of a notification service. Insufficient expressiveness can lead to unnecessary broad subscriptions stressing the network and raising the need for additional consumer-side filtering. On the other hand, scalable implementations of more expressive description models require complex delivery strategies [ ].

Content-based filtering allows subscriptions to evaluate the whole content of a notification, leveraging finer notification selection both inside the notification service and at the clients. Therefore, it provides a more powerful and flexible notification selection than it is possible for channel- or subject-based notification services where the content of a notification is opaque.

Centralized solutions of content-based notification services do not scale and the use of a distributed implementation that is built upon a set of cooperating event brokers is the key for scalability. Besides flooding, content-based routing is known from the literature. Here, a broker forwards a notification that it processes to some other brokers that is determined by a filter-based routing table. Unfortunately, almost all approaches dealing with content-based routing assume that each broker has global knowledge about all active subscriptions [,]. In our view, flooding and content-based routing that assumes global knowledge degrade the scalability of notification services because the former may waste network resources while the latter generates overly large routing tables.

As an alternative approach Carzaniga [ ] has shown that global knowledge about all active subscriptions is not necessary in order to implement a routing algorithm that solely forwards notifications that match active subscriptions. He proposed to use covering tests among filters to reduce the amount of information that is needed by a broker to determine the set of brokers to which an incoming notification must be forwarded. However, his work has only considered some predefined constraints on primitive data types (e.g., comparisons among integers). In a previous paper we have presented how more complex data types and constraints can be supported and also how filters can be merged [ ]. We also presented preliminary ideas how to apply covering tests and merging to semistructured data and objects [ ].

In this paper we combine and build on previous results and describe a set of routing algorithms that exploit filter similarities by applying identity and covering tests as well as carrying out filter merging. We show how to support these routing optimizations if the underlying data and filter model is based on structured records.

The remainder of this paper is organized as follows: Section 2 presents our system model and describes some routing algorithms that exploit filter similarities. In section 3 we show how to support identity and covering tests as well as filter merging for structured records. In the final sections we give an overview of some related work and briefly depict our notification service called REBECA.

2   Content-Based Routing

2.1   System Architecture

Clearly, a notification service that relies on a centralized broker cannot be scalable. It may match a notification against a large set of subscriptions very fast [,], but it will not be able to communicate with millions of clients. Moreover, a centralized broker is a single point of failure. In consequence, an implementation is needed that distributes the functionality of the service.

The key for a scalable notification service is to use content-based routing. In a publish/subscribe system that is based on *content-based routing* a set of cooperating *brokers* is arranged in a distributed topology. The *topology* of a distributed broker network is a connected undirected graph $G = (V, E)$ with a set of nodes $V = \{B_1, \ldots, B_n\}$ corresponding to the brokers and a set of edges $E \subseteq \{(B_i, B_j) \mid 1 \le i < j \le n\}$ representing connections among them. For convenience, we define a function $e(B_i, B_j)$ that returns (B_i, B_j) if $i < j$ and (B_j, B_i) otherwise.

In general, a topology is not static but it changes when new connections are established or existing connections are closed. One can distinguish between acyclic and generic topologies. In an *acyclic* topology between any two brokers exactly one path exists. In this case each broker is a single point of failure because if a single broker fails the topology is partitioned into two disconnected sub-topologies. Contrary to that, cycles can exist in a *generic* topology allowing for multiple paths between two brokers. Hence, a broker may not be a single point of failure but special care must be taken to avoid duplicated notifications and passing notifications and control messages in cycles. A simple and well-known method [,] to support generic topologies is to define for each broker B a (minimal) spanning tree of G that is used to route notifications originating from B. With this approach every broker is still a single point of failure but if a broker fails the spanning trees can be adapted accordingly. In order to resiliently tolerate broker failures multiple independent paths must exist between any two brokers [, ,]. In this paper we concentrate on acyclic topologies. In first approximation, routing algorithms are independent of the underlying transport mechanisms (e.g., multicast and unicast). They only specify the flow of notifications. Please refer to [,] for a detailed overview showing how to efficiently use multicast to disseminate notifications.

Each broker B has a set of *neighbor brokers* $N_B = \{H \mid e(B, H) \in E\}$ and manages an exclusive set of *local clients* L_B. Each client X has a set of active subscriptions S_X that changes if X subscribes or unsubscribes to a filter. Each broker B delivers a notification that it processes to all of its local clients that have a matching subscription, i.e., $\{X \mid X \in L_B \wedge \exists F \in S_X . n \in N(F)\}$. Additionally, every broker forwards a notification to a subset of its neighbors by evaluating a filter-based routing table.

Formally, a *filter* F is a stateless boolean function that maps a notification n to the boolean values *true* and *false*. A notification n *matches* a filter F iff $F(n)$ evaluates to *true*. We denote by $N(F)$ the set of all notifications that match F.

In our model the *routing table* T_B of a broker B consists of a set of *routing entries* (F, U) where F is a filter and U is a neighbor of B. Let $F_B^N(n)$ be the set of neighbors of B for whom there exists a routing entry that matches a given notification n, i.e., $\{U \mid U \in N_B \land \exists (F, U) \in T_B. n \in N(F)\}$. Then B forwards a notification that it processes to all neighbors in F_B^N if n has been published by a local client of B and to all neighbors in $F_B^N \setminus \{H\}$ if B has received n from a neighbor H. Finally, the brokers exchange *control messages* in order to keep their routing tables up to date.

2.2   Flooding vs. Filtering

Flooding   The technique of *flooding* can be seen as the simplest approach to implement content-based routing. In this case the routing tables of all brokers are initialized with constant routing entries such that $F_B^N(n)$ evaluates to N_B for all notifications n. Brokers do not exchange any control messages and therefore, they have no knowledge about active subscriptions of clients of other brokers and solely perform filtering on behalf of their local consumers. Hence, every broker simply forwards a notification that is published by one of its local clients to all of its neighbors and if a broker receives a notification from a neighbor it simply forwards it to all other neighbors. In consequence, each published notification is eventually processed by every broker and a lot of notifications may be forwarded unnecessarily. On the other hand, flooding may be a rather good choice if subscription profiles are equally distributed among the clients [21].

Filtering at Intermediate Brokers   Alternatively to flooding, filtering can be performed at intermediate brokers to reduce the number of notifications that are unnecessarily forwarded. In order to determine the minimal set of neighbors to which a broker must forward a notification assume for a moment that the set of active subscriptions is static and that the edge between a broker B and one of its neighbors U is removed from E. In this case the graph G is partitioned into two not connected subgraphs. Let $V_{U,B}$ be the set of all brokers that are nodes of the subgraph that contains the broker U. We denote by $\eta_{U,B}$ the set of all notifications that are of interest to any local consumer of a broker in $V_{U,B}$, i.e., $\cup_{H \in V_{U,B}} I_H$ with $I_H = \cup_{X \in L_H} \cup_{F \in S_X} N(F)$. Let $\phi_B(n)$ be the set of all neighbors of B for which n is in $\eta_{U,B}$, i.e., $\{U \mid U \in N_B \land n \in \eta_{U,B}\}$. Since G is acyclic a routing algorithm must ensure that $F_B^N(n)$ is a superset of $\phi_B(n)$ for all notifications. We call a routing algorithm *perfect* if $F_B^N(n) = \phi_B(n)$ for all notifications. Otherwise it is called *imperfect*. In general, a perfect routing algorithm requires that each broker has a more detailed knowledge about the active subscriptions but it also minimizes notification forwarding.

In a real system however, the set of active subscriptions changes as clients issue new or cancel existing subscriptions. The problem with this is that the set of notifications a client is interested in changes instantly while the routing tables cannot reflect this immediately. This means that the delivery of notifications which are exclusively matched by a new subscription is not guaranteed until all necessary updates to the routing tables have been carried out. Besides the delivery of matching notifications a routing algorithm should try to minimize unnecessary forwarding of notifications. For example, the routing tables should be updated in reaction to cancellations of subscriptions, too.

In the next subsections we describe some routing algorithms that are based on *control message forwarding*: For each new and canceled subscription the broker that manages the corresponding client sends an individual control message to some of its neighbors. A broker that receives a control message from a neighbor updates its routing table (if necessary) and sends an individual control message to some of its other neighbor. Brokers process incoming control messages serially and in FIFO-order.

2.3   Routing Based on Global Knowledge

A simple approach is to incorporate a routing entry for every active subscription into the routing tables of all brokers. To achieve this, the broker that manages the subscribing/unsubscribing client sends a control message that contains the new/canceled subscription S to all of its neighbors. A broker that receives such a control message from one of its neighbors H adds/extracts a corresponding routing entry (S, H) to its routing table and forwards the control messages unchanged to all of its other neighbors.

2.4   Routing Based on Filter Identity

The simple routing algorithm described in the previous subsection enforces that all brokers have knowledge about all active subscriptions. Clearly, this is not feasible in a large scale system because this would result in huge routing tables and costly coordination. Therefore, it is crucial to minimize the number of routing entries that is needed in the routing table of a broker to determine F_B^N while still retaining the same quality of filtering. This can be achieved by taking into account *similarities* among the filters, i.e., the subscriptions. Of course, this requires that it is possible to detect a relation between the sets of matched notifications among filters.

For example, assume that we are able to detect that two filters match the same notifications. Formally, two filters F_1 and F_2 are *identical*, denoted by $F_1 \equiv F_2$, iff $N(F_1) = N(F_2)$. A broker does not need to forward a new/canceled subscription S_2 to a neighbor if another identical subscription S_1 has already been forwarded to that neighbor for that no corresponding unsubscription has been received yet. This reduces the size of the routing tables because routing entries with identical filters regarding the same neighbors are avoided. Moreover, the number of exchanged control messages is reduced, too.

2.5   Routing Based on Filter Covering

The direct extension of identity-based routing is to apply more complex similarity tests among subscriptions. The next step is to exploit covering among

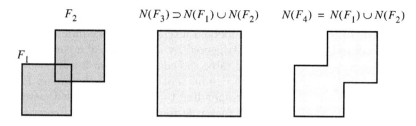

Fig. 1. Illustrating perfect and imperfect merging

filters. Let F_1 and F_2 be two arbitrary filters. We say that F_1 *covers* F_2, denoted by $F_1 \sqsupseteq F_2$, iff $N(F_1) \supseteq N(F_2)$. It is easy to see that if $F_1 \sqsupseteq F_2$ then $n \in N(F_2)$ implies $n \in N(F_1)$ and $n \notin N(F_1)$ implies $n \notin N(F_2)$. The pair $(\mathcal{F}, \sqsupseteq)$ defines a partial order over the set of all filters $\mathcal{F}$ and can be illustrated by a Hasse diagram.

Covering tests can be used to reduce the number of routing entries in routing tables as well as the number of control messages that must be forwarded. A broker B does not need to forward a subscription/unsubscription S_2 to a neighbor H if B has already forwarded a subscription S_1 to H that covers S_2 for which B has not received a corresponding unsubscription yet. Moreover, if B receives a new subscription S from a neighbor U it can drop those routing entries regarding U whose filters are covered by S. But this implies that in the case that B forwards an unsubscription S to a neighbor H then also all subscriptions that are covered by S of those routing entries regarding all brokers except H must be forwarded to H again.

In the context of notification services the use of covering was first described by Carzaniga [,]. Computing covering tests is in general very expensive or even intractable. For example, computing covering tests for relational expressions or linear context-free grammars is NP-complete [ ]. Fortunately, in practice special cases exist for which covering can be determined quite efficiently [,].

2.6   Routing Based on Filter Merging

In this subsection we describe how to extend the routing algorithm outlined in the previous section in order to exploit filter merging in addition to covering. In contrast to covering, merging does not merely rely on the filters that have been issued by the clients. Instead, new filters are derived from existing ones such that each new filter covers the set of filters it was generated from. We say that F is a *merger* of (or covers) a set of filters $\{F_1, \ldots, F_n\}$, denoted by $F \sqsupseteq \{F_1, \ldots, F_n\}$ iff $N(F) \supseteq (\cup_i N(F_i))$. The merger F is *perfect* if the equality holds and *imperfect*, otherwise (see Fig. 1).

The basic idea of merging-based routing is that each broker can merge filters of existing routing entries and forward the generated merger to a subset of its neighbors. As a merger covers the filters it was generated from, a broker that receives a merger from a neighbor will drop those routing entries that belong to this neighbor and represent the merged filters. Hence, the number of routing entries is reduced. Periodically or triggered by the receipt of a control message every broker investigates its routing table and checks whether it can generate new mergers and if the existing mergers can be kept. After that the broker forwards subscriptions/unsubscriptions corresponding to each new/canceled merger to a specific subset of its neighbors. If it forwards an unsubscription corresponding to a canceled merger, the broker also embeds the subscriptions that were covered by the merger into the control message.

The following example illustrates that generating a perfect merger is not sufficient to guarantee that no notifications will be forwarded unnecessarily. In fact, the subset of neighbors to which a merger is forwarded plays an important role. Consider a broker B_3 with two neighbors B_1 and B_2. The routing table of B_3 consists of two routing entries (F_1, B_1) and (F_2, B_2) with $N(F_1) \neq N(F_2)$. Now, B_3 decides to forward a perfect merger of F_1 and F_2 to all of its neighbors, i.e., B_1 and B_2. In this example, broker B_1 will also forward notifications that match F_2 but not F_1 and broker B_2 will forward notifications that match F_1 but not F_2 to B_3 although B_3 will not forward any of these notifications to B_1 or B_2. In fact, the set of neighbors to which a merger can be forwarded without raising this problem depends on the routing entries from which it was generated: a merger can be forwarded to all neighbors if for each routing entry (F, H) from which it was generated there exists another routing entry (G, I) such that $N(F) = N(G)$ and $H \neq I$.

At a first glance, imperfect merging seems to be less promising, but in situations in which perfect merging cannot be applied it might be a good compromise. On one hand, imperfect merging results in notifications being forwarded that do not match any of the original subscriptions and one must be careful to avoid that the effects of imperfect merging are chained along delivery paths such that the routing degenerates to flooding. But on the other hand, imperfect merging can greatly reduce the amount of subscriptions that must be dealt with.

In order to apply merging it must be possible to efficiently compute mergers and if imperfect merging is performed the fraction of the irrelevantly matched notifications must be sufficiently small. Merging is powerful but also complex and its usability needs further investigation.

2.7   Use of Advertisements

Advertisements are filters that are issued by producers to indicate their intention to publish notifications. In our model each notification that is published by a producer must match one of its active advertisements. Advertisements can be used as additional mechanism to further optimize content-based routing [ ]. For this purpose they are propagated through the broker network in the same way as described for subscriptions in order to route subscriptions more efficiently: a subscription is only forwarded to a neighbor if it overlaps with an advertisement that has been received from this neighbor. The only underlying assumption is that it is possible to detect whether a given advertisement A and a given subscription S are *overlapping*, i.e., whether or not $N(S) \cap N(A) \neq \emptyset$. All routing algorithms presented in the former sections can be easily extended in such a way that advertisements are used.

2.8   Discussion

The routing algorithms are getting more complex by applying the proposed routing optimizations such as covering and merging. But on the other hand, these improvements reduce the size of the routing tables and may also reduce the number of exchanged control messages. If they are used, the efficient evaluation of these optimizations will be crucial for the load induced on the brokers. Normally, a more expressive data and filter model tends to make these optimization more complex, too. Moreover, there exists a trade-off between network and computing resource usage/wastage and in our view there will be no static solution that is optimal for all application scenarios. We propose to use statistical online evaluation of connection and filter selectivity as a basis to adapt routing algorithms: the forwarding broker disables filtering if the matching rate exceeds a certain threshold while the receiving broker can request to turn filtering on again if the relative amount of forwarded notifications that do not match is too large.

3   Supporting Filter Similarities for Structured Records

Many systems model notifications similar to structured records consisting of a set of name/value pairs called attributes. Examples are SIENA [4], Gryphon [1,2], REBECA [8], and the CORBA Notification Service [20]. In this model attributes are addressed by their unique name and constraints are imposed on the values of the respective attributes. Besides *flat* records in which values are atomic types, *structured* records in which attributes may be nested can also be supported by using a dotted naming scheme (e.g., *Position.x*).

Some systems restrict constraints to depend on a single attribute (e.g., $x = 1$) while other systems allow them to depend on multiple attributes which are combined by operators (e.g., $x+y = 5$). Multiple constraints can be combined by boolean operators (e.g., $y < 3 \land x = 4$). SIENA and REBECA limit constraints to depend on a single attribute and the combination of constraints to conjunctions in order to allow for efficient evaluation of routing optimizations. In the following we present some of the basics that underlie the proposed routing optimizations such as covering and merging.

3.1   Notifications

Formally, a notification n is a set of attributes $\{A_1, \ldots, A_n\}$ where each A_i is a *name/value pair* (n_i, v_i) with *name* n_i and *value* v_i. We assume that names are unique, i.e., $i \neq j$ implies that $n_i \neq n_j$, and that there exists a function that uniquely maps each n_i to a type T_k that is the type of the corresponding value v_i

(e.g. *Integer*). Moreover, a notification has a mandatory attribute with name *type* that indicates the type of the notification (e.g., *StockQuote*) in order to enable *type-based filtering* based on a type hierarchy. For each type a set of additional *mandatory attributes* is defined that may be empty. An example of a notification in this model is $\{(type, StockQuote), (name, "Foo Inc."), (price, 45.0)\}$.

3.2   Filters

A filter consisting of a single atomic predicate is a *simple filter* or *constraint*. Filters that are derived from simple filters by combining them with boolean operators are *compound filters*. A compound filter that is a conjunction of simple filters is called a *conjunctive filter*. Any compound filter can be converted into its *DNF (disjunctive normal form)* that consists of a disjunction of a set of conjunctive filters whose size may be exponential in the worst case. As multiple subscriptions of a single client are interpreted disjunctively this implies that it is sufficient to support conjunctive filters. Therefore, we restrict the discussion to conjunctive filters for the rest of this paper.

3.3   Attribute Filters

We model filters as conjunctions of attribute filters that are simple filters and impose a constraint on the value of a single attribute (e.g., $\{name = "Foo Inc."\}$). Hence, a notification n matches a filter F iff it satisfies all attribute filters of F. Moreover, a filter with an empty set of attribute filters matches any notification.

An *attribute filter* is defined as a tuple $AF_i = (n_i, Op_i, C_i)$ where n_i is an attribute name, Op_i is a test operator and C_i is a set of constants that may be empty. The name n_i determines to which attribute the constraint applies. If the notification does not contain an attribute with name n_i then AF_i evaluates to *false*. Therefore, each constraint implicitly defines an existential quantifier over the notification. Otherwise, the operator Op_i is evaluated using the value of the addressed attribute and the specified set of constants C_i. We assume that the types of operands are compatible with the used operator. The outcome of AF_i is defined as the result of Op_i that evaluates either to *true* or *false*. We also provide an attribute filter that simply checks whether a given attribute is contained in n. For the sake of simplicity we use the more readable notation $\{price > 10\}$ instead of $\{(price, >, \{10\})\}$. An example for a conjunctive filter consisting of attribute filters is $\{(type = StockQuote), (name = "Foo Inc."), (price \notin [30, 40])\}$. Note, that this filter potentially matches also all notifications whose type is a subtype of *StockQuote*.

By $L(AF_i) \subseteq dom(T_k)$ we denote the set of all values that cause an attribute filter to match an attribute, i.e., $\{v_i \mid Op_i(v_i, C_i) = true\}$. We assume that $L(AF_i) \neq \emptyset$. An attribute filter AF_1 covers an attribute filter AF_2, written $AF_1 \sqsupseteq AF_2$, iff $n_1 = n_2 \wedge L(AF_1) \supseteq L(AF_2)$. For example, $\{price > 10\}$ covers $\{price \in [20, 30]\}$.

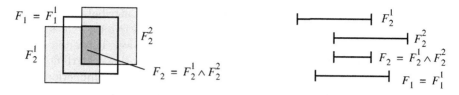

Fig. 2. $F_1 \sqsupseteq F_2$ although neither $F_1^1 \sqsupseteq F_2^1$ nor $F_1^1 \sqsupseteq F_2^2$ (two examples)

3.4 Covering of Conjunctive Filters

Here, we investigate covering of filters that are conjunctions of attribute filters.

Proposition 1. *Given two filters $F_1 = AF_1^1 \wedge \ldots \wedge AF_1^n$ and $F_2 = AF_2^1 \wedge \ldots \wedge AF_2^m$ that are conjunctions of attribute filters, the following holds: $\forall i \exists j.\ AF_1^i \sqsupseteq AF_2^j$ implies $F_1 \sqsupseteq F_2$.*

ASSUME: $\forall i \exists j.\ AF_i^1 \sqsupseteq AF_j^2$
PROVE: $F_1 \sqsupseteq F_2$
PROOF: If an arbitrary notification n is matched by F_2 then n satisfies all AF_2^j. This fact together with the assumption implies that n also satisfies all AF_1^i. Therefore, n is matched by F_1, too. Hence, $F_1 \sqsupseteq F_2$. $\square$

If several attribute filters can be imposed on the same attribute then $\forall i \exists j. AF_1^i \sqsupseteq AF_2^j$ is not a necessary condition for $F_1 \sqsupseteq F_2$ (see also Fig. 2). If we restrict conjunctive filters to have at most one attribute filter for each attribute then we can strengthen Proposition 1 to an equivalence:

Proposition 2. *Given two filters $F_1 = AF_1^1 \wedge \ldots \wedge AF_1^n$ and $F_2 = AF_2^1 \wedge \ldots \wedge AF_2^m$ that are conjunctions of attribute filters with at most one attribute filter for each attribute, the following holds: $F_1 \sqsupseteq F_2$ implies $\forall i \exists j.\ AF_1^i \sqsupseteq AF_2^j$.*

ASSUME: $\neg(\forall i \exists j.\ AF_1^i \sqsupseteq AF_2^j)$
PROVE: $\neg(F_1 \sqsupseteq F_2)$
PROOF: We construct a notification n that matches F_2 but not F_1 to prove that F_1 does not cover F_2. The assumption implies that there is at least one AF_1^k that does not cover any AF_2^j. If there exists an AF_2^l that constrains the same attribute as such an AF_1^k then choose for this attribute a value that matches AF_2^l but not AF_1^k. Such a value exists because $L(AF_1^k) \neq \emptyset$ and $AF_1^k \not\sqsupseteq AF_2^l$. Add name/value pairs for all other attributes that are constrained in F_2 such that they are matched by the appropriate attribute filters of F_2. The constructed notification matches F_2 but not F_1. Therefore, F_1 does not cover F_2. $\square$

Corollary 1. *Given two filters $F_1 = AF_1^1 \wedge \ldots \wedge AF_1^n$ and $F_2 = AF_2^1 \wedge \ldots \wedge AF_2^m$ that are conjunctions of attribute filters with at most one attribute filter per attribute, $F_1 \sqsupseteq F_2$ is equivalent to $\forall i \exists j.\ AF_1^i \sqsupseteq AF_2^j$.*

PROOF: by Proposition 1 and 2. $\square$

The limitation to at most one attribute filter for each attribute is not severe because our system provides complex data types as attribute values and an extensible set of constraints that can be imposed. Moreover, it is often possible to merge several conjunctive constraints imposed on a single attribute into a single constraint on the same attribute. If the result of a conjunction of two constraints of some constraint type always yields another constraint of the same type then this set of constraints is either contradicting or can be replaced by a single constraint of the same type. We call such types of constraints and their corresponding attribute filters *conjunction-complete*. For example, constraints testing whether a point is in a given rectangle in a two-dimensional plane are conjunction-complete. If a constraint type is not conjunction-complete it is often possible to substitute a set of such constraints by a single constraint of a more general type. For example, a set of ordering constraints defined on a totally ordered set (e.g., integer numbers) are either contradictory or can be replaced by a single interval constraint. In a previous paper [ ] we have presented an algorithm that determines the possibly empty set of filters that cover a given filter which is derived from the predicate counting matching algorithm [ ].

3.5   Identity and Overlapping of Conjunctive Filters

The following two propositions show how identity and overlapping of conjunctive filters can be reduced to their respective attribute filters. The proofs are left out due to space reasons.

Proposition 3. *Two filters $F_1 = AF_1^1 \wedge \ldots \wedge AF_1^n$ and $F_2 = AF_2^1 \wedge \ldots \wedge AF_2^m$ that are conjunctions of attribute filters with at most one attribute filter for each attribute are identical iff they contain the same number of attribute filters and $\forall AF_1^i \exists AF_2^j. \left(n_1^i = n_2^j \wedge L(AF_1^i) = L(AF_2^j) \right).$*

Proposition 4. *Two filters $F_1 = AF_1^1 \wedge \ldots \wedge AF_1^n$ and $F_2 = AF_2^1 \wedge \ldots \wedge AF_2^m$ that are conjunctions of attribute filters with at most one attribute filter for each attribute are overlapping iff $\nexists AF_1^i, AF_2^j. \left(n_1^i = n_2^j \wedge L(AF_1^i) \cap L(AF_2^j) = \emptyset \right)$*

3.6   Merging of Conjunctive Filters

In the general case purely algebraic merging techniques have exponential time complexity. Alternatively, a predicate proximity graph can be used to implement a greedy algorithm [ ]. For many practical cases (e.g., the set operators) efficient algorithms exist.

An algorithm that determines the possibly empty set of filters which are candidates to be merged with a given filter was depicted in a previous paper [ ]. From the set of merging candidates the set of attribute filters to be merged can be easily extracted. This set is used as input of a merging algorithm which has a specialized implementation for each type of constraint. Only in rare cases it is necessary to use an exhaustive combinatorial or a suboptimal greedy algorithm.

Perfect Merging A set of conjunctive filters with at most one attribute filter for each attribute can be perfectly merged into a single conjunctive filter if for all except a single attribute their corresponding attribute filters are identical and if the attribute filters of the distinguishing attribute can be merged into a single attribute filter. For example, the two filters $F_1 = \{x = 5 \wedge y \in \{2,3\}\}$ and $F_2 = \{x = 5 \wedge y \in \{4,5\}\}$ can be merged to $F = \{x = 5 \wedge y \in \{2,3,4,5\}\}$.

The characteristics of the constraints that are used to define attribute filters are important for merging. Constraints which only exist in a normal and a negated form can be directly merged by using some basic laws of boolean algebra. For example, a filter $F_1 = P_1 \wedge P_2$ can be merged perfectly with a filter $F_2 = P_1 \wedge \bar{P}_2$ to a filter $F = P_1$. Although these cases also exist for more complex constraints (e.g., $x = 5$ and $x \neq 5$) constraints are not restricted to be the negated form of each other. Better merging can be achieved by taking the specific characteristics of the imposed constraints into account.

A class of constraints that is *complete under disjunction* allows to merge a set of constraints of this class into a single constraint of the same class. Examples for disjunction-complete constraints are *set inclusions* (e.g., $x \in \{2,3,7\}$) and *set exclusions* (e.g., $x \notin \{2,3,7\}$) while *comparison constraints* (e.g., $x < 4$) are not disjunction-complete. If a constraint class is not disjunction-complete it may still be possible to carry out merging if a specific *merging condition* is met. For example, a set of *interval tests* (e.g., $x \in [2,4]$ and $x \in [3,5]$) can be merged into a single interval test (here, $x \in [2,5]$) if the intervals form a connected set. Otherwise, merging may be possible if a more general constraint is considered as merging result. For example, two comparison constraints (e.g., $x < 4$ and $x > 7$) can be merged to an interval test (here, $x \notin [4,7]$).

Imperfect Merging In order to use imperfect merging a set of heuristics is necessary that define in what situations and to what degree imperfect merging should be carried out. For example, filters that differ in few attribute filters could be merged imperfectly by imposing on each attribute a constraint that covers all original constraints. This could also be accomplished by explicitly replacing an attribute filter with another that only tests for the existence of the given attribute or by simply dropping the attribute filter. Note, that an existence test is equivalent to no constraint if the attribute is mandatory for the corresponding type of notification.

4   Related Work

Answering Queries Using Views Covering relations are known from the database theory and in particular from the area of answering queries using views [12,25]. There, the question is whether the result set of a given query Q can be solely obtained from a set of predefined views V whose elements can be combined by the usual relational operators, i.e., whether Q is covered by some combination of the views in V. Answering this question for relational expressions is *NP*-hard even without comparison operators. If only the union operator is allowed, this is still a more general scenario than ours. Although special cases have been investigated, we were not able to find an approach that is closely related to ours.

Semantic Caching Lee and Chu [ ] describe a semantic caching algorithm for conjunctive point queries that exploits covering between conjunctive predicates to find cache entries which cover a given query. However, this work is restricted to point queries involving the equivalence and the like operator. Godfrey and Gryz [ ] depict an architecture for predicate-based caching that is similar to answering queries using views. Therefore, it is not surprising that their algorithms are *NP*-complete, too. Keller and Basu [ ] propose a predicate-based caching scheme for client/server database architectures. They perfectly merge predicates in the cache to obtain a more compact cache description and to speed up query processing. Their algorithm has exponential time complexity.

Query Merging Crespo et al. [ ] propose merging of queries that are evaluated periodically against a database. As example, they use geographical queries represented by a rectangle. Before the queries are processed a merging algorithm is run that combines similar queries and outputs a set of merged queries whose answers contain all tuples of the original query. Their aim is to find a set of mergers which is cost optimal. They show that in the general case query merging is *NP*-complete and discuss optimal and heuristic algorithms.

Geometrical Algorithms In the context of geometrical algorithms [ ], for example, polygon inclusion, intersection, and containment of convex polygons are investigated. These algorithms can be integrated with our work to support efficient matching, covering, and merging of notifications containing geometric objects. Such objects are, for example, prevalent in geographical information systems.

Notification Services SIENA [ ] exploits covering relations between filters and applies them to subscription and advertisement forwarding, but their support for data types and constraints is very limited. Moreover, they do not support merging. Elvin [ ] supports quenching in which notifications are first evaluated against a broader subscription that covers the disjunction of all subscriptions but no algorithms are described.

5 Implementation

In the context of our research project REBECA [,] we investigate event-based architectures for E-commerce applications. We have realized a prototype of a content-based publish/subscribe middleware that relies on content-based routing and exploits covering and merging. The routing algorithms are implemented on top of a flexible routing framework in order to enable the testing of various routing algorithms. Optionally, our system can use subscription and advertisement leasing in order to be more fault-tolerant. We also implemented support of notifications about new/canceled subscriptions and advertisements.

We have implemented a stock trading application based on real-time quotes to test the system under an observable load. At the moment we investigate the effects of using different data models and routing algorithms on the performance of the system. Moreover, we are developing another application dealing with meta-auctions that are a generalization of normal Internet auctions.

6   Conclusion

In this paper we outlined a set of content-based routing algorithms that exploit similarities among filters. In particular, we have described how identity and covering tests as well as filter merging can be used in order to reduce the size of routing tables and the number of exchanged control messages. We have also presented the basic mechanisms and assumptions that underly these optimizations and how they can be supported if the underlying data and filter model uses structured records. We suggested to use statistical on-line adaption of the filtering strategy to cope with the trade-off between network resource waste and processing cost overhead. Future work will include detailed studies of the effects of different filtering strategies based on our prototypical publish/subscribe middleware and the implemented applications.

References

1. M. Aguilera, R. Strom, D. Sturman, M. Astley, and T. Chandra. Matching events in a content-based subscription system. In *PODC: 18th ACM SIGACT-SIGOPS Symposium on Principles of Distributed Computing*, pages 53–61, 1999. 226, 231
2. G. Banavar, T. Chandra, B. Mukherjee, J. Nagarajarao, R. E. Strom, and D. C. Sturman. An efficient multicast protocol for content-based publish-subscribe systems. In *Proceedings of the 19th IEEE International Conference on Distributed Computing Systems*, pages 262–272, 1999. 225, 226, 231
3. C. Bornhövd, M. Cilia, C. Liebig, and A. Buchmann. An infrastructure for meta-auctions. In *Second International Workshop on Advance Issues of E-Commerce and Web-based Information Systems (WECWIS'00)*, San Jose, California, June 2000. 224
4. A. Carzaniga. *Architectures for an Event Notification Service Scalable to Wide-area Networks*. PhD thesis, Politecnico di Milano, Milano, Italy, Dec. 1998. 225, 226, 229, 230, 231, 236
5. A. Carzaniga, D. S. Rosenblum, and A. L. Wolf. Design and evaluation of a wide-area event notification service. *ACM Transactions on Computer Systems*, 19(3):332–383, 2001. 225, 226, 229
6. A. Crespo, O. Buyukkokten, and H. Garcia-Molina. Efficient query subscription processing in a multicast environment. In *Proceedings of the 16th International Conference on Data Engineering (ICDE)*, 2000. 236
7. F. Fabret, A. Jacobsen, F. Llirbat, J. Pereira, K. Ross, and D. Shasha. Filtering algorithms and implementation for very fast publish/subscribe. In *SIGMOD 2001*, pages 115–126, 2001. 226

8. L. Fiege and G. Mühl. Rebeca Event-Based Electronic Commerce Architecture, 2000. http://www.gkec.informatik.tu-darmstadt.de/rebeca. 231

9. L. Fiege, G. Mühl, and F. C. Gärtner. A modular approach to build structured event-based systems. In *ACM Symposium on Applied Computing (SAC)*, 2002. 236

10. M. R. Garey and D. S. Johnson. *Computers and Intractability A guide to the Theory of NP-Completeness.* W. H. Freeman and Company, New York, 1979. 229

11. P. Godfrey and J. Gryz. Answering queries by semantic caches. In *Database and Expert Systems Applications (DEXA) LNCS Vol. 1677*, pages 485–498. Springer, 1999. 236

12. A. Y. Halevy. Theory of answering queries using views. *SIGMOD Record*, 29, Dec. 2000. 235

13. Y. Huang and G.-M. Hector. Exactly-once semantics in a replicated messaging system. In *Proc. of the 17th International Conference on Data Engeneering (ICDE)*, 2001. 226

14. Y. Huang and G.-M. Hector. Replicated condition monitoring. In *Proc. of the 20th ACM Symposium on Principles of Distributed Computing (PODC)*, 2001. 226

15. A. M. Keller and J. Basu. A predicate-based caching scheme for client-server database architectures. *VLDB Journal*, 5(1):35–47, 1996. 234, 236

16. D. Lee and W. W. Chu. Conjunctive point predicate-based semantic caching for wrappers in web databases. In *Workshop on Web Information and Data Management*, 1998. 236

17. G. Mühl. Generic constraints for content-based publish/subscribe systems. In *Proceedings of the 6th International Conference on Cooperative Information Systems (CoopIS)*, pages 211–225. Springer, 2001. 225, 229, 234, 236

18. G. Mühl and L. Fiege. Supporting covering and merging in content-based publish/subscribe systems: Beyond name/value pairs. *IEEE Distributed Systems Online (DSOnline)*, 2(7), 2001. 225, 229

19. G. Mühl, L. Fiege, and A. Buchmann. Evaluation of cooperation models for electronic business. In *Information Systems for E-Commerce, Conference of German Society for Computer Science / EMISA*, pages 81–94, Nov. 2000. ISBN 3-85487-194-5. 224

20. Object Management Group. Corba notification service. OMG Document telecom/99-07-01, 1999. 231

21. L. Opyrchal, M. Astley, J. Auerbach, G. Banavar, R. Strom, and D. Sturman. Exploiting ip multicast in content-based publish-subscribe systems. In J. Sventek and G. Coulson, editors, *Middleware 2000*, volume 1795 of *LNCS*, pages 185–207. Springer-Verlag, 2000. 225, 226, 227

22. F. P. Preparata and M. I. Shamos. *Computational Geometry: An Introduction.* Springer, 1985. 236

23. W. Segall and D. Arnold. Elvin has left the building: A publish/subscribe notification service with quenching. In *Proceedings of the 1997 Australian UNIX Users Group, Brisbane, Australia, September 1997.*, 1997. http://elvin.dstc.edu.au/doc/papers/auug97/AUUG97.html. 236

24. A. C. Snoeren, K. Conley, and D. K. Gifford. Mesh-based content routing using xml. In *18th ACM Symposium on Operating System Principles*, 2001. 226

25. J. D. Ullman. Information integration using logical views. In *6th Int. Conference on Database Theory; LNCS 1186*, pages 19–40. LNCS 1186, Springer, 1997. 235

26. T. W. Yan and H. Garcia-Molina. Index structures for selective dissemination of information under the Boolean model. *ACM Transactions on Database Systems*, 19(2):332–334, 1994. 234

Session VI

Networking 2

A Bluetooth Remote Control System

Fridtjof Feldbusch, Alexander Paar, Manuel Odendahl, and Ivan Ivanov

Institute for Computer Design and Fault Tolerance (Prof. Dr. D. Schmid),
University of Karlsruhe, 76128 Karlsruhe, Germany
feldbusch@informatik.uni-karlsruhe.de
AlexPaar@Technologiefabrik.de
Manuel.Odendahl@hadiko.de
ueh2@rz.uni-karlsruhe.de

Abstract. Emerging radio technologies like WLAN and Bluetooth enable electronic devices of any kind to communicate with one another. A simple and easy to implement application layer protocol called BTRC protocol was developed allowing devices to exchange data of any kind and format over different protocols like TCP/IP or Bluetooth. Based upon this protocol a universal remote control system was implemented. Software applications simulating cellular phones and personal digital assistants (PDA) were developed as remote control devices. BTRC server devices send their graphical XML based user interface to the remote control. This way the use of devices is simplified significantly.

1   Introduction

The Internet revolution of the nineties has concentrated mainly on the communication of Personal Computers. While these developments were based mainly on wire connections between the computers, wireless technologies like WLAN and Bluetooth are offering new possibilities. These technologies will eventually be more than just a replacement of wires. Electronic devices of any kind like household, audio and video devices will be able to exchange information. To make this future come true, applications running on these devices must obey certain standards of communication to understand each other and to make access to peer devices uniform.

These ideas enlarge upon the concept of a conventional remote control. Unfortunately, today every device has its own proprietary infrared remote control. This is why we developed the Bluetooth remote control (BTRC) system, which allows devices to send requests to one another in a standard way, to describe the commands they support and to provide a flexible user interface description. Using the BTRC system, it is possible to use various existing devices (e.g. mobile phones, personal digital assistants, web pads or even web browsers) as a universal remote control.

When a user enters a room, every device that can be controlled remotely identifies itself to the remote control's gadget list. Depending on the size of the display and the computing capacity of the remote control, these devices are

H. Schmeck, T. Ungerer, and L. Wolf (Eds.): ARCS 2002, LNCS 2299, pp. 241–255, 2002.

shown as a list of strings or as icons. When the user chooses a device, a request is sent to the device to query its user interface. This way the remote control obtains all commands that are supported by this device and supplementary online help files to guide the user. XML (extensible markup language) and XSL (extensible stylesheet language) are used for the description of the user interface.

The BTRC system uses the application layer BTRC protocol, which permits devices to send commands over various transport protocols. The simplicity of the protocol permits its implementation on small wearable devices with limited computational resources. Furthermore, BTRC protocol messages can be embedded in Universal Resource Identifies (URIs), as proposed by several RFCs [ ],[ ],[ ]. To show the applicability of the BTRC protocol, both clients and servers using Bluetooth and TCP/IP were implemented. An HTTP proxy enabling a conventional web-browser to access BTRC devices was also implemented.

2   System Overview

Figure 1 shows the overview of the entire remote control system. An application simulating a Bluetooth PDA remote control was developed as a reference implementation (right top of figure 1). This application is equipped with a speech recognition interface to demonstrate a highly user-friendly system.

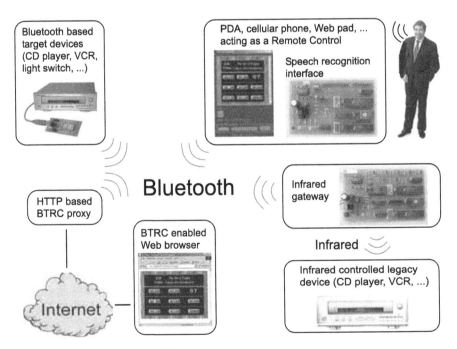

Fig. 1. System overview

In the left top of figure 1 there is an example for a controlled device. In the near future these devices will contain a cheap Bluetooth transmitter and a controller for analyzing protocol strings, operating the device and delivering stored XML pages on demand. Due to the fact that various types of remote controls offer different displaying capabilities and therefore seek different graphical user interfaces a controlled device provides a set of several XML based GUIs.

A BTRC enabled Web browser and a HTTP based BTRC proxy were implemented to show how easy conventional Web and Internet applications can be integrated into a BTRC environment (left bottom of figure 1). To prove the applicability of the BTRC approach, various types of server applications were developed. Several Bluetooth based multimedia applications were implemented to demonstrate the collaboration of BTRC and Bluetooth.

A BTRC-to-RC5-Infrared relay application that consists of both software and hardware components was designed to integrate legacy devices into a BTRC system (right bottom of figure 1). The BTRC approach is particularly pervasive because the BTRC protocol is scalable down to pieces of equipment even with very restricted computing and networking capabilities. All implementations were tested to prove the compliance with the BTRC protocol specification.

3   The BTRC Protocol

The BTRC protocol is a simple request/response based protocol. Its pursuit is to provide a simple, uniform and scalable way of information exchange between embedded as well as higher scaled devices. It allows the transfer of device commands and device information, as known from existing remote controls, and targets every device platform that offers accessible and controllable functionality. To ease the integration of BTRC into a wide range of existing device and communication technologies (e.g. consumer devices, existing applications), BTRC messages are very easy to parse, and can be mapped to hyperlinks, to which many users are already accustomed from their Web browser. Moreover, we will present some extensions of the BTRC core protocol, enlarging its remote control capabilities.

3.1   Protocol Design

Request/Response Scheme The BTRC protocol is trying to provide a simple protocol allowing the user to send device commands as he used to with a normal remote control. The BTRC protocol is request/response based: each request encapsulates a whole command to the target device. Furthermore, it is an application protocol (on OSI layer 7), and is thus transport protocol independent, requiring the implementation to use a reliable channel to transmit protocol messages. Flow control is done using a stop and wait scheme. While highly inefficient in data transmission protocols, this model is adequate for a remote control protocol, as under normal conditions few requests are send, and they mostly represent independent device commands, requiring individual acknowledgement. More complex schemes such as transmission windows are neither applicable nor necessary.

An Application Protocol Before sending BTRC requests to a target device, a client device has to establish a reliable channel using the underlying transport protocol. This can be quite resource expensive, so the BTRC protocol allows the underlying channel to be reused by making it possible to send another request after receiving a response. It is up to the specific implementation to choose reasonable timeout values if necessary, and to close the underlying channel when appropriate so as not to waste resources. As multiple devices can be attached to one communication controller (for example a radio and a cd player sharing one Bluetooth controller), BTRC requests to different target devices can be multiplexed over the underlying channel using BTRC IDs (see subsection 3.1).

Gatewaying the BTRC Protocol As the BTRC protocol does not require a BTRC message to be delivered in a special way, it can easily be gatewayed over different nodes using various transport protocols. The delivery and forwarding of a BTRC message as well as the discovering of BTRC devices has to be handled appropriately by the underlying transport protocol (see subsection 3.3 and subsection 3.3). Furthermore, the BTRC protocol can be gatewayed over other application protocols. As we designed BTRC messages so that BTRC requests could be serialized into URIs (see subsubsection 3.2), it was quite natural to implement a HTTP gateway (see subsubsection 3.3).

BTRC IDs The multiplexing of BTRC requests is achieved using BTRC IDs, which uniquely identify the receiving and the sending end of a BTRC request. BTRC IDs have to be unique in order to precisely identify a device in different networks where no common reliable characteristic can be found. 64 bit hexadecimal, permanent and uniquely assigned numbers meet these requirements. Padding up Ethernet MAC adresses or Bluetooth IDs can easily generate such an ID. This temporary solution is used up to now. In the future BTRC IDs could for example be assigned by a central instance, just as ranges of Ethernet MAC addresses are granted to network hardware manufacturers. As the BTRC protocol is a text-based protocol, switching to bigger BTRC IDs is seamless.

Device Independency The purpose of the BTRC protocol is not to provide command handling in place of the device. The BTRC protocol knows nothing about possible states of the underlying device, and cannot enforce interrequest dependencies and error handling of out of state requests. As with existing remote controls, the device has to handle inconsistent commands (a VCR still has to handle the command to play a VCR while recording in a reasonable way). However, the BTRC protocol can be used to negotiate the use of other protocols, for example to set quality of service parameters for streaming protocols.

Device Naming and Discovery Another issue which is not adressed directly by the BTRC protocol is the discovery and naming of BTRC devices. The first issue is addressed by the transport protocol, either using available functionality (see subsubsection 3.3) or storing device references into a database (see subsubsection 3.3). Moreover, a 64 bit BTRC ID, even if presented in hexadecimal form, may not be easily memorized. There is an evident need for a name service that enables the user to use symbolic names. A name service can be used to map class names or manufacturer names to the locally available devices conforming to their classes (the locally available CD player could for exemple be referenced by "cd-player" as well as his exact name). Such a name service was implemented using the DNS (Domain Name System), as described in subsubsection 3.3.

3.2   BTRC Commands

BTRC Messages The BTRC protocol is intended to be simple and its messages easy to parse. We chose a message format similar to the format of messages in the HTTP protocol. Each message is divided in a header, which uses the 8 bit ASCII encoding, and a body, which can contain any kind of data. The header contains connection, command and additional information, consisting of text lines divided into an attribute name and an attribute value, as in HTTP.

Every message header includes connection information: a source ID, identifying the source device issuing the command and a destination ID, identifying the device which has to receive the message. BTRC devices can implement additional features such as XML parsing/generation, speech control or encryption/authentication. These additional features are specified in the header as boolean attribute/value pairs. Additional information such as the body encoding is also specified in the header.

Every BTRC message is either a command request or a command response: a command attribute/value pair has to be present in the header. Most commands take parameters, which are given in additional attribute/value pairs. In case of a command response message, the parameters of the executed command are repeated in order to simplify message handling by the requesting device.

An example of a request is given below.

```
Srcid: 0x12345678
Destid: 0x87654321
Cmd: cd-play-track
Track: 01
```

Standard BTRC Commands Each BTRC device, regardless of its actual functionality, has to supply a mandatory set of standard commands: device-commands and device-attributes. This permits the client device to build a custom user interface and allows the BTRC protocol to scale well, allowing existing BTRC clients to interface correctly with new devices. When a BTRC client encounters a new device, its commands are inquired via device-commands. This request is answered with a list of all supported commands, their description and their specification. The description allows human users to directly understand the command, and allows generic clients to support unknown devices and provide online help. The `device-attributes` request is answered with an extensive description of the device, containing manufacturer information, model, type, name, production year as well as the device class (see subsubsection Device Classes).

A possible `device-commands` answer is given below.

```
cd-play-track: Play a CD Track,track,required,integer,0,99
cd-pause-duration: Pause the CD for,duration,optional,integer,0,99
xml-interface: Get an XML interface,style,required,string
device-attributes: Get the device attributes
device-commands: Get the device commands
device-description: Get the device description
```

The BTRC URI Scheme BTRC messages can be serialized to the BTRC URI scheme, which fully complies with the hierarchical subset of URIs defined in RFC 2396. Here is an example for an URI for playing the first track of a CD on a device named cd-player:

```
btrc://cd-player?cmd=cd-play-track&track=01
```

The BTRC URI scheme has been kept simple, just containing the identification of the remote device, the command and the command's parameters. As the BTRC URI scheme can be understood and remembered by humans, it is quite easy to write such URIs by hand and embed them in hyperlink documents or emails. The BTRC scheme is a "generic scheme" ("Uniform Resource Identifiers (URI): Generic Syntax", [ ]). Thus it uses an identifier for the host (either the BTRC ID or the name provided by the naming system). BTRC further supports hierarchical based resource addressing (which is not yet used). We want to emphasize that a BTRC URI is not an URL; as such an URI does not identify a resource through its location in a network but by its name. In order to test the correctness of the design decisions, the guidelines defined in RFC 2718 were applied ("Guidelines for new URL Schemes", [ ]). To demonstrate the applicability of the BTRC URI scheme a HTTP based BTRC proxy was implemented as proposed in RFC 2718 (see subsubsection 3.3). This proxy enables access to BTRC devices through the Internet.

Device Classes Several BTRC devices that offer a common set of commands create a device equivalency class (i.e. [CD player, tape recorder]). In order to simplify the handling of these commands and to avoid command clashing (many manufacturers tend to reimplement standard commands), this common set of commands is not to be modified and should be supplied whenever possible. Manufacturer consortiums could for example issue "device class specifications" on which they agree, so that generic interfaces could be integrated in control devices. Device classes, as they are standard sets of commands, enable BTRC remote controls to store standard interfaces for these devices and thus permit reuse of existing software components. For example, one could build a standard cd-player interface and use it with every device conforming to the class `cd-player`. In the future, a device class name could be mapped to the BTRC ID of an available device belonging to that device class via a BTRC name service.

Security and Privacy The BTRC protocol can be used to control security sensitive services like gates or resource consuming devices (i.e. heating, fridge). Such functionality is solely to be accessed in a secure environment. The BTRC protocol therefore has to possess some encryption and authentication mechanism. In the implementation, the OpenPGP package, using an hybrid key architecture for encryption and a public key architecture for authentication, was preferred since it is widely used and freely available. In a secure BTRC communication, each side has a private/public key pair, which it uses for both authentication and encryption. In order to set up a secure communication, the devices must trust each other. This can basically be achieved by doing manual or user controlled key exchanges. Secure BTRC communications make use of a challenge/response scheme to avoid replay attacks: the challenge is changed by the server on each message, the client then has to send it back to the server. BTRC messages can be crypted with the public key of the other side, and signed with the own secret key. This way, services requiring a secure access can request both an encrypted channel and make sure the commands are coming from an authenticated client.

3.3   Protocol Implementation

Bluetooth Integration In a Bluetooth wireless network, the reliable transport channel is provided by the Logical Link Control and Adaption Protocol (L2CAP), which provides protocol multiplexing, packet fragmentation and reliable transfer of data. However, a Bluetooth network is a moving network: it is possible for BTRC devices to move out of range of a client device, and for new ones to move in range. The inquiry procedure used for the discovery of new devices is quite time-expensive. Fortunately, periodic piconet browsing and clock resynchronization with reachable devices can improve the mean access and response time. This strategy is used in the reference implementation of a HTTP based BTRC proxy and of a BTRC remote control (see subsection 3.3 and section 4). Moreover, device discovery in a Bluetooth network can be achieved using the Bluetooth Service Discovery Protocol (SDP). Therefore, it is reasonable to map the information and attributes of a BTRC service normally provided as response to `device-attributes` and `device-commands` requests into SDP Service Records. SDP can also be used as a name service, allowing the client to refer to BTRC devices using the information found in SDP Service Records.

TCP/IP Integration The BTRC protocol can also be used over the TCP/IP transport protocol, hence BTRC messages can be transported over the entire Internet. Location and naming information can be kept in DNS databases, using a special query type and a special query class. A BTRC device can thus be found by querying the appropriate directory server. As the BTRC protocol is mostly used in order to control a small group of devices (e.g. household, home office), there is no need to provide a self-propagating, worldwide directory service. Such a service would permit users to locate and gather information about other people's property, which would be rather useless and probably unwanted by most users.

A HTTP Based BTRC Proxy There is an obvious desire to control consumer devices through the Internet. To accomplish this, BTRC messages have to be delivered using Internet protocol standards (i.e. the HTTP protocol and the browser concept as it is used in the World Wide Web). Every web browser is inherently a possible BTRC client. For that reason if must be capable of recognizing an entered BTRC URI (starting with `btrc://`). A BTRC enabled browser can deliver such a URI via a HTTP GET or PUT request to a HTTP based BTRC proxy. Such a browser was implemented both using an Internet Explorer ActiveX Control and using an embedded Mozilla component. Whenever the navigation target is a BTRC scheme URI, the browser forwards the complete URI to the BTRC proxy using a HTTP request. The appropriate BTRC proxy was implemented as well, supporting the BTRC protocol both over the Bluetooth L2CAP protocol and over the TCP/IP transport protocol. In case the BTRC request addresses a Bluetooth based device or a TCP/IP based device, the message is sent to the destination device. Otherwise, the proxy could again forward the BTRC message to a further proxy server. As HTTP is used as a transport protocol for BTRC requests, the proxy has to enforce appropriate error handling if the request cannot be sent to the end device.

Suppose now the use case example of accessing a BTRC video recorder at home while being at work. Moreover the VCR is supposed to be part of a Bluetooth piconet and the office PC connected to the Internet and running a BTRC enabled web browser. A BTRC request that is sent from the office has to be conveyed to the VCR: the web browser sends the request to the BTRC proxy at home, which will contact the VCR over Bluetooth, delivering the request and sending back the answer over HTTP to the web browser.

Protocol Requirements The BTRC protocol is a low bandwidth protocol. In fact, measurements conducted on the protocol implementation came up with following data:

Table 1. Average message length

Message type	Request	Answer
Text-only protocol	80 bytes	120 bytes
GUI (XML, XSL, Jpeg, ...)	100 bytes	6080 bytes
GUI (compressed)	90 bytes	1950 bytes

BTRC messages tend to be sent in short, high-rate bursts (when the user actually sends commands to the device, for example when setting the right volume). Even in those cases, the underlying protocol's bandwidth is left nearly untouched by the BTRC protocol.

BTRC messages were designed to be very easy to parse, while allowing for extension if the communicating devices can provide support for more elaborated formats like XML. A complete BTRC service (switching a LED on and off) using a serial transport protocol was successfully implemented on a PIC microprocessor with 2 Mhz clock frequency, 1024 words of ROM and 128 bytes of RAM, showing that the BTRC protocol requires only minimal computing resources. The virtual service implemented on a PC (switching a virtual light on and off) was able to saturate a 10 Mbps ethernet link. Even when XML is used, precalculated documents for often occuring requests can be returned, thus allowing even very simple computers to provide flexible GUIs.

4   Implementation

4.1   PDA Simulator

The BTRC protocol is to a great extent independent of the underlying hardware platform. However, to demonstrate the practicability of our approach an instance of a BTRC device representing a wireless PDA simulator extended with BTRC remote control capabilities was implemented [5]. For the purpose of a vivid impression the specification is explained below by visualizing the sequential control flow of a typical use case (see Fig. 2).

Switching on the PDA simulator via <ON/OFF> enables the <Browse Piconet> button. This function inquires the local Piconet of all BTRC devices in reach. The application internally maintains an array of all discovered Bluetooth transceivers. These devices are displayed as root nodes in the above services <Tree View Control>. A double-click on such a device expands the node and lists the services on hand by this device. These services are also internally held in a dynamic array. Certain BTRC service properties such as flags whether the service performs communication via XML or supplies a certain speech recognition vocabulary were mapped directly onto Bluetooth Service Record Attributes to minimize request/response transmission traffic. When a service is selected within the <Tree View Control> the application automatically displays a URI in the <Address Field>. The user has just to complete this string with the apposite command. All right, but: How to know what functionality a BTRC device provides? Both cases specified by the BTRC protocol were implemented:

Supposing the selected appliance does not speak XML; yet it will support the BTRC command `device-commands`. This command is applied to the device instantly when it has been selected. Since the result of this call is a list of all device commands in plain text this catalog is put out directly to the <Main Display> area (Fig. 2).

Fig. 2. PDA simulator

In case the device knows XML the command `xml-interface` will lead to a complete XML based GUI for this device displayed on the <Main Display> (Fig. 3).

For that reason the <Main Display> area is implemented by means of an Internet Explorer ActiveX Control. Because a GUI Web page comprises several items and files several distinct transmissions would be necessary. Again to reduce networking overhead all these file objects are compressed into one zip-file (so specified in the BTRC extended protocol). The BTRC device determines in advance which files are needed for its XML response. It then builds a zip-file containing exactly this collection. The BTRC remote control receives this item and extracts it. Thus obtaining the original files. In this way the number of discrete broadcasts as well as the total amount of transmitted data is reduced significantly. To finally send a command string you can submit the string contained in the <Address Field> with <ENTER>. You can of course also click

Fig. 3. XML GUI on PDA

on a BTRC hyperlink that is embedded in the XML based GUI. We want to emphasize that our PDA simulator application supports both input methods known from common Web browsers: You can both enter a URI directly and you can rely on embedded hyperlinks. In case the addressed BTRC device supports XML communication the BTRC remote control even gets a response through an updated XML based GUI. For such a use case please refer to section 4.2.

4.2 BTRC CD Player

The BTRC CD Player simulator is a potential counterpart to the BTRC remote control simulator. Basically it is a windows application able to play CDs via an ActiveX Control and beyond capable of Bluetooth communication. This BTRC CD player is derived from a generic BTRC server application that was developed before. This generic server can easily be extended to implement a concrete device,

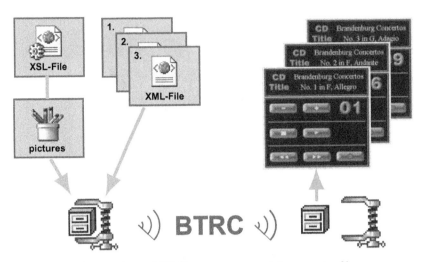

Fig. 4. Several XML pages are sent in one zip-file

which then provides its functionality to clients in that way that it acts as a BTRC server. This implies that it exports Bluetooth properties indicating it is a BTRC device. An own Class Of Device [ ] and dedicated device and service names were defined to enable a purposeful service search for each device since there is interest only in finding a possible BTRC functionality of a certain device. Of course such Bluetooth specific definitions are as usual subject to the approval of an official instance (e.g. Bluetooth SIG members). The packaging of a BTRC device can be extremely simple. The screenshot of figure 5 shows an example of a BTRC device. Actually you can completely omit any LEDs, switches and buttons that have made the manufacture of consumer devices tremendously expensive until now. Access to a BTRC device is completely wireless. These devices will appeal

Fig. 5. BTRC CD-Player

to prospective buyers with a well developed XML based GUI set that adapts to a wide range of BTRC remote control devices. Our CD Player simulator fully complies with the BTRC protocol specification and provides the functionality of a very simple real life CD Player. The `device-commands` BTRC request delivers a plain text response as seen in Fig. 2. The output as seen in Fig. 3 is a result of an `xml-interface` request. Supposing now that the CD Player has been discovered by a BTRC remote control and has already sent its XML based GUI. Then the BTRC command

    btrc://0x123456781234?cmd=cd-play-track&track=07

will start the device playing track number seven and send an updated XML based GUI to the remote control that contains for instance the refreshed number, remaining time and title of the current track.

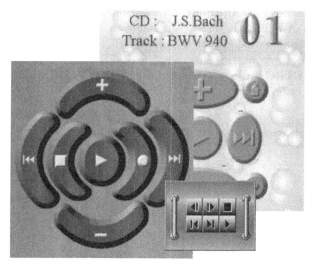

Fig. 6. Different XML GUIs

4.3   Legacy Infrared Devices under the Control of BTRC

Until now the power of the BTRC protocol has only been demonstrated by either Bluetooth wireless technology or a complex HTTP and TCP/IP based protocol stack. But there are billions of infrared controlled consumer devices. They can neither run a Bluetooth stack nor will they ever join the Internet via an IP based network connection. Instead they are accessed by an infrared remote control. This was taken into account when BTRC was developed. Due to the fact that there are already several established infrared remote control standards we decided to implement a BTRC-to-RC5 gateway since RC5 is by far the most widely used one. The basic idea of such a relay is that there are, as we think of a home automation environment, accumulations of consumer devices in certain rooms (e.g. in a living room there may be a TV set, a VCR, a CD player and a tape recorder). They all seek infrared commands. These commands are supplied by a BTRC-to-RC5 gateway that is for example attached to the living room ceiling. This relay may either be connected to the Internet or possessing a Bluetooth transceiver and thus be accessible by BTRC clients using the methods and technologies already introduced above. The relay must only be set up once with a mapping of BTRC commands onto infrared codes. Since a single BTRC-to-RC5 gateway might be responsible for more than one legacy device multiplexing incoming requests to several infrared receivers was also taken into consideration. In case of addressing RC5 devices this is pretty easy because the RC5 protocol specification already provides a scheme of device "addresses". Consequently distinguishing between BTRC IDs and identifiers of underlying transport protocols avoids ambiguities in case of a 1:n relation between a relay and its infrared receivers. It is possible to supply several Bluetooth Service Records with information about numerous BTRC services from one Bluetooth transceiver. The reference implementation of such a BTRC-to-RC5 gateway is a normal MS Windows application. Again this instance (of a BTRC server!) is derived from the same generic BTRC server application just like the also Bluetooth based BTRC CD player (section 4.2).

5   Summary

The objective of this work was to realize a universal remote control system. An application layer protocol was developed to provide uniform access to devices. A complete remote control system was developed based on this specification. This system consists of the following implementations:

- Bluetooth based PDA simulator
- Speech recognition interface
- BTRC enabled Web browser
- HTTP based BTRC proxy
- Generic BTRC server template
- Several BTRC server applications (CD player, MS Power Point, etc.)
- BTRC-to-RC5-Infrared gateway

The BTRC approach is pervasive, scalable, uniform, completely wireless and by means of speech recognition highly user-friendly. Its simplicity makes development of BTRC devices fast and easy. Even infrared controlled legacy devices were integrated into our remote control system. The range of a Bluetooth based remote control was extended to the entire Internet. We expect that in the near future Bluetooth based remote control systems will replace other existing solutions.

References

1. T. Berners-Lee (CERN) "Universal Resource Identifiers in WWW" Network Working Group Request for Comments: 1630 242, 246
2. T. Berners-Lee (MIT/LCS), R. Fielding (U. C. Irvine), L. Masinter (Xerox Corporation) "Uniform Resource Identifiers (URI): Generic Syntax" Network Working Group Request for Comments: 2396 242
3. L. Masinter (Xerox Corporation), H. Alvestrand (Maxware), D. Zigmond (WebTV Networks, Inc.), R.Petke (UUNET Technologies) "Guidelines for new URL Schemes" Network Working Group Request for Comments: 2718 242, 246
4. http://www.bluetooth.com/developer/specification/core.asp Document: Bluetooth_11_PartH1_HCI.pdf 252
5. F. Feldbusch, G. Bocksch, G. Dummer, I. Ivanov, M. Odendahl, A. Paar: "The Universal BTRC Remote Control System"; IEEE Computer Science International Design Competition (CSIDC) 2001, Washington, 23.7- 25.7.2001 249

Rendezvous Layer Protocols for Bluetooth-Enabled Smart Devices*

Frank Siegemund and Michael Rohs

Distributed Systems Group, Institute of Information Systems
Swiss Federal Institute of Technology (ETH) Zurich, 8092 Zurich, Switzerland
{siegemun,rohs}@inf.ethz.ch

Abstract. Communication platforms for ubiquitous computing need to be flexible, self-organizing, highly scalable and energy efficient, because in the envisioned scenarios a large number of autonomous entities communicate in potentially unpredictable ways. Short-range wireless technologies form the basis of such communication platforms. In this paper we investigate device discovery in Bluetooth, a candidate wireless technology for ubiquitous computing. Detecting new devices accounts for a significant portion of the total energy consumption in Bluetooth. It is argued that the standard Bluetooth rendezvous protocols for device detection are not well suited for ubiquitous computing scenarios, because they do not scale to a large number of devices, take too long to complete, and consume too much energy. Based on theoretical considerations, practical experiments and simulation results, recommendations for choosing inquiry parameters that optimize discovery performance are given. We propose an adaptive rendezvous protocol that significantly increases the performance of the inquiry procedure by implementing cooperative device discovery. Also higher level methods to optimize discovery performance, specifically the use of sensory data and context information, are considered.

1 Introduction

Ubiquitous computing [,] envisions that information technology is present throughout the physical environment, integrated in a broad range of everyday objects. Thereby, information technology becomes omnipresent but at the same time also invisible to users. Everyday items are augmented with self-awareness and awareness of their surroundings in order to provide new functionality and novel interaction patterns.

A first step towards this vision is to attach small computing devices to everyday objects. Smart things sense their surroundings and cooperate with one another. Information processing takes place autonomously in the background, unsupervised by human beings. To collect information about their surroundings,

---

* Part of this work was conducted in the Smart-Its project, which is funded by the European Commission (contract No. IST-2000-25428) and the Swiss Federal Office for Education and Science (BBW No. 00.0281).

H. Schmeck, T. Ungerer, and L. Wolf (Eds.): ARCS 2002, LNCS 2299, pp. 256–273, 2002.

smart artifacts need to be equipped with sensors for various physical parameters. To cooperate with other entities, e.g. to distribute collected sensor data or to use services offered by other entities, smart artifacts need to be able to communicate.

The communication of smart objects poses several challenging problems: the communication technology must be unobtrusive; the scarce radio resources must be used effectively in order to achieve scalability; communication must happen without mediation, spontaneously and without administration; previously unknown devices have to be discovered automatically; a wide range of communication patterns and traffic volumes must be accommodated for; and the least energy possible must be used.

In the Smart-Its project [ ] small computing devices – so-called *Smart-Its* – were developed that are attached to everyday items providing them with collective awareness and supporting intelligent collaborative behavior. As a communication platform we investigate low-power fixed-frequency modules as well as Bluetooth [ ], which is a frequency-hopping system. Fig. 1 shows a Smart-It equipped with a Bluetooth module and an attached sensor board [ ].

One reason for using Bluetooth in the Smart-Its project is that frequency-hopping as a spread-spectrum technique offers higher robustness and scalability than fixed-frequency systems. Smart-Its are designed to operate in areas with dozens of devices in range and are going to be equipped not only with standard sensors for temperature and acceleration but also with more data intensive sensors such as low resolution cameras. Hence, scalability in terms of number of devices in communication range and volume of data traffic is crucial.

The issue we focus on in this paper is the discovery of new devices, which is a necessary task for each device in an ad hoc network. Device detection is an essential part of the rendezvous layer. The challenge is to find all potential communication partners present in communication range using the shortest time and the least amount of energy possible. This issue is critical if a huge number of devices are present as in the scenarios envisioned. Although Bluetooth seems to be a promising technology for ubiquitous computing, the insufficient scalability and high energy consumption of its rendezvous layer limit its applicability.

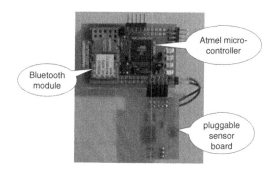

Fig. 1. A Bluetooth-enabled Smart-Its prototype

While investigating Bluetooth, we found that the Bluetooth modes for device detection – INQUIRY and INQUIRY SCAN – consume significantly more energy than normal receive and transmit modes. For the modules used in the Smart-Its project, energy consumption in INQUIRY mode is approximately twice as high as in transmit mode [12, 1]. Therefore, our goal in this paper is to reduce the energy consumption of Bluetooth's rendezvous layer during device discovery, while at the same time increasing its scalability. This is achieved through appropriate settings for the inquiry parameters, an adaptive protocol for cooperative device discovery, and the utilization of context information.

Due to a limited number of available Bluetooth modules and their restricted functionality, the performance evaluation of Bluetooth's rendezvous layer and of the proposed adaptions are based on simulation results with the Network Simulator (ns-2) [15] and BlueHoc [10], an open-source Bluetooth simulator provided by IBM. Considerable extensions of BlueHoc were necessary to carry out the simulation experiments described in this paper.

The remainder of the paper is structured as follows: Section 2 motivates the need for a rendezvous layer in ad-hoc networks in general. Section 3 introduces the Bluetooth inquiry procedure in particular, while section 4 evaluates its performance in terms of time to complete, energy consumption, and scalability. Section 5 discusses how to set the Bluetooth inquiry parameters in order to optimize performance. In section 6 we present an adaptive rendezvous layer protocol that optimizes discovery performance in settings with many devices present. In section 7 several possibilities for the utilization of context information in device discovery are explored. We conclude with a general judgement of the Bluetooth discovery process and give some suggestions for improvements.

2   The Rendezvous Layer

In mobile ad hoc environments of smart devices, units initially posses no information about nearby devices, and no centralized instance exists where devices can acquire information about their environment. Therefore, protocols are needed that provide energy-efficient means for detecting new devices and enable peer communications in mobile environments. The rendezvous layer contains such protocols. A rendezvous layer for fixed-frequency systems introduced in [4] provides a mechanism for node discovery using a beaconing approach and implements power saving meachnisms that allow units to be put in sleep modes between communication periods. Our approach to the rendezvous layer is different in that we concentrate on Bluetooth's device discovery and try to minimize power consumption by minimizing the time units have to stay in power-consuming device detection modes. Scheduled rendezvous are not an issue of this paper.

The rendezvous layer enables devices to communicate with each other by helping them to find potential communication partners. The actual data traffic after connection establishment, however, does not flow through the rendezvous layer. The term "layer" might therefore be misleading, but it emphasizes that the results of rendezvous layer protocols are a precondition for communication

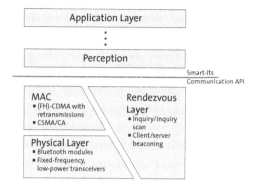

Fig. 2. Communication platform architecture for smart devices

and that every mobile node generally needs to use rendezvous protocols to be able to connect to other devices.

Fig. 2 shows a possible communication platform architecture for smart devices. The actual position of the rendezvous layer strongly depends on the concrete design. It is possible that it reaches down to the hardware layer, e.g. when low-power RF detection circuits are used to detect other devices. For fixed-frequency systems, [1] distinguishes between client and server beaconing. In the envisioned ubiquitous computing application scenarios there are no fixed client/server roles. Hence, it seems advantageous to distinguish between dynamically assigned roles such as service provider and service consumer. In general each device acts both as service provider and service consumer.

The rendezvous layer for frequency hopping systems is more complicated than for fixed-frequency solutions. This is mainly due to an initial frequency discrepancy between devices. Frequency hopping systems also result in a much higher energy consumption of the rendezvous layer compared to fixed-frequency systems. In Bluetooth, the rendezvous layer mainly consists of the INQUIRY and INQUIRY SCAN procedures.

3   Bluetooth's Inquiry Procedure

The Bluetooth standard introduces an INQUIRY procedure for device detection and a PAGE procedure for connection establishment. Both are asymmetric processes initiated by the unit that wants to collect device information or create a connection. The initiating unit spends significantly more energy than the unit that is inquired or paged, because it stays in INQUIRY or PAGE mode for a long time whereas the other device enters a scanning mode only periodically for short time intervals. The PAGE and INQUIRY procedures resemble each other in that they both have to overcome an initial frequency discrepancy between devices. However, the paging unit has an estimate of the scanning unit's current clock which was acquired during a preceding inquiry.

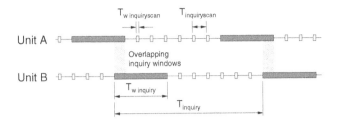

Fig. 3. Important inquiry parameters

During the inquiry process, the unit that wants to find devices in communication range periodically enters the INQUIRY state. Devices that want to advertise their presence and thereby agree to be found by other devices enter the IN-QUIRY SCAN state regularly. Typically, in the envisioned application scenarios devices enter both states, INQUIRY and INQUIRY SCAN, in certain time intervals. But in order to ensure that two devices find each other, one has to be in INQUIRY and the other in INQUIRY SCAN state simultaneously. To prevent devices from synchronizing their inquiry states, the time between the start of two consecutive inquiries, $T_{inquiry}$, has to be randomly distributed in an interval $[T_{inquiry}^{min}, T_{inquiry}^{max}]$. Fig. 3 and Tab. 1 show the parameters influencing Bluetooth's inquiry procedure.

The device in INQUIRY state broadcasts ID packets on different frequencies at twice the usual hopping rate. That is, it sends two ID packets in a 625 μs wide slot, and afterwards listens for 625μs for responses from other devices. This is repeated for the duration of the entire inquiry window, $T_{w\ inquiry}$, which is typically in the range of several seconds. There exists a unique inquiry hopping sequence comprising 32 frequencies[1] on which an inquirer sends out ID packets. This sequence is the same for all devices, only the phase within the sequence is determined by the native clock $CLKN$ of the inquiring unit and therefore specific for each device. Furthermore, for each 1.28 s the inquiry hopping sequence is divided into two disjunct, consecutive trains A and B, each containing 16 frequencies. The inquirer needs $T_{train} = 10\ ms$ to both send on all frequencies in a single train and check for potential responses. According to the Bluetooth specification [ ], the frequencies in "a single train must be repeated for at least $N_{inquiry} = 256$ times before a new train is used". The phase X_p in the inquiry hopping sequence that determines the frequency at which ID packets are transmitted is calculated as follows:

$$X_p = [CLKN_{16-12} + k_{\text{offset}} + (CLKN_{4-2,0} - CLKN_{16-12})\,mod\,16]\,mod\,32 \quad (1)$$

In equation 1, $CLKN_{x-y,z}$ denotes bits x to y and bit z of the inquiring unit's native clock. $k_{\text{offset}} \in \{24, 8\}$ selects the active train A or B of the inquirer. k_{offset}

---

[1] This paper concentrates on Bluetooth's 79 hop system because it is applied in the vast majority of countries in the European Union and in the USA. In case of the reduced hop system, the inquiry hopping sequence contains only 16 frequencies.

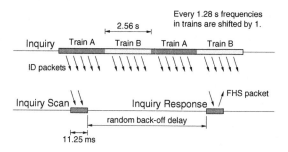

Fig. 4. Overview of the inquiry procedure

is changed after a single train is repeated $N_{inquiry}$ times. The frequencies within each train are shifted by one phase every 1.28 s, since after this time $CLKN_{16-12}$ changes. CLKN has a resolution of 312.5 μs. $(CLKN_{4-2,0} - CLKN_{16-12}) \, mod \, 16$ determines the phase within each train. The expression $CLKN_{16-12}$ is necessary to avoid omitting a frequency when $CLKN_{16-12}$ changes, since this could lead to a repetitive mismatch between inquiring and scanning unit.

The device that agrees to be found enters the INQUIRY SCAN state periodically. The time between two consecutive inquiry scans is determined by the inquiry scan interval $T_{inqscan}$. The inquiry scan window, $T_{w\,inqscan}$, specifies the time a unit stays in INQUIRY SCAN mode. During that time the unit listens at a single frequency in the inquiry hopping sequence for ID packets from the inquirer. The current phase in the inquiry hopping sequence is determined by its native clock [ ]:

$$X_p = CLKN_{16-12}. \tag{2}$$

The Bluetooth standard defines $T_{w\,inqscan} \geq T_{train} = 10 \, ms$ in order to ensure that a frequency synchronization between inquiring and scanning unit takes place when the scanning frequency is in the currently active train of the inquirer. Also, the condition $T_{inqscan} \leq 2.56 \, s$ must hold. When the unit in INQUIRY SCAN mode receives an ID packet, it leaves the INQUIRY SCAN mode for a random backoff delay which is evenly distributed between $[0, \ldots, 639.375] \, ms$. This reduces the probability that units simultaneously transmit response packets on the same frequency. Afterwards, the unit enters INQUIRY RESPONSE state and again listens for ID packets of the inquiring unit. When the unit in INQUIRY RESPONSE state achieves frequency synchronization, it transmits a packet containing device information such as its current clock timing and its Bluetooth device address to the inquirer.

4   Performance of Bluetooth's Inquiry Procedure

A characteristic feature of ubiquitous computing settings is the presence of many highly autonomous, mobile devices with distinctive resource restrictions in a

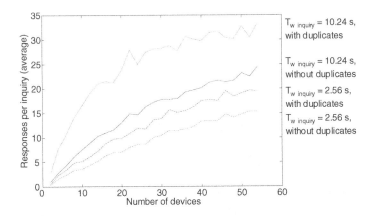

Fig. 5. Responses during inquiry subject to the number of devices in range considering different inquiry windows

relatively small area. The aspects of scalability, energy consumption, and device detection delay are therefore crucial when evaluating Bluetooth's rendezvous protocols.

According to datasheets [14] and experimental measurements [12], the energy consumption in INQUIRY and INQUIRY SCAN state is approximately twice as high as in normal receive and transmit modes. The Bluetooth standard suggests that devices could enter INQUIRY mode for 10.24 s every minute. This means that Bluetooth devices would spend approximately 17% of their lifetime in INQUIRY mode. Besides an unacceptably high energy consumption, this also leads to poor performance if many devices are present. Above all, in INQUIRY mode a Bluetooth unit cannot actively exchange application data with other devices. Fig. 5 shows the average number of responses during inquiry subject to the number of potential communication partners in range. It indicates that in the presence of only a limited number of devices practically all units are found, when $T_{w\,inquiry}$ is chosen as suggested in the standard. It also indicates that performance deteriorates as the number of devices grows, in that a smaller and smaller portion of devices are discovered. The reasons are manifold and are discussed in more detail in the following sections:

- Because of a long random backoff delay, $T_{w\,inqscan}$ must be very large when the scanning unit is supposed to answer more than once during one scan window. Large scan windows are undesirable because they are repeatedly blocking the device.
- Since the relative clock differences of Bluetooth units remain unchanged, a unit tends to answer the same device in consecutive INQUIRY SCAN intervals (cf. equations 1 and 2). Fig. 5 shows that the overall number of responses is sufficiently high, but the same device often answers the same inquirer in consecutive inquiry scan intervals. This prevents the device from responding to other devices. Only in INQUIRY RESPONSE state an offset is added to the

scanning frequency after each response. However, multiple responses during a single inquiry scan window are only possible when the window is relatively large, which is undesirable in the envisioned application scenarios.

- Large $\frac{T_{w\,inquiry}}{T_{inquiry}}$ values lead to high numbers of overlapping inquiry windows where the devices cannot find each other.

Regarding scalability and energy consumption the rendezvous layer must be designed to support inquiry parameter settings such that

- the overall time a unit has to stay in INQUIRY and INQUIRY SCAN modes is minimized,
- the probability for overlapping INQUIRY and INQUIRY SCAN states is maximized,
- the probability for overlapping INQUIRY modes in different units is reduced, and
- the time for the frequency synchronization delay between inquiring and inquired device is as low as possible.

Decreasing the value of $\frac{T_{w\,inquiry}}{T_{inquiry}}$ leads to fewer overlapping inquiry intervals. Since $T_{inquiry}$ cannot be predetermined but generally depends on sensory input and application restrictions, one purpose of the rendezvous layer is to decrease $T_{w\,inquiry}$, the inquiry window. Small $T_{w\,inquiry}$ values reduce the energy consumption and decrease the number of duplicate responses and overlapping inquiry intervals. However, $T_{w\,inquiry}$ cannot be decreased arbitrarily. Fig. 5 shows the average number of devices found during a 2.56 s compared to a 10.24 s inquiry window subject to the number of devices in range. In 2.56 s the inquirer can probe only at a single train, which limits the number of responses. But compared to $T_{winquiry} = 10.24$ s, in the presence of many devices fewer duplicate responses are received, much less energy is consumed, and proportionally more devices are found. In settings with many devices, increasing $T_{w\,inquiry}$ will not result in the discovery of significantly more devices, because the devices will block each other. Even with large inquiry windows, in settings with many devices not all devices in range are found.

5 Inquiry and Inquiry Scan Settings

Device discovery in Bluetooth is performed in the INQUIRY and INQUIRY SCAN procedures which are controlled by various parameters. These are shown in Fig. 3 and Tab. 1. $T_{inquiry}$ and $T_{inqscan}$ denote the interval between the start of two consecutive inquiries and inquiry scans, respectively. $T_{w\,inquiry}$ and $T_{w\,inqscan}$ specify the duration of a single inquiry and inquiry scan, respectively. $N_{devices}^{max}$ depends on the memory restrictions of a device in that it restricts the number of inquiry responses that are processed. As pointed out before, $T_{inquiry}$ depends on specific applications and sensory input. Therefore, the rendezvous layer does not influence $T_{inquiry}$ and $N_{devices}^{max}$ settings. The train repetition number $N_{inquiry}$

Table 1. Inquiry and inquiry scan parameters

Parameter	Description
$T_{inquiry}$	inquiry interval
$T_{w\,inquiry}$	inquiry window, $T_{w\,inquiry} \leq T_{inquiry}$
$T_{inqscan}$	inquiry scan interval, $T_{inqscan} \leq 2.56\ s$ [ ]
$T_{w\,inqscan}$	inquiry scan window, $T_{train} = 10\ ms^2 \leq T_{w\,inqscan} \leq T_{inqscan}$
$N_{devices}^{max}$	maximum number of responses processed in a single inquiry
$N_{inquiry}$	train repetition number, $N_{inquiry} \geq 256$ (predefined, fixed)

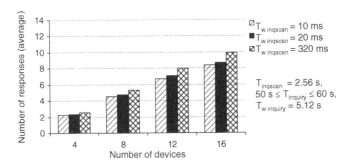

Fig. 6. Average number of devices found during inquiry subject to $T_{w\,inqscan}$ and number of devices in range, $T_{inqscan} = 2.56\ s$

defines the number of times a single train is repeated by the inquirer before a new train is used.

5.1 The Inquiry Scan Window

A suitable value for the inquiry scan window is the minimal setting $T_{w\,inqscan} = T_{train} = 10\ ms^2$. Here, T_{train} is the time period for the inquirer to send at all $N_{train} = 16$ frequencies in the active train. $T_{w\,inqscan}$ should only be increased when $N_{inquiry}$ is noticeable smaller than 256 (which is not the case in Bluetooth), because the inquirer consecutively sends on more than N_{train} frequencies only when it switches between different trains. This happens just every $T_{train} * N_{inquiry}$ seconds and would not justify the additional time a unit would have to spend in INQUIRY SCAN mode.

In an error-free environment, $T_{w\,inqscan} = T_{train}$ seems to be the best choice. However, in ubiquitous computing application scenarios where the probability of packet loss is relatively high, we suggest to choose $T_{w\,inqscan} = 2 * T_{train} = 20\ ms$ to ensure that an inquirer can send ID packets at each frequency in its active train twice. If the ID packet that was sent at the scanning frequency gets lost, the inquirer can send it again at this frequency. Fig. 6 and 7 show

---

[2] The definition of the Write_Inquiry_Scan_Activity HCI command says that $T_{w\,inqscan} \geq 11.25\ ms$.

the average number of devices found during inquiry considering inquiry scan windows of varying length in an error-free environment. Noticeably more devices are only found when $T_{w\,inqscan}$ is substantially increased, because in this case the probability that a train switch takes place during scanning is significantly higher. However, since all connections have to be suspended during scanning, substantially increasing $T_{w\,inqscan}$ is not recommendable. Instead, as Fig. 6 and 7 suggest, decreasing the inquiry scan interval is much more effective regarding both energy consumption and the number of devices found. Increasing $T_{w\,inqscan}$ by a factor of 32 from 10 ms to 320 ms is not as effective as lowering $T_{inqscan}$ from 2.56 s to 1 s regarding the number of devices that are found during inquiry and the energy consumed.

5.2   The Inquiry Scan Interval

The inquiry scan interval, $T_{inqscan}$, denotes the time between the start of two consecutive inquiry scans. The condition $T_{inqscan} \leq 2.56\ s$ must hold. $T_{inqscan}$ is chosen such that the overall energy consumption of the whole system of participating nodes is reduced. Consequently, the scan interval can be shortened when in return the inquiry window of other devices can be reduced. Since every unit generally attains both inquiry and inquiry scan modes regularly, this is beneficial for the whole system of smart devices as well as for single units. A module in continuous INQUIRY mode consumes significantly more energy than in periodic INQUIRY SCAN mode when the inquiry scan window is sufficiently small as suggested in section 5.1.

$T_{inqscan}$ can be used to control the accessibility of single devices. A short inquiry scan interval entails that the device can easily be found by other devices. On the other hand, a low value of $T_{inqscan}$ also means that the device might respond more often to the same device during consecutive inquiry windows.

In order to decrease the time a unit has to stay in continuous INQUIRY mode it is desirable that the first and second frequency synchronization before and after the random backoff delay (cf. Fig. 4) take place before a train switch in the inquiring unit occurs. Since a train switch takes place every $T_{train} * N_{inquiry}$ seconds, a first approximation for a suitable $T_{inqscan}$ is

$$T_{inqscan} \leq T_{train} * N_{inquiry} - RB_{max} - T_{train} \qquad (3)$$

Here, $RB_{max} = 639.375\ ms$ is the maximum random backoff delay. For the standard settings and $N_{inquiry} = 256$ this results to $T_{inqscan} \leq 1910.625\ ms$.

The above settings ensure that when there are only two devices and one of them enters INQUIRY mode, the inquirer has to stay in inquiry mode for only $5.12\ s$ (instead of $10.24\ s$) to find the other device with high probability. Especially in the presence of many devices it is worthwhile to decrease $T_{inqscan}$ further. A lower value than $1910.625\ ms$ leads to a higher energy consumption for scanning. But on the other hand, $T_{w\,inquiry}$ can be reduced to $N_{inquiry} * T_{train} + T_{inqscan} + RB_{max} + T_{train}$. Furthermore, a device with a short inquiry scan interval can respond to other devices more frequently.

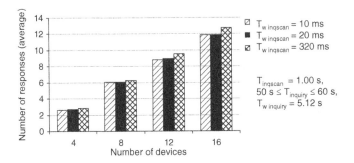

Fig. 7. Average number of devices found during inquiry considering a different value for $T_{inqscan}$ (1.00 s) compared to Fig. 6 (2.56 s)

5.3   The Inquiry Window

The inquiry window, $T_{w\,inquiry}$, denotes the time a unit continuously stays in INQUIRY mode. Since INQUIRY is a mode with very high energy consumption, $T_{w\,inquiry}$ should be as low as possible. In settings with a low number of Bluetooth devices, a unit might prolong the inquiry window until no new devices are found for a certain amount of time. However, as shown before (cf. section 4) in environments with a large number of devices, prolonged inquiry windows make the rendezvous layer inefficient because of overlapping inquiry windows, high energy consumption, and decreased accessibility of inquiring devices. Furthermore, even in settings with large inquiry windows it cannot be assured that all potential communication partners are found.

When equation 3 holds for all devices $d \in D$ in communication range, a good lower bound for the inquiry window parameter would be $T_{w\,inquiry} = \max_{d \in D}\{(\lfloor \frac{T_{train}*N_{inquiry}}{T_{inqscan}(d)} \rfloor + 1) * T_{inqscan}(d)\} + RB_{max}$, where D is the set of devices in range and $T_{inqscan}(d)$ the inquiry scan interval of device d. This setting ensures that without overlapping inquiry windows and only a few devices in range all potential communication partners can be found with high probability.

A generally appropriate setting for $T_{w\,inquiry}$ is $T_{w\,inquiry} = 2 * N_{inquiry} * T_{train} = 5.12$ s, when $T_{inqscan}$ and $T_{w\,inqscan}$ are selected as recommended in the previous sections. This enables the inquiring device to probe at frequencies in both trains for an equal amount of time and provides sufficient time to select responses. On the other hand the number of duplicate responses is relatively low and the energy consumption is much lower than for the suggested 10.24 s in the Bluetooth standard.

However, $T_{w\,inquiry} = 5.12$ s might be a suboptimal choice for environments with only few devices and is still very energy consuming. The next section deals with an adaptive protocol for Bluetooth-enabled smart devices that performs well independently of the number of devices present and further reduces $T_{w\,inquiry}$ to save energy.

6 An Adaptive Rendezvous Layer Protocol for Cooperative Device Discovery

The performance of the standard Bluetooth inquiry procedure is sufficient for settings with a limited number of devices in communication range. But the performance decreases significantly with a rising number of units. In such environments only a fraction of the potential communication partners are found – even when $T_{w\,inquiry}$ is high. Unfortunately, large values for $T_{w\,inquiry}$ result in many duplicate responses, overlapping inquiry windows, and poor overall performance (cf. section 4).

In settings with many devices, it is more appropriate to discover devices in a cooperative fashion. Cooperative device discovery splits up the task of finding communication partners between multiple units. One idea is to let only one or two units per piconet [5] handle rendezvous tasks on behalf of the whole piconet; another is to utilize inquiry results of other devices that responded during inquiry. The goal of such measures is to reduce the overall number of devices that take part in inquiry and the overall time units have to stay in INQUIRY mode in order to discover more devices in less time using less energy.

In the adaptive protocol proposed here, a unit starts inquiry for a certain time window and accumulates responses from other devices. Although units do not know how many devices are in range, they can estimate their number considering the number of devices that responded during the first seconds of an inquiry. When, after a given time interval, more devices than a predetermined threshold were discovered, it concludes that many devices are in range, stops the inquiry, builds up connections to some of those devices, and gets further discovery information from them. By selecting devices with appropriate clock values, this can be done in such a way that a large subset of the available devices is covered, as explained below.

The advantage of this approach is that it splits up the responsibility for inquiry between different nodes and, more importantly, that the time interval after which inquiry is canceled when a sufficient number of responses are accumulated can be very short. In fact, we suggest a value of only 2.56 s. During this interval an inquirer only inquires at frequencies in a single train since $T_{train} * N_{inquiry} \geq 2.56\ s$ (cf. section 3). That is, in the average case only 50% of devices in range can be found during the first phase of the protocol. However, the timing information transferred during inquiry responses enables the original inquirer to identify devices that during their inquiries discover a subset of devices not found by direct inquiry. It might seem that connecting to another device consumes the energy saved by a shorter inquiry for the paging process – which is also very energy intensive. But since the timing information of this device were transferred during a recent inquiry response, connection establishment is almost instantaneous. The simulation results show that the overall execution time for the adaptive protocol is only slightly longer than the interval after which the actual inquiry is stopped.

In the following, the algorithm for the inquirer is depicted. The inquiry scan settings in participating Bluetooth units should be chosen as described in section 5. The protocol can be implemented on top of Bluetooth's Host Controller Interface (HCI) without changing lower layers of Bluetooth. An initialization for all Bluetooth-enabled smart devices should include enabling page and inquiry scans (HCI_Write_Scan_Enable) and setting the inquiry and page parameters (HCI_Write_Inquiry_Scan_Activity, HCI_Write_Page_Scan_Activity). Furthermore, the page timeout should be chosen as low as possible in order to prevent a device from paging a unit that left its communication range for a long time (HCI_Write_Page_Timeout). After sending inquiry responses, units should enter PAGE SCAN state to ensure fast connection establishment.

BRLP (Bluetooth Rendezvous Layer Protocol)
Input:
　　Inquiry settings for inquirer: $T_{inquiry} \in [T_{inquiry}^{min}, T_{inquiry}^{max}]$, $T_{w\,inquiry}$, $N_{devices}^{max}$
　　Time interval for normal inquiry: BRLP_timeout
　　Threshold for device responses: BRLP_size
　　Number of devices to retrieve discovery information from: N_{select}
Output:
　　Bluetooth device addresses and clock settings of devices

```
ensure(T_inquiry^min > T_w inquiry)
inqtimer = random(T_inquiry^min, T_inquiry^max)
do forever
    if time_over(inqtimer) then
        responses.delete()
        HCI_Inquiry(ALL_DEVICES, T_w inquiry, N_devices^max)
        inqtimer = random(T_inquiry^min, T_inquiry^max)
        BRLP_timer = BRLP_timeout
    end if
end do


inquiry_response_event_handler(Inquiry_Response_Event e)
begin
    response = e.getResponse()
    responses.add(response)
        if not time_over(BRLP_timer) and responses.size > BRLP_size then
            HCI_Inquiry_Cancel()
            selected_responses = responses.select(N_select)
            for all sr in selected_responses do
                HCI_Create_Connection(sr)³
            end for
        end if
end
connection_complete_event_handler(Connection_Complete_Event e)
begin
    get_assembled_devices(e.connection_handle);
end
```

The suggested protocol decreases the level of confidence in the obtained results, because they are partially retrieved indirectly from other devices and might refer to units outside the communication range. This is not a severe problem, because direct results might also be inaccurate – e.g. obsolete because of mobility – and the algorithm has to deal with uncertain results anyway. Section 7 shows how sensory input can be used to decrease this uncertainty. Also, in order to inhibit error propagation, a unit is only allowed to pass on discovery information that it learned from its own most recent inquiry procedure. A low value for BRLP_size means that only a few inquiry results are available to be transferred to other devices. This entails that this parameter should be adapted after each inquiry process. A variation of the described protocol is to carry out normal inquiry for a certain amount of time (for example 2.56 s) regardless of the number of devices found during this inquiry window. When more than a given threshold of units have been found after this period, connections to some of these devices are established and discovery information is requested.

To clarify the performance of the adaptive part of the algorithm, Fig. 8 shows the average number of devices found considering a very low value for BRLP_size. It considers only the cases in which after 2.56 s inquiry connections to other devices are established to request discovery information. From the set of inquiry results two devices are selected to retrieve further discovery information from ($N_{selected} = 2$). The selection criteria are explained below. The average total time for the initial 2.56 s inquiry, connection establishment, and transfer of discovery information from the two selected devices was 3.44 s. Compared to normal inquiry with $T_{winquiry} = 10.24\ s$ a better performance regarding the number of responses is achieved, and the time a unit has to stay in inquiry mode is reduced significantly. Therefore, the adaptive protocol results in substantial energy savings, enables units to enter energy-saving modes more frequently, and leaves more time for application specific tasks.

The selection of units to retrieve discovery information from is important for the performance of the adaptive algorithm. The retrieved discovery information is only useful if it contains inquiry results from devices not already found by direct inquiry. The probability for this is highest, when devices with appropriate clock offsets are selected. The clock offsets are part of the inquiry results.

When the timeout for the initial inquiry, BRLP_timeout, is lower than or equal to $T_{train} * N_{inquiry} = 2.56\ s$ – which is desirable regarding energy consumption – only the frequencies of a single train are inquired. Let I be the inquiring and S a scanning unit that responded to I during the initial inquiry window. $CLKN^I_{16-12}$ and $CLKN^S_{16-12}$ shall be bits 12 to 16 of the native clock of I and S, respectively. The frequencies at which I inquires and S scans only depend on $CLKN^I_{16-12}$ and $CLKN^S_{16-12}$ (cf. equations 1 and 2). Let the first active train during inquiry be train A. Then, the phases of the frequencies in the active train are $[CLKN^I_{16-12} - 8, \ldots, CLKN^I_{16-12} + 7]$ (mod 32). When $CLKN^S_{16-12} \in [CLKN^I_{16-12} - 8, \ldots, CLKN^I_{16-12} + 7]$ during one inquiry scan interval this will also be the case during all successive inquiry scan

---

[3] See the definition of HCI_Create_Connection for the exact sequence of parameters.

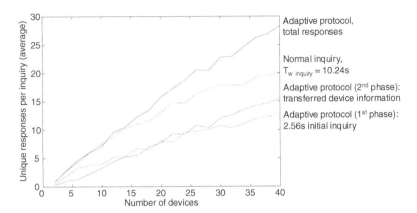

Fig. 8. Average number of discovery responses accumulated with the adaptive protocol ($N_{selected} = 2$)

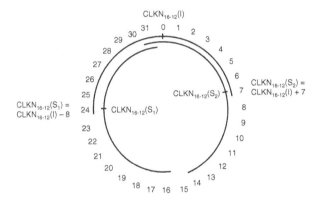

Fig. 9. Phases covered by different units relative to $CLKN_{16-12}^{I}$ during inquiry in train A

intervals due to constant clock differences. This is important: because of given constant clock differences it does not matter when a device enters inquiry state. It will always find the same devices scanning at frequencies in the same train, because the frequencies in a train also depend on $CLKN_{16-12}$. This implies that I should select a device S to obtain discovery information from, such that $|CLKN_{16-12}^{I} - CLKN_{16-12}^{S}|$ is maximal.

Fig. 9 illustrates this in the light of a concrete example. The semicircles show the frequency phases covered by units I, S_1, and S_2 during inquiry in train A relative to $CLKN_{16-12}^{I}$. The inquiry of I results in the discovery of two units, S_1 and S_2. The clock offset of S_1 is $CLKN_{16-12}^{S_1} - CLKN_{16-12}^{I} = -8$; that of S_2 is $CLKN_{16-12}^{S_2} - CLKN_{16-12}^{I} = 7$. These relative clock differences remain constant over a longer period of time, although the $CLKN_{16-12}$ change every 1.28 s, possibly at different times, rotating the halfcircles right. Fig. 9 shows that S_1 and S_2 in their inquiries cover frequency phases relative to $CLKN^I_{16-12}$ that are not traversed by I. Units scanning at these phases with a relative distance larger than 7 or lower than -8 are never found by I, regardless of the current value of $CLKN_{16-12}$. Since the clock offsets of S_1 and S_2 are maximal, they cover the maximal number of phases relative to $CLKN^I_{16-12}$ not traversed by I. By transitively selecting devices from the discovery information of S_1 and S_2 it is possible for I to choose devices that have optimal clock offsets in order to cover a large area of phases. In the same way that a device S_{opt} is an optimal choice for I, I vice versa is an optimal choice for S_{opt} – the relationship is symmetric. Therefore in a setting with a large number of devices present, a few devices can form stable subgroups to cooperatively perform device discovery. They complement each other, and the whole system as well as individual units profit in terms of energy savings, number of devices discovered, and shorter discovery delays.

7   Using Sensory Input to Improve Rendezvous-Layer Protocol Performance

When everyday items are augmented with information processing capabilities they will provide information about their environment to other devices, thus enabling collaborative perception of the environment. In the Smart-Its project, smart devices are equipped with a wide variety of different sensors for physical parameters like temperature, acceleration, etc. An interesting question is how sensory data that is accumulated independently from the communication platform can be used to improve rendezvous layer protocol performance. The idea to take advantage of context information – especially location – in communication protocols has also been used to improve other protocol layers, e.g. routing protocols [ ].

If sensory input from acceleration or general location sensors are available, the inquiry parameter settings are adapted when a device moves. Since it is more probable that a moving device enters a new environment, the inquiry window is prolonged or the inquiry interval is shortened in order to discover new devices. In this case only individual devices increase their inquiry window; this does not lead to a deterioration of the rendezvous layer protocol performance of the whole system. Alternatively, the inquiry scan interval is reduced to ensure that other units can access the device faster. In general, all sensory input that could lead to an increased access to the device could result in the same adjustment of inquiry setting parameters.

Context information can also be used to implement the *select* routine in the adaptive rendezvous layer protocol. The purpose of the *select* statement is to choose such devices among all units that responded during inquiry, for which the uncertainty of transferring obsolete device information is as low as possible. When no sensory input is available, devices are selected as shown in the previous section or randomly from the set of devices that already responded during inquiry. But when context information is available, then it should be used to select devices that are as near as possible, that inquired at different frequencies, and that started inquiry most recently. In the Bluetooth 1.1 standard there exists a link manager protocol (LMP) command to determine the signal strength to other Bluetooth devices. This information could be used to evaluate whether the device is suitable to get device information from.

8   Conclusion

The standard inquiry procedure of Bluetooth consumes much energy which is problematic for communicating smart devices in ubiquitous computing settings. This paper showed how the standard inquiry parameters can be adapted to decrease power consumption and increase the scalability of the inquiry procedure. Since typically smart devices perceive their environment through sensors, we also presented ways for using sensory input to improve the performance of Bluetooth's rendezvous layer.

Furthermore, it was pointed out that the scalability of Bluetooth's inquiry procedure is not sufficient if many devices are present. As a result from this observation, an adaptive protocol for cooperative device detection was introduced that reduces energy consumption and improves scalability for environments with many devices.

The properties of Bluetooth's rendezvous layer that have the strongest impact on device detection delay are a relatively high random backoff delay and the existence of two separate frequency trains. In terms of the rendezvous layer for general frequency hopping systems there should be only a single train comprising all 32 frequencies of the inquiry hopping sequence. Alternatively, $N_{inquiry}$ could be reduced to one, and the minimum inquiry scan window should be increased to 20 ms. It is important to note that even with these adaptations the majority of parameter selection rules and the adaptive rendezvous layer protocol presented in this paper are still applicable.

References

1. Mattisson, Sven: *Low-Power Considerations in the Design of Bluetooth.* International Symposium on Low Power Electronics and Design, ISLPED 2000, Rapallo, Italy, 2000.
2. Salonidis, T.; Bhagwat, P.; Tassiulas, L.; LaMaire, R.: *Distributed topology construction of Bluetooth personal area networks.* In: Proceedings of INFOCOM 2001, IEEE, Volume: 3, 2001, pp. 1577-1586.
3. Salonidis, T.; Bhagwat, P.; Tassiulas, L.: *Proximity awareness and fast connection establishment in Bluetooth.* First Annual Workshop on Mobile and Ad Hoc Networking and Computing, MobiHOC, 2000.
4. Girling, Gray; Wa, Jennifer Li Kam; Osborn, Paul; Stefanova, Radina: *The Design and Implementation of a Low Power Ad Hoc Protocol Stack.* In: IEEE Personal Communications, Vol. 4, No. 5, pp. 8-15, October 1997. 258, 259

5. Bluetooth Special Interest Group: *Specification of the Bluetooth System, Core. Version 1.1*, February 2001. 257, 260, 261, 264, 267
6. Haartsen, Jaap C.: *The Bluetooth Radio System*. In: IEEE Personal Communications, February 2000.
7. Gomie, N.; van Dyck, R. E.; Soltanian, A.: *Interference of Bluetooth and IEEE 802.11: Simulation Modeling and Performance Evaluation*. ACM MSWiM 2001, The Fourth ACM International Workshop on Modeling, Analysis and Simulation of Wireless and Mobile Systems 2001, July 2001, Rome, Italy, 2001.
8. Ko, Young-Bae; Vaidya, Nitin H.: *Location-Aided Routing (LAR) in Mobile Ad Hoc Networks*. MOBICOM 98, Dallas, Texas, USA, 1998. 271
9. Feeney, Laura Marie; Nilsson, Martin: *Investigating the Energy Consumption of a Wireless Network Interface in an Ad Hoc Networking Environment*. IEEE INFOCOM 2001, Anchorage, Alaska, April 2001.
10. Mattern, Friedemann: *The Vision and Technical Foundations of Ubiquitous Computing*. In: Upgrade European Online Magazine, pp. 5-8, October 2001. 256
11. Weiser, Mark: *The Computer for the Twenty-First Century*. In: Scientific American, pp. 94-100, September 1991. 256
12. Kasten, Oliver; Langheinrich, Marc: *First Experiences with Bluetooth in the Smart-Its Distributed Sensor Network*. Workshop on Ubiquitous Computing and Communications. In: Proceedings PACT 2001, October 2001. 258, 262
13. Moser, Thomas; Karrer, Lukas: *The EventCollector Concept, Distributed Infrastructure for Event Generation & Dissemination in Ad Hoc Networks*. Diploma thesis, ETH Zurich, March 2001. 257
14. Ericsson Microelectronics: *ROK 101 007 Bluetooth Module Datasheet Rev. PA5*. April 2000. 258, 262
15. The Network Simulator - ns-2: *http://www.isi.edu/nsnam/ns/*. 258
16. BlueHoc, An Open-Source Bluetooth Simulator: *http://oss.software.ibm.com/developerworks/opensource/bluehoc/*. 258
17. The Smart-Its Project: *http://www.smart-its.org*. 257

A Robust Header Compression Simulator & Visualizer

Xiaoyuan Gu[1], Hannes Hartenstein[2], and Stefan Fischer[3]

[1] Panasonic European Laboratories GmbH
Monzastr. 4c, 63225 Langen, Germany
egu@panasonic.de
[2] NEC Europe Ltd., Network Laboratories Heidelberg
Adenauerplatz 6, 69115 Heidelberg, Germany
hannes.hartenstein@ccrle.nec.de
[3] Technical University of Braunschweig
Institute of Operating Systems and Computer Networks
Mühlenpfordtstr. 23, 38106 Braunschweig, Germany
fischer@ibr.cs.tu-bs.de

Abstract. IP-based realtime multimedia communication provides for a large Layer-3 and Layer-4 header overhead due to usually small payload sizes of single packets in a realtime flow. Because of the restricted bandwidth of wireless links, header compression represents an essential prerequisite for the Mobile Internet, i.e., whenever an IP-based mobile end device has to communicate with an IP-based infrastructure. RFC 3095 on Robust Header Compression (ROHC) represents the state-of-the-art header compression proposal. It provides a complex framework that allows to fine-tune compression *efficiency* versus *robustness* against link errors. We present a Java-based simulator/visualizer currently running ROHC Profile 2 (UDP/IP) in Uni-directional Mode that allows experimentation with all relevant ROHC parameters (like state transition timers and repeat counters) as well as with various link conditions. We present the implementation and report on simulation results. An average header length of about 2.8 bytes is achieved. In general, the tool is useful as an educational tool for assessing ROHC performance and to see Robust Header Compression 'at work', i.e., to explore the underlying parameter space. For the future, the simulator will be also used to generate realistic audio/video packet flows for evaluation with respect to audio/video decompression handling in the presence of packet losses.

1 Introduction

When a streaming application sends UDP/IPv4 packets with a packet rate of 50 packets/s, the bandwidth needed solely for the UDP/IPv4 headers amounts to 11.2 kbits/s. With RTP, IPv6, or tunneling approaches the overhead gets even larger. Since the air interface in a wireless system represents a scarce resource, header compression techniques are of utmost importance in order to make 'IP over air' economically feasible. The basic assumption for header compression is that the link over which IP headers

H. Schmeck, T. Ungerer, and L. Wolf (Eds.): ARCS 2002, LNCS 2299, pp. 274-286, 2002.

are compressed is a point-to-point link. IP headers in packet flows over the link will not change much from packet to packet, thus, this 'temporal' redundancy can be exploited by compression techniques. The main idea is that both end points of the link – in a 3G system, for example, the Radio Network Controller and the mobile terminal – maintain a copy of a *context* containing all the fixed fields of the header (static part of context) as well as reference values for fields with predictable changing patterns (dynamic part of context). In subsequent (compressed) headers, the fixed fields can be entirely omitted and for the predictable fields only some delta-information with respect to the reference values has to be sent. However, to keep contexts at both end point of the link in sync is a challenge for lossy links. Here, the engineering trade-off involves compression efficiency versus robustness of the method. The state-of-the-art in header compression for wireless links is RFC 3095 *Robust Header Compression* (ROHC) [1]. ROHC will be used in UMTS from Release 4 onwards (see [2]) and represents an enabling technology for IP-based wireless communications.

The field of header compression came to life with Van Jacobson's header compression scheme for TCP/IP [3] developed for slow modem lines. Degermark et al. designed a general IP header compression framework [4] for compressing IPv6 base and extension headers, IPv4 headers, TCP and UDP headers, and encapsulated IPv6/IPv4 headers. Degermark's et al. framework was extended to RTP/UDP/IP header compression in [5]. This so-called CRTP mechanism was analyzed for appropriateness for wireless links in [6]. The analysis showed significant drawbacks with respect to robustness. Several improvements were proposed, most notably *ROCCO* (Robust Checksum-based Header Compression) [7] and ACE [8] that very much influenced the ROHC proposal.

The ROHC proposal represents a complex framework for header compression where complexity comes from various sources: *i)* in order to maximize *compression efficiency* various special cases have to be taken into account, *ii)* it provides a general framework for a large number of header types, and *iii)* it provides a high degree of adaptivity to various links and their respective error characteristics. Since ROHC presents a very recent approach to header compression, only very few performance results can be found in the literature today. In order to study the effects of changing the various ROHC parameters as well as to check the corresponding compression performance, we have seen the necessity to come up with a ROHC simulator/visualizer. The simulator currently supports ROHC Profile 2 (UDP/IP) in Unidirectional Mode. The simulator allows us to tune ROHC parameters, serves for educational purposes, and will be extended in the future in order to study ROHC effects on various audio/video codecs.

2   A Brief Introduction to Robust Header Compression

Header Compression aims at reducing the header overhead by exploiting the redundancy inherent in a sequence of UDP/IP (or other types of) headers stemming from a flow of packets. The redundancy is due to the fact that within a flow of packets, several fields in the header do not change at all or change predictably. Table 1 indicates the static and inferable fields in IPv4 and UDP headers.

Table 1. UDP/IPv4 header fields and their ROHC classification (static, inferable, irregular)

Field	Type	Field	Type
Version	Static	Header Checksum	Irregular
IHL	Static	Source Address	Static
Type of Service	Static	Dest. Address	Static
Total Length	Inferable		
Identification	Irregular	Source Port	Static
Flags	Static	Destination Port	Static
Fragment Offset	Static	Length	Inferable
Time to Live	Static	Checksum	Irregular
Protocol	Static		

The static fields are constant for the complete packet stream while the inferable fields (length information) can be computed from link layer header information. The IP header checksum as well as the UDP checksum are discarded at the compressor and restored at the decompressor using the well-known checksum mechanism. Thus, only the IP Identification (IP ID) field is left over for compression. The IP ID is assumed to follow the Sequential Allocation Policy, therefore, it changes predictably and can be coded efficiently.

In an 'ideal' scenario where the link between compressor and decompressor can be assumed to be error-free, header compression works as follows. When the compressor gets the first packet of a packet flow, it stores all the static fields as well as reference values of predictably changing fields in a *context*. The compressor assigns a currently unused *context identifier* (CID, a small integer) to the context and sends the uncompressed header together with the CID to the decompressor. The decompressor generates an identical context with the same CID. All following packet headers can now be sent only with the CID and without the constant and inferred fields, and the remaining fields can be coded efficiently. When the context has to be changed, a packet of appropriate type that contains the necessary context updating information is sent to the decompressor.

Clearly, the challenge of header compression is to deal with non-perfect links where packets can get damaged or lost. In this case, the contexts at compressor's and decompressor's side can get out of sync. In other words, the decompressor's context might no longer be correct and needs to be repaired, e.g., by sending a full header or some partial update. The extent to which a header compression algorithm is able to deal with such loss/error situations determines its *robustness*. The efficiency of header compression and its robustness are directly related, and a ROHC operator has to find a tradeoff between the two by tuning the scheme's parameters. One of the goals of the simulator described in this paper is to help in finding good parameter settings for specific link characteristics.

There are three operating modes of the ROHC Protocol, namely Unidirectional Mode (U-Mode), Optimistic Mode (O-Mode), and Reliable Mode (R-Mode).

U-Mode is designed for links with no return path (path from the decompressor to the compressor), or where a return path is not desired. Thus, there is no means or need for the decompressor to communicate with the compressor.

The Optimistic Mode is aiming at maximizing compression efficiency and makes sparse usage of the feedback channel when running in an environment of relatively low bit error rates and low irregularities. The feedback channel is used to send error recovery requests and (optionally) acknowledgments of significant context updates from decompressor to compressor.

The Reliable Mode, finally, aims at maximizing the robustness against loss propagation and damage propagation, i.e., minimize the probability of context invalidation even under header loss/error burst conditions. It may have a lower probability of context invalidation than O-mode due to the fact that context invalidation is almost immediately feedbacked to the compressor. R-Mode has a more intensive usage of the feedback channel and a stricter logic at both the compressor and the decompressor that prevents loss of context synchronization except for very high residual bit error rates. Feedback is sent to acknowledge all context updates, including updates of the sequence number field.

A ROHC implementation should be able to support all three modes of operation, and all operation must start at U-Mode. Transition to any of the bi-directional modes can be performed as soon as a packet has reached the decompressor and it has replied with a feedback packet indicating that a mode transition is desired. In the rest of the paper we restrict ourselves to U-mode as the ROHC base mode.

Both compressor and decompressor are described as state machines with 3 main states each. The compressor states are 'Initialization and Refresh State' (IR State), 'First Order State' (FO State), and 'Second Order State' (SO State). The compressor states dictate what kind of headers are allowed to be sent by the compressor: in IR state, full headers together with additional information like CIDs has to be sent, in FO state partial updates and a specific compressed header (UOR2, see below) can be sent additionally, and in SO state the smallest compressed headers (UO1, UO0, see below) can be sent in addition. A state transition diagram is given in Figure 1.

The states of the decompressor indicate whether the decompressor has *i)* no context, or *ii)* a partial context, or *iii)* a full context available. At each state only packets of certain type(s) are given decompression permission. A state transition diagram for the decompressor is given in Figure 2.

As mentioned above, ROHC defines a number of different packet formats for the exchange between compressor and decompressor (see Table 2). The Initialization and Refresh (IR) header sets up contexts and is 27 bytes long for UDP/IPv4. The IR_DYN header is used to update the total dynamic part of the context and is 13 bytes long. There are three compressed header formats (UOR2, UO1, and UO0 are the official names of RFC 3095) that differ slightly in their fields and field lengths, respectively, and their respective lengths are 4, 3, and 2 bytes. The compressed headers only contain information on the 'irregular' UDP/IPv4 header fields. All the packets contain also CRC fields (see below) and a CID that refers to its context.

The decompressor needs to be able to decide whether a decompressed packet is correct, i.e., the context that has been used for decompressing the compressed header is up-to-date. In ROHC this is done using Cyclic Redundancy Checks (CRC). At the compressor side, CRCs for IR and IR_DYN packets are computed over their respective structures that contain rearranged header fields and some other information. CRCs for compressed header packets are computed over the original header fields. The CRC is then performed again after all header fields are restored at the decompressor. The results of the two CRC calculations are checked to see whether they match. If yes, there is a good chance that the piece of data before compression and the restored piece of data after decompression are identical. A CRC mismatch might be caused either by a damaged context or by a bit error. In the first case, the decompressor typically tries to repair the context, e.g., by decompressing it with a previously used context, in the second case, it usually discards the packet and remains in its current state.

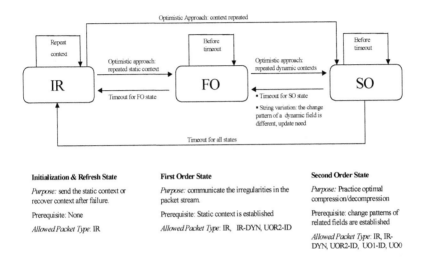

Fig. 1. State transition diagram of compressor in U-Mode

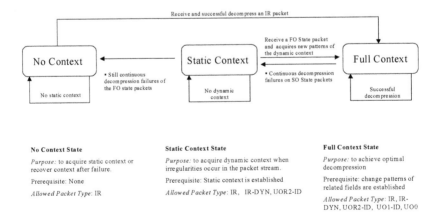

Fig. 2. State transition diagram of decompressor in U-Mode

Table 2. ROHC packet types used in U-Mode

Packet Name	Packet Function	Packet Size [bytes]
IR	Initialization / Refresh	27
IR_DYN	Partial context update	13
UOR2-ID	Compressed header	4
UO1-ID	Compressed header	3
UO0	Compressed header	2

3   Simulator/Visualizer Implementation

Our ROHC simulator for UDP/IPv4 in U-mode allows to set operational parameters of repeat counters, timers, options, packet delay, link packet loss rate, and link bit error rate for performance evaluation and tuning. The corresponding visualizing component allows us to view original headers together with their compressed and reconstructed counterparts. Monitoring information like current compressor/decompressor states, state transition events, current packet type, and context update events are also shown. In addition, we provide evaluation results like bandwidth consumption, compression gain, and average header length as well as statistics on packet type distributions. Furthermore, the ROHC simulation tool provides for debugging facilities.

The ROHC simulator/visualizer has been written in Java to avoid a split-level implementation with two programming languages. In addition, Java enforces good object-oriented design practices in order to produce solid and extensible applications and it ensures portability. We encountered two (tractable) problems when using Java for our purposes. First, Java has no support for unsigned data types, thus, mapping between signed values and their unsigned equivalent binary representations has to be done. Second, in order to write and read ROHC packet headers of different types (in form of Java class objects) to and from a data stream, the mechanism of Object Serialization is used to significantly simplify the task of passing data. However, since the serialization mechanism automatically deals with the process of saving and restoring the state of a class, regardless of where the stream points, packet type indication suffers. The reason is that the decompressor cannot locate the exact position of the packet type indication byte inside a received packet, and therefore the decompression based on packet type halts. To fix this problem, an additional layer of encapsulation is introduced. A ROHC header object is defined as member of object of a common class Uniform. Packet Type Indication bytes are separated from the ROHC packet header to avoid the location problem.

The simulations testbed is presented in Figure 3: two Windows 2000 PCs on a Fast Ethernet provide us with a compressor and decompressor facility, respectively. The compressor uses as input a recorded sequence of packet headers. The compressor/decompressor are structured into a back-end and a front-end: the back-end is responsible for protocol operations while the front-end allows interactions between the user and the back-end. Screenshots of the compressor and decompressor GUIs are shown in Figure 4. The main parameters to experiment with are as follows.

The screenshot of the Compressor GUI shows four timers: *Delay* determines the inter-arrival times of packets, *TIME_ALL* determines after which time interval the compressor has to transit back to IR state, and *TIME_SO* and *TIME_FO* correspondingly determine after which time interval the compressor has to transit back from second order to first order and from first order to IR state, respectively. Not shown in the current view are the counters for repeats (successive transmissions) of significant context update packets like *IR Repeat, IR_DYN Repeat,* and *UOR2 Repeat*. The minimum values are 2 for these counters (otherwise there is no repeat of packets). Higher values lead to higher reliability but less compression efficiency.

At the decompressor side, *failure thresholds* that decide when to fall back to a lower state in case of continuous decompression failures have to be set. Examples are *threshold_FC* that decides when to trigger a downward transition from Full Context State to Static Context State, and *threshold_SC* that decides when a backward transition is triggered from Static Context State to No Context State. The thresholds are common for all modes, and the exact values are subject to link characteristics.

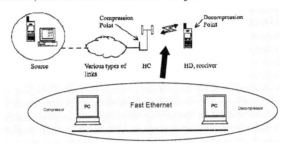

Fig. 3. Testbed scenario

4   Experimental Results

In this section we present experimental results obtained with the proposed simulator. We show what compression efficiency can be optimally achieved and then give an example for the exploration of the parameter space as it is enabled by the simulator. For the first, 'optimal' scenario we have set the repeat values for IR, IR_DYN, and UOR2 packets to 2, and the timers TIME_ALL and TIME_SO to 9s and 3.3s, respectively. For a second, 'more reliable but less efficient scenario' we have increased the repeat values to 6 and have the timers TIME_ALL and TIME_SO decreased to 3s and 1.1s. Compression gain and average header length vs number of packets are given in Figures 5 and 6 for a packet stream of about 2000 packets where a packet is sent every 100ms.

The optimal scenario shows a compression gain of 83.04% after 20 packets, and the compression gain reaches about 90.0% after 2000 packets. However, if the repeat counters for IR, IR_DYN and UOR2 are set to 3 times larger, and the timers for TIME_ALL, TIME_SO are adjusted to 3 times smaller, the compression gain drops immediately by more than 20%.

The corresponding header lengths for the 'optimal' scenario are 4.75 bytes after 20 packets and 2.84 bytes after 2000 packets. For the 'less efficient but more reliable' scenario the compression performance measured by average header length is significantly affected., i.e., eventually more than three times higher than in the 'optimal' case.

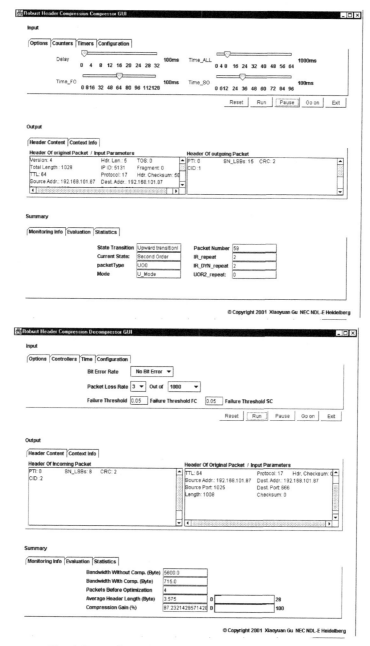

Fig. 4. Screenshots of compressor and decompressor GUI

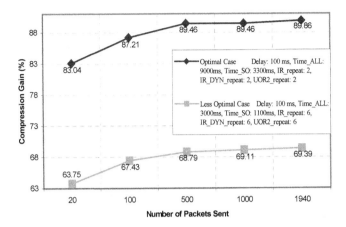

Fig. 5. Compression gain (in % compared to original header size) vs packet numbers

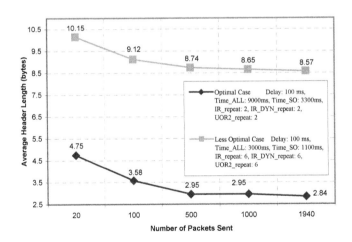

Fig. 6. Average header length (in bytes) vs packet numbers

Figure 7 shows the packet distribution for the two scenarios at the level of 2000 packets sent. For the 'optimal' scenario, the packet with minimum-sized header-UO0 packets is in the vast majority, it occupies about 88% of the overall packet numbers. The packets with biggest header, IR packet, is below 1%. This leads to an average header length of only 2.84 Bytes.

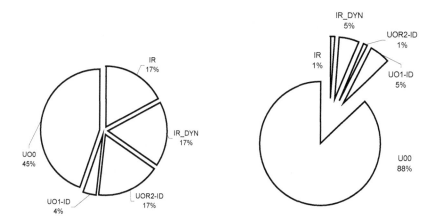

Fig. 7. Distribution of ROHC packet types for the 'more robust but less efficient' scenario (left) and the 'optimal' scenario (right)

Figure 8 presents a study on the robustness of ROHC in U-mode. We show how a damaged or lost header can affect the successive packet stream due to a damaged context on the compressor's side.

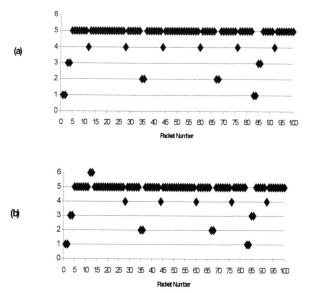

Fig. 8. A study on the robustness of ROHC. Shown are packet numbers for a stream of packets vs corresponding packet header types (1: IR; 2: IR_DYN; 3: UOR2-ID; 4: UO1-ID; 5: UO0; 6: lost or damaged). Ideal case (no packet losses) is shown in (a), (b) shows the loss of a UO1-ID packet that leads to the loss of the following packet, (c) shows the loss of 2 UO0 packets that does not lead to successive losses, (d) shows that loss of UO2 packets might result in successive losses (continued on next page)

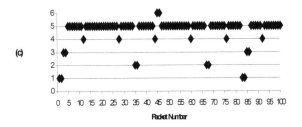

(c)

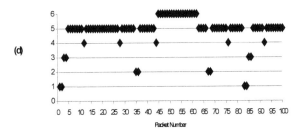

(d)

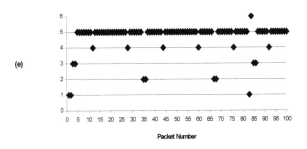

(e)

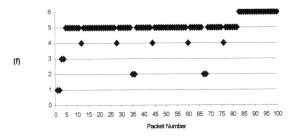

(f)

Fig. 8 (cont'd). (e) shows that loss of a single IR packet does not effect the system, while (f) indicates that a loss of 'number of repeats' IR packets results in a loss of successive packets until the context is repaired again by a context-updating packet

Figure 8(a) shows the pattern of changing header types when no loss/damage is present. Figure 8(b) illustrates the case where a UO1-ID packet is damaged and a following packet is discarded until the context is repaired again. Figures 8(c) and (d) show that the loss of UO0 packets might or might not lead to successive packet losses depending on whether the *sequence number least significant bits* (SN LSB) field wraps around or not. If it is just wrapping around the finite number space when a UO0 packet gets lost, the decompressor's context gets irritated and a number of subsequent packets will be discarded until a context repair procedures adjusts the sequence number again. Figures 8(e) and (f) show the importance of the repeat counters for major context updates like IR packet headers: the loss of a single IR packet does not affect the packet stream, while the loss of two (number of repeats) IR packets leads to successive packet losses until the context is repaired again, in the worst case when the next IR packet is periodically sent.

The purpose of the above discussion has been to demonstrate the tuning of the trade-off between compression efficiency and robustness. Of course, as input parameter also the distribution of the bit errors should be taken into account.

Quantitative results with respect to packet loss rate depending on residual bit error rate are presented in Figure 9. Again, the error distribution is a uniform distribution. Only errors in the packet headers were considered.

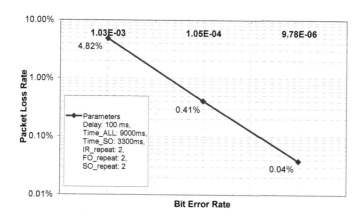

Fig. 9. Relationship between residual Bit Error Rate and Packet Loss Rate

5   Discussion & Future Work

We have presented a ROHC simulator and visualizer for Profile 2 (UDP/IP) in U-mode in order to facilitate exploration of the ROHC parameter space as well as ROHC evaluation, i.e., the trade-off between efficiency and robustness. Experimental results show that optimimum compression in U-mode leads to an average header length of 2.84 bytes. We have also shown the effects of damaged headers on the packet loss rate. The simulator/visualizer is implemented in Java and allows easy replacement and extensions of modules, e.g., for error modeling or input packet types.

Furthermore, we use the outlined tool also for determining which ROHC parameters should be configurable via SNMP, thus, should be included in the Management Information Base [9]. Finally, we plan to perform experiments on the effects of packet losses due to decompression failures on several audio and video codecs.

References

1. Bormann, C., et al.: Robust Header Compression (ROHC): Framework and four profiles: RTP, UDP, ESP, and uncompressed. RFC 3095, July 2001
2. 3GPP TS 25.323, V4.2.0: Packet Data Convergence Protocol (PDCP) Specification (Release 4). September 2001
3. Jacobson, V.: Compressing TCP/IP Headers for Low-Speed Serial Links. RFC 1144, Feb. 1990
4. Degermark, M., Nordgren, B., and Pink, S.: IP Header Compression. RFC 2507, Feb. 1999
5. Casner, S., Jacobson, V.: Compressing IP/UDP/RTP Headers for Low-Speed Serial Links. RFC 2508, February 1999
6. Degermark, M., Hannu, H., Jonsson, L., Svanbro, K.: Evaluation of CRTP Performance over Cellular Radio Networks. IEEE Personal Communication Magazine, vol. 7, no. 4, August 2000, pp. 20-25
7. Svanbro, K., Hannu, H., Jonsson, L., and Degermark, M.: Wireless Real Time IP-services enabled by header compression. Proc. IEEE VTC, May 2000
8. Liu, Z. et al.: ACE: A Robust and Efficient IP/UDP/RTP Header Compression Scheme. Internet Draft (work in progress), "draft-ace-robust-hc-01.txt", March 2000
9. Quittek, J., Hartenstein, H., Stiemerling, M.: Definitions of Managed Objects for Robust Header Compression. Internet Draft (work in progress), "draft-quittek-rohc-mib-00.txt", November 2001

Author Index

Lecture Notes in Computer Science

For information about Vols. 1–2221
please contact your bookseller or Springer-Verlag